CAREERS IN DIVING

A guide to careers in diving.

Steven M. Barsky,
Kristine C. Barsky
Ronnie Lynn Damico

BEST PUBLISHING COMPANY

Photography by Steven M. Barsky, unless otherwise noted.

FIRST EDITION
Designed by Carolyn Gibbs, Best Publishing Company

ISBN 0–941332–37–3
Library of Congress Catalog Number 93–071479

Composed and printed in the United States of America.

Best Publishing Company
2355 North Steves Boulevard
P.O. Box 30100
Flagstaff, AZ 86003–0100 USA

WARNING

Diving is a potentially hazardous occupation. No matter what type of diving you do, there is always some risk involved, even if you only go sport diving. Certain types of diving careers are especially hazardous, such as military diving and commercial diving.

The authors make no recommendations for career choices in this book. Each of the authors has known people who have died or been seriously injured while diving. Making a choice of a diving career is a personal decision. Only you can evaluate whether you have the mental and physical abilities to be a diver. A physical examination is a prerequisite for any type of diving activity.

Should you elect to pursue a career in diving then you must assume the risks and responsibility for that choice.

TABLE OF CONTENTS

ACKNOWLEDGMENTS

As we sat down to write this book, we thought about the people who have influenced our careers. As you will learn in the stories in this book of the people who work in diving, mentors have been important to most of them. Certainly they have been important to us. First and foremost, we would like to thank the people who helped us to get where we are today. For Steve Barsky that list includes Bob Christensen, Dick Long, Jim Parker, and John Wozny. Kristine Barsky is especially grateful to Dr. Jake Houck, who encouraged her studies in marine biology. Élise and Paul Henderson, Kristine's parents, gave her the support and confidence to achieve her goals. Ronnie Damico thanks Drs. Ron & Sue Bangasser, Mark Flahan, Homer Fletcher, Dr. Robert Given, and Jon Hardy.

This book would not have been possible without the many divers who you will meet in this book that shared their careers with us. Their stories are what make this book special.

Many people helped us bring this project to completion and provided us with introductions and ideas. Carol McCann of Diving Unlimited Intnl. gave us many introductions to military divers and made this entire section of the book possible. Frank Clark, formerly of the Naval Explosive Ordnance Disposal Technology Center provided us with extensive information on the tasks of EOD divers. Ed Stetson, friend, diving instructor and law enforcement officer with the Santa Barbara Harbor Patrol has frequently modeled for photos.

Jay Jeffries, also of Diving Unlimited, provided us with introductions and contact numbers for many of the people we interviewed. Bob Clark and Laurie Clark Humpal of SSI reviewed the section on diving instruction and made many suggestions for improvements. Sam Jackson and Jed Livingstone at NAUI also checked the text for accuracy. Frankie Wingert at the YMCA updated our information on their excellent program. Drew Richardson of PADI gave us a great deal of insight to the PADI organization and philosophy. Jon Hayes and Scott McIntyre of Oceanic USA made it possible for us to shoot photos at their facility.

Although we shot most of the photos in the text, we were provided with many outstanding photographs by friends and colleagues. These photographers include Lee Peterson, Jim Church, Diane Pleschner, Michael Weinberg, Lt. Scott Hill, Steve Linton, Joe Packi, Larry Murphy (National Park Service), Peter Ellegard, and Jeff McConnel of Ocean Sports Waikoloa. Organizations that provided photos include Diving Systems International, Petersen Publications Staff, Scuba Schools International, and Scripps Institution of Oceanography. Special thanks go to Doug Kesling for his photos of scientific divers and newspaper photographer Dennis R. Floss for his photos of Lt. Scott Hill.

John Wozny, long time diving instructor and close friend, reviewed the text and made numerous suggestions for improvements. As John never lets us forget, "Practice doesn't make perfect. Only perfect practice makes perfect."

Finally, we would like to thank our publisher, Jim Joiner. Jim saw the value in this project from the beginning and gave us the support we needed.

STEVE BARSKY, KRISTINE BARSKY, RONNIE DAMICO
MARCH, 1993

Chapter One

INTRODUCTION

What you achieve depends upon how badly you want it.

If you're reading this book, chances are that you're already an avid scuba diver. You've also probably wondered how you could make diving your career. Many people have asked that same question, numerous times, to each of the three authors of this book. We've done it and you can do it, too! It's just a matter of making up your mind about what you really want to do with your life.

This book is designed for both the young person who is starting out in their career, and for the older person who is looking to make a career change. It is our goal to give you the straight facts, both good and bad, about what it takes to succeed in a career in diving. We have tried to present the truth about the day to day demands of each job. We have included interviews with successful people in each of the areas covered in this book so you can get an idea of what it took them to get where they are today.

One of the things that we have found out about life is that everything is a question of ambition. You may talk to people who tell you that it is terribly difficult to get a job as a marine biologist, or how long it takes for an apprentice or "tender" to become a commercial diver. These things are usually true, but the reality of life is that you can achieve whatever it is you want to do, it is strictly a question of desire. That question can be simplified very easily. *How badly do you want to do what it is you say you want to do?*

We have met many people who tell us that they want to be a marine biologist. Usually, they have a somewhat romantic notion of what marine biologists do, and picture themselves aboard the *Calypso,* working with the Cousteaus. Yet, how many people would have the determination that Kristine Barsky had when she set out to be a marine biologist? After graduating from Humboldt State University in Northern California she worked in six other biology jobs for a total of six years before she achieved her goal of becoming a marine biologist for the California Department of Fish and Game. During those six years she worked as a range biologist in Nevada for the federal government, as a water quality biologist for the state of California, and cloned ferns for a botanical company. She also worked as deputy game warden and as a staff member of the biology department of a museum.

Fig. 1.1 – It took Kristine Barsky over six years to get a full time job as a marine biologist.

Ultimately, Kristine was hired as a biologist/diver with the Department and went on to become an associate marine biologist based in Santa Barbara. During the course of her employment with the Department she has worked on abalone and sea urchin research projects, made numerous research dives under a variety of conditions, and participated in underwater surveys with the National Park Service. In some years she made as many as 250 dives for the various research projects in which she participated. If she had not been persistent in her goals, however, she never would have had the opportunity she worked so hard to achieve.

We also meet many young divers today who want to be commercial divers. Yet when you tell most of them about the conditions they must work under as a tender, very few of them are willing to make the sacrifices necessary to have a well paying career.

Because so many people want to work in diving or diving related occupations, there is stiff competition for the jobs that do exist. This doesn't mean that you can't get the job you want. What it does mean is that you will probably have to make some sacrifices to get where you want to go.

How many people do you know who hate to go to work each morning? We firmly believe that your job should be something you enjoy. We have found that most of the people who work in diving do so because they genuinely enjoy what they do. On the other hand, after reading some of the accounts in this book you may decide that a career in diving is not for you. We hope not, but if that's true we may have saved you a lot of time and trouble.

A major trend that has started in the past few years is that many people with successful careers are leaving their traditional jobs to work in an occupation they believe will be more fulfilling and enjoyable. This rejection of traditional jobs and values has become more and more common. In addition, there are many people who have been forced out of their jobs because of changes in the economy or through technological changes in their field. It's been estimated that up to 90% of all executives will suffer at least one job loss!

Fig. 1.2 – Most people who work in the diving field thoroughly enjoy what they do.

Working in diving isn't always fun.

Making a career change is a very personal decision. One thing you should keep in mind, especially if you are successfully employed, is that very few people "get rich" in diving. There are many people who work in diving who make reasonable incomes, but few people become truly wealthy through diving. Again, this is not to say that it can't be done, but these people tend to be the exception rather than the rule. Most people who work in diving do so because they are committed to the field and take great satisfaction from what they do. For them, money is usually a secondary issue and not their primary motivation.

To be successful in diving, as in most things in life, you must be the type of person who takes initiative. You have to make things happen, rather than sitting on the sidelines waiting for an opportunity.

Whether you want to be an underwater photographer, a commercial diver, or a marine biologist, to be successful you must have creative energy and imagination. You must learn to see the possibilities in every situation, and learn how to make positive experiences work for you and the other people with whom you work.

We have found that virtually everyone that we interviewed for this book loves their job. They were all motivated people who did not need anyone to tell them what they should do.

As a professional in the diving field you must also learn how to get along with other people and be a team player. While this is important in most jobs, it's essential in diving since you must often rely upon other people for your safety. Many times in commercial diving, the divers who get the most opportunities and make the most money are not necessarily the most talented. Frequently you'll find that the divers who are friendly and pleasant to be with, under the stress of living aboard an offshore oil rig, end up being the most successful.

Keep in mind, too, that although working in diving sounds glamorous, it is still a job just like any other job. There are ups and downs in

Fig. 1.3 – No matter what career path you choose in diving you must be able to work as part of a team. This crew is launching a diving bell on a commercial diving job.

every job and you will find them in the diving field, too. If you've left the security of a well paying office job, you may be unhappy with the unpleasant conditions that frequently exist in life at sea. A novice marine biologist will discover that not all research vessels are comfortable, and you may have to share a cabin with several other people. Search and rescue divers sometimes find they are not up to the task of recovering dead bodies in zero visibility water. Seafood divers often learn that they must dive when a sport diver would not consider entering the water.

If you've grown accustomed to a 9 to 5 job you may not be happy with the long hours that many diving jobs demand. Diving at a tropical resort may be fun and exciting, but you may not enjoy having to make every night dive, or filling tanks after your guests have gone off to the local night spots for some fun. Working for a diving equipment manufacturer may be fascinating to you, but the long hours and travel involved in visiting dealers and attending trade shows can take a toll on your marriage or other relationships. Search and rescue divers are usually on call twenty-four hours a day, seven days a week.

Also, as we've mentioned before, very few people make the kind of money in diving that allows them to live a lavish lifestyle. This is particularly true for people who are just starting out in the field. If making lots of money is essential to you, you may want to consider another line of work.

The positive side of working in diving.

Of course, there are many positive things about working in diving, and that's what makes the field so competitive. The most obvious positive thing about a career in diving is the opportunity to do something you enjoy and to get paid for doing it. Not everyone gets the chance to have fun while they work!

A big advantage to working in most positions in diving is the chance to work outdoors rather than be seated behind a desk all day long. For many people, the feeling of freedom gained by working outdoors or on the ocean is irresistible. Most people who enjoy this are also attracted by the physical activity involved in diving.

The reasons why people enjoy working in diving are as varied as the reasons why people dive. Just as some people love to dive for the excitement they find in the sport, some people get the same enjoyment from working at diving as a career. This is probably one of the driving factors for many commercial divers.

Another big attraction to the diving field is the opportunity to travel. Although all three of the authors currently reside in California, diving jobs have taken them to various locations around the world. Our collective dive travel for the purposes of work includes dives in Florida, Hawaii, Washington, Louisiana, Texas, and Rhode Island in the U.S., and Scotland, Holland, Norway, the Bahamas, Mexico, Puerto Rico, and the Cayman Islands.

Fig. 1.4 – People who work in diving frequently get the chance to travel and do special things.

Perhaps the most special thing about your career in diving will be the opportunities you will have to dive in special places and situations that most divers never get the chance to experience. For example, between the three authors we have had the fortune to dive on the *U.S.S. Arizona* in Pearl Harbor, shoot photos inside the Monterey Bay Aquarium, participate in the experimental dives that helped develop the Edge decompression computer, work as a stunt diver in numerous films and television shows, and dive with white sharks.

Which career is right for you?

There are numerous career opportunities in the diving field. Some of them, such as dive shop management, require little formalized training to be successful. Other areas, like marine biology, require a college degree at a minimum.

We have selected 14 of the most popular career areas in diving to cover in this book. These are the jobs we get asked about most frequently.

The information you find here is based upon our personal experiences, as well as interviews with top professionals in each of these categories. In each chapter we will describe what training you need to work in a particular area and what you can expect from the job. In our interviews with the professionals in each category we will describe how they got to where they are today. Whether you want to be a resort dive guide or work as a diving archaeologist, you'll find the answers to your career questions in this book.

No one can tell you which career choice is right for you. However, we have found that most of the people who work in diving knew what they wanted to do with their lives from very early on and did whatever they needed to do to pursue the career path they chose.

One thing that we have found to be true is that your career is an accumulation of your experience. The more areas you have skills in, the greater your chances of success. Given a choice between hiring a scuba instructor with a business degree and one who just knows diving, a diving equipment manufacturer will probably pick the one with the degree. If you are a commercial diving school graduate with a background as a diesel mechanic you are more likely to be hired than a person who has graduated from dive school but has no other training.

Fig. 1.5 – Nobody can tell you which career choice is right for you. It's a personal decision.

We sincerely hope that this book will give you special insights into the varied and interesting careers in diving. We have tried to portray both the positive and negative aspects of each job. Keep in mind that there is no such thing as the "perfect job." Every job has certain negative aspects, and any job is what you make it.

Chapter Two

SCUBA INSTRUCTION

Many of the people in top positions in the diving industry got their start as scuba instructors. Probably more than any other job in diving, this career provides one of the best stepping stones for divers who aspire to positions of responsibility. Diving instructor training and experience provides you with two very important skills, leadership training and public speaking experience. Both these skills are essential to success, no matter which career path you choose.

Scuba instruction can be an extremely rewarding career in itself. The main ingredient in choosing this type of work is that you must have a real aptitude for teaching.

Preparing to Become a Scuba Instructor

One of the keys to becoming a successful scuba instructor is to gain as much diving experience as possible, under as varied conditions as possible. It's not reasonable to expect to be able to teach a course in deep diving, or any other specialty, if you only have made a few dives in that specialty area. Similarly, it's unreasonable to expect that a diver with limited overall diving experience will be able to judge whether conditions are truly "safe" to take a class of novices in the water.

Many people are becoming diving instructors today with limited amounts of diving experience. This is a mistake, especially if you plan to make this your career. While most training agencies require only a year of diving experience, with as little as 50-100 dives, we recommend a minimum of two year's experience with a minimum of 150-200 dives. While there are certainly people who have become instructors with less experience, it is not recommended.

Fig. 2.1 – To prepare to become an instructor you need to get as much diving experience as possible. You should also log all your dives.

To be accepted at an instructor training course, most training agencies will also require certification as an advanced diver at the very least, or as a divemaster or assistant instructor. Dive rescue certification is required by all agencies so you are properly prepared to rescue any student who might need assistance.

Aside from gaining diving experience, there are two other important things that you should do to prepare yourself for a career in scuba instruction. First, you should take as many specialty diving courses as possible. These will increase your knowledge and confidence, and they will also show you all the things that you don't know.

You should also work as an assistant with as many different instructors as possible. This is especially important, so you can see a variety of teaching techniques and get a feeling for what works and what doesn't. If you only work with one or two instructors you won't receive much of an exposure to varied styles of instruction and teaching ideas. Even if you happen to find an instructor with outstanding abilities, you should still work with other instructors to help you put things in perspective. There is even some value in assisting with a poor instructor, in that you'll learn some things that you shouldn't do or that you want to avoid.

Current CPR (cardiopulmonary resuscitation) and First Aid certification by nationally recognized agencies (American Red Cross, American Heart Association, etc.) are required by all training agencies to become a diving instructor. Depending on the agency, you will

Fig. 2.2 – Working with an instructor is one of the best ways to prepare yourself to become a scuba instructor. Here, one assistant helps a student with a loose fin while another monitors entries.

either be required to have these certificates before entering the ITC (Instructor Training Course), or before you complete the course. It's not a bad idea for the instructor candidate to look into becoming certified as a CPR and/or First Aid instructor as well. Besides giving you a head start on getting some teaching experience, it will make your teaching of these subjects in your scuba courses that much better. Some training agencies require current certification in CPR and First Aid throughout the entire time an instructor is teaching, and some will require it only at the time the instructor becomes certified. It is highly recommended that every diving instructor maintain current skills and certification in both of these areas.

Of course, you must also be in good physical condition to be an instructor. You must have the capability to take care of yourself as well as other divers. You must be strong enough to make a rescue of another diver in full open water scuba equipment.

Finally, you should read everything that you can about diving to increase your knowledge and to expose yourself to different ideas and theories. The world of diving is especially broad and there is no one who is an expert in all phases of it. No matter where you live there will be specialty areas of diving that are unavailable to you unless you travel. For example, if you live in Southern California there is no cave diving, no coral reefs, and few deep, intact wrecks like those found on the east coast. Reading will allow you to at least familiarize yourself with these areas even if you are unable to gain firsthand experience with them.

Another important aspect of reading about diving is that it will help you to put many aspects of diving into historical perspective. This is especially true if you can manage to find old copies of diving magazines or older diving texts. These documents will help you to understand the evolution of diving, so that you understand how and why things are the way they are in the diving industry today.

Selecting a Training Agency to Join

Once you decide to become a diving instructor, your next major decision is to choose which agency you want to join. This is an important decision since not all agencies are alike. You should spend a good deal of time in evaluating which agency, or agencies, you want to certify your students through. Just because you were initially certified through one agency doesn't mean that you can't become an instructor with a different agency.

You need to evaluate the philosophy of the agency and compare it with your personal philosophy about diving and teaching. You also need to evaluate where you want to teach and the type of program you want to teach. Some agencies have very structured teaching requirements while others are more liberal about where, how, and what you can teach.

Different agencies run their instructor training programs in different ways. One method, used by PADI, is to divide the program into two main parts. The first part is known as the IDC – Instructor Development Course. The purpose of this course is to train divers to the instructor level using the PADI system. The program stresses the development of knowledge and skills. Upon completion of the PADI IDC you are then qualified to attend the PADI Instructor Evaluation or "IE." This course consists entirely of testing of your water skills, knowledge, teaching ability, and professionalism.

Other instructional agencies have a pre-testing program that you must complete prior to attending the actual instructor course. The pre-testing is designed to ensure that you have the physical capability and knowledge level to be an instructor. For example, NAUI designates theirs with the title, "Instructor Qualification Course." During this course you will be required to demonstrate your swimming skills and endurance, your diving skills, teaching ability, and your knowledge. You will be expected to perform these skills as an instructor would perform them. If you don't pass the qualification course, you won't be allowed to attend the training course. Don't go to the qualification course or the instructor course unprepared! You are only wasting your time and money if you do.

The majority of instructor training programs are divided up into several phases. The core areas of these programs usually include instruction in how to teach, expanding your knowledge of diving, teaching ability, and your ability to perform successful diver rescues. You are evaluated and graded on your knowledge, rescues, and teaching ability. Most of the agencies require you to achieve a passing grade in each of these areas. Everything you do while you are at the instructor course will be scrutinized by the staff.

Most instructor training courses last for anywhere from eight to ten days, although some are longer. If you have the time, you may want to consider enrolling in an instructor program at a university or community college. These programs tend to offer more comprehensive training. Since they are more spread out they allow you more time to learn and are generally less stressful than the more concentrated programs.

If you live in Southern California, one of the agencies you might want to consider is the L.A. County Underwater Instructors Association. In its abbreviated form, you may see this agency referred to by the acronym LACO UIA. The L.A. County program is the oldest in the United States and offers an excellent program of instruction. They also offer a cross certification weekend that allows you to become an instructor with NAUI (National Association of Underwater Instructors). You can also earn YMCA instructor certification through the L.A. County Program

Fig. 2.3 – A scuba instructor's skills must be excellent.

The L.A. County Underwater Instructors Association is a small, tightly knit organization. The program grooms its new instructors from the ranks of its Advanced Diver Program (ADP) which is held once a year. The LACO ADP program is one of the most comprehensive programs of its kind. It is run largely by the same staff that run the instructor course, so you can get a good idea of the sort of training you will receive in the instructor course.

The L.A. County program is administered by County employees and is funded by taxpayer dollars. Although the Instructor Association makes most of the decisions regarding the curriculum of the program, the county has a say in anything that affects the finances of the program.

The YMCA is another excellent national certification program, particularly for those who want to make a career within the structure of the "Y" organization. Like most of the other national certifications, if you are certified through the YMCA you can offer a scuba course anywhere you choose. The YMCA is a not–for–profit agency and trains divers all over the world.

The YMCA scuba instructor's program is run by the National YMCA headquarters located in Georgia. Regional instructor courses are sanctioned by YMCA headquarters under the direction of local instructors. YMCA Headquarters holds an annual instructors' conference with special education programs each year. There are approximately 1300 YMCA instructors worldwide.

NAUI is a not-for-profit educational association, where all the money that is not used for the direct operation of the organization is plowed back into the development of new training materials and other products that will benefit the members. The board of directors that provides the planning for the association takes no salary for their work.

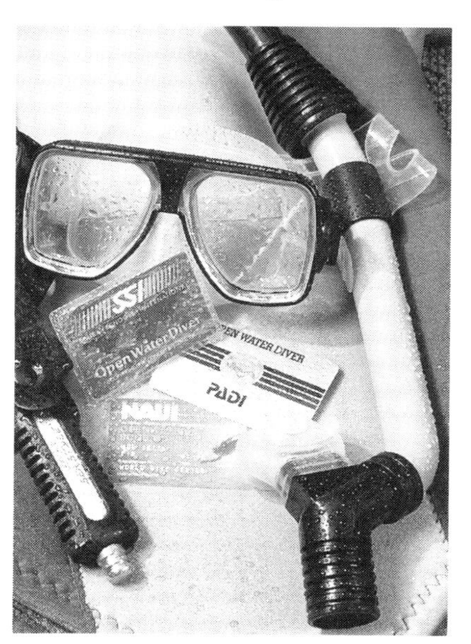

Fig. 2.4 – Different training agencies have different philosophies about diving instruction.

NAUI is unique among all scuba instructor programs in that NAUI is the only agency that is governed by a board of directors that is elected by its membership. This means that every NAUI instructor has a say in how the organization is governed and the membership has direct input on the development of standards and their revisions.

At NAUI, as well as the YMCA, if the staff of your instructor course does not feel you have the proper attitude towards diving instruction they have the option to not certify you. At the end of an instructor course, the staff evaluates each candidate on their overall attitude and performance. If there is any question about a candidate's abilities, the question is asked, "Would you allow this person to teach your loved ones, i.e., wife, children, parents, etc., to dive?" If the staff does not feel that they would trust you with this responsibility, they will not certify you.

Although NAUI started in the U.S. with their first instructor course in Houston in 1960, they now certify instructors all over the world. NAUI courses are offered in Japan, Australia, Canada, Mexico, and many other locations.

NAUI annually runs the International Conference on Underwater Education, also known as "IQ." This conference is designed to bring together diving educators from around the world to discuss the latest in diving and teaching techniques. NAUI has run this program since the 1970's.

PADI (the Professional Association of Diving Instructors) is the largest instructor certifying organization in the world. Like most of the other certifying organizations, PADI offers instructors training programs in many foreign countries. They have developed extensive training materials in numerous languages. The quality of their materials is excellent.

PADI also has a very strong network of dive stores with support programs for their retailers. They have a complete system of sales training and materials. The organization is heavily involved in dive travel through the PADI International Resort Association.

PADI is owned and operated by John Cronin, former president of U.S. Divers, along with several other share holders. PADI is run for the profit of its owners. While PADI members do not have a vote in the operation of PADI, they are routinely consulted by PADI headquarters, both formally and informally, on the operations, standards, and protocols of PADI.

One of the biggest advantages of being a PADI instructor is that there are more dive stores affiliated with PADI than with any other agency. This provides more ready opportunities for PADI instructors to teach than with the other agencies. PADI has also developed many resources to help dive store owners train their staff and manage their stores.

SSI (Scuba Schools International) is another privately held certifying organization, located in Ft. Collins, Colorado. SSI was started by CEO Bob Clark. Bob's son Gary, and his two daughters Linda and

Laurie are also part of the SSI staff. SSI employs 30 people at their headquarters. The president and executive director of SSI is Ed Christini, who has been with the association for many years.

SSI is supported by a strong membership network that consists of over 300 retail stores in the United States. SSI has over 400 international stores and resorts on five continents and in more than 50 countries. SSI's regional centers in countries such as Australia and Brazil each provide services, products, and training to the stores, schools, and resorts in their part of the world. The size of SSI is limited by its policy of working only through professional schools, stores, and resorts. As an SSI instructor you must be affiliated with, and work through an SSI retail member, educational member, or resort member.

SSI has developed their extensive line of student, instructor, and business support products through their parent company, Concept Systems, Inc. SSI has their own in-house video production company and their diver training materials are excellent. SSI materials are available in many foreign languages.

Some of the training agencies are more strict in their requirements than others. For example, some agencies will allow you to teach your course in any way you see fit, as long as it meets their national standards. Other agencies will require you to use their lesson plans and training aids with no deviations.

There are a variety of other instructor organizations in the United States at this time. These include IDEA (International Diving Educators Association), NASDS (the National Association of Scuba Diving Stores), NASE (National Association of Scuba Educators, MDEA (Multinational Diving Educators Association), and PDIC (Professional Diving Instructors Corp.). These associations have structures similar to those already discussed and are worth your consideration when you are deciding which agency you want to join. See the directory at the end of this chapter for contact information on all the dive certification agencies.

Taking the Instructor Training Course

Before you attend any instructor course, take the time to find out who will be running the course. The philosophy, attitude, and capability of the course director will have a large impact on your experience at the course. Try to find other instructors who have attended an instructor course taught by this person to see how they rate the course director and their staff. You need to know what the course director expects and any personal biases that may affect your completion of the course.

Attending an instructor certification course is a demanding experience, but it can be fun if you are properly prepared. For it to be enjoyable you must be in good physical condition, well rested, and mentally prepared. If you are not, the experience will be extremely stressful and unpleasant.

You should arrive at the instructor course with all the materials specified by the course director. This includes all your diving equipment and any teaching materials you are expected to provide. For example, most agencies will provide an instructor's teaching manual and every instructor candidate is expected to own a copy and be familiar with it.

In addition to the items that you are instructed to bring, there are several extra items that will help ensure your success at the course. Most candidates find it helpful to bring along at least a portion of their diving technical library, including books on diving physiology, marine life, oceanography, and similar topics.

Some agencies expect you to teach using their training aids exclusively, such as slides or videos. Other agencies, such as L.A. County, the YMCA, and NAUI will want to see your creativity as an instructor and will expect you to develop your own training aids. If you choose to join one of these agencies, you not only should develop your own training aids prior to the course, but also bring the materials to make up training aids on the spot should you need them. Some of the items you should bring with you to do this include a small blackboard, clear acetate for preparing transparencies for use on an overhead projector, colored marking pens, and poster board.

If there are written exams given at the course you should be totally prepared for the exams prior to your arrival at the course. There is usually little or no time to prepare for any exams at the course itself. Study the recommended texts before the course and know the material in them inside and out.

Instructor candidates will be given the tools to construct and deliver lectures on all topics to be covered in an entry level scuba course. Throughout the course each candidate will have the opportunity to practice, and eventually present for graded evaluation, specific oral presentations on different topics within the scuba course curriculum. This aspect of the ITC takes lots of practice. The skills acquired here will carry over and determine how well the individual can teach in all areas of an entry level course (classroom, confined water, and open water).

An example of such an exercise might be: *Give a seven minute oral presentation on the features, function, selection and care of a mask*, or, *in ten minutes highlight the definition, cause, symptoms, first aid, treatment and prevention of air embolism.* (Some topics will be so complex, the candidate will need to narrow down how much information can be adequately and effectively covered within the time allowed.)

As with the oral presentations, instructor candidates are usually given specific pool teaching skills to teach a simulated group of students (usually other candidates in the program). They will be evaluated on their ability to organize the group, introduce the skill to be taught, effectively teach that skill to the students, give the students a chance to practice the skill, and critique and review their mastery of the skill afterward.

There is a strong emphasis on *control* of the group anytime in-water exercises are being taught, for reasons of safety. Many other things come into play such as, effective use of time, effective use of the pool or facility, most effective placement of students during the introduction and demonstration of a skill, as well as during the execution of the skill. Students must be able to hear and see the instructor well, and the instructor must be able to see all the students. Consideration must be given to keeping students busy enough to remain interested, and so they do not get too cold. Safety must always be foremost in the instructor-candidate's mind when having students practice skills in the water. A lecture on the subject of confined water or pool teaching is usually offered sometime during the ITC.

Open water instruction is perhaps the most critical time an instructor spends with students, and therefore, the same is true for the

Fig. 2.5 – This instructor is demonstrating good control of his group of students.

instructor candidate during training. Again, candidates are usually asked to teach all or part of a typical training dive to a group of simulated students. Every aspect of this phase is carefully evaluated, from the predive briefing on the beach, to the entry, surface swim, buoyancy checks, descent, underwater activity, ascent, exit and debriefing. This is the highest risk environment a student will face during a scuba course, and therefore the most important for the instructor candidate to handle well. This is the place where the candidate's own watermanship comes into play.

If you complete the instructor course satisfactorily you are free to begin teaching as soon as you want, provided you have the required liability insurance for teaching in the U.S. If you have a slight weakness in one area, some agencies will designate you as a "*provisional instructor*," with the requirement that you make up the deficiency in a specified manner within a specific period of time. There is nothing to be embarrassed about if you are certified as a provisional instructor. Some of the top instructors in the country today started their career this way.

Fig. 2.6 – Teaching in the open water environment is the most demanding location where diving instructors work. Here an instructor evaluates a student during a simulated out-of-air emergency.

Tools of the Trade

As a full time diving instructor you will need to equip yourself with several items that are specific to dive instruction. Aside from your personal diving equipment you will need some specialty items including safety gear, training materials, administrative items, and insurance. You should have these items on hand from the first day you start to teach.

Your personal diving equipment should be in excellent condition, and you should have sufficient spares to cover most normal situations.

Every instructor should carry a spare regulator, mask and snorkel, and extra weights. These are essential in the event any of your personal equipment is damaged, lost, or forgotten, or a student forgets or loses equipment.

Safety gear is very important to help prevent accidents and to help ensure the health of your students in the event of an accident. Every instructor should have at least one safety float with an anchoring system. These are used for surface support and rescue. You should also have an oxygen system, a tool and spares kit, and a complete first aid kit.

If you are working as an independent instructor you will probably want your own slide projector and/or VCR with monitor. You will also need training aids, whether you make them yourself or buy them from your agency. If you work for a dive shop or other organization this equipment is usually supplied by them.

Fig. 2.7 – There are many different tools available to help today's instructors teach diving.

One of the major considerations for independent instructors is providing diving equipment for their students. This can be very expensive. Some independents choose to purchase the gear to teach their courses while others rent theirs from a local shop. If you choose to provide your own equipment then you are responsible for all repairs and maintenance records on this gear.

You cannot teach without liability insurance because all certification agencies require this today before they will allow you to renew your membership or issue cards to students. While professional teaching liability insurance has been increasing every year, it is still a bargain compared to the insurance that doctors and other professionals must carry. Liability insurance is used to pay for your defense in court in the event one of your students has an accident and is injured, and you are sued.

If you are an independent instructor and want to teach full time, you will need additional materials to support your business. For example, you will probably want a personal computer to help prepare support materials, such as course schedules and handouts. In addition, the computer can be used to handle all your business correspondence, create a database for mailings to past students, and to do your bookkeeping.

Teaching Environments for the Diving Instructor

Diving instructors work in many different environments today. Some work in dive stores, others work as independents, and still others work in academic environments and resorts. Each different teaching environment presents different challenges and opportunities.

Working and teaching in a dive store usually presents the most entry level situations for the new instructor. If you work for a store, your pay rate for teaching will usually be a bit higher than you make on an hourly basis for sales. Your in-store hours will be adjusted to suit your teaching load and schedule.

Diving instruction through a dive store provides a great deal of variety. You may teach both large and small groups and private lessons, too. Your classes will be made up of a wide range of people, from high school students to housewives. Some people will be in excellent physical condition, while others are not. Your students will have varying intellectual ability. This can be a challenging teaching situation.

Retail dive stores are the most common place to find work as a diving instructor. There are hundreds of dive stores across the country, almost all of whom offer diving instruction. Which training agency you choose may affect which stores you will be able to work with, as some retail stores affiliate with only certain training agencies.

The average retail store will pay an instructor between $50 - 100/per student for entry level courses. There is a wide range, so you need to ask the right questions when seeking work. Some stores will offer additional "perks," such as discounts on purchases of dive gear, discounts or free space on boat dives, and some will even pay for your instructor liability insurance. Be sure to find out everything you will be given as part of your contract with a retail store. Also, be sure to find out what kind of schedule you will be expected to teach under.

Some stores are more flexible than others, while some will only allow instruction for so many hours, on certain days, no more or less. Frequently stores will have their own curriculum of what is to be covered during which session, so that students who miss a class or do not pass can "drop-in" for make-ups.

Be sure to find out what your responsibility is for make-up dives or lectures for students who miss class. If you aren't careful, you could spend a lot of your own unpaid time doing make-ups. Also be sure to find out if the store expects you to certify every student who enrolls in a class. It is extremely important to realize from the start that *not everyone should be certified* - and once you sign that card, you have a moral and legal obligation to decide if that card should be issued. Be sure that all the terms and conditions of your employment are spelled out before you begin any contract arrangement. This will help to avoid any unexpected surprises, and help ensure a good relationship with the store for years to come.

Working as an independent instructor offers the most freedom, but also puts the burden of promoting your courses and handling all the administrative functions on you. When you work for a shop, the shop will usually sign up students for the classes, order the textbooks, schedule classrooms and boat dives, and perform other similar chores. When you're on your own, the responsibility is entirely yours.

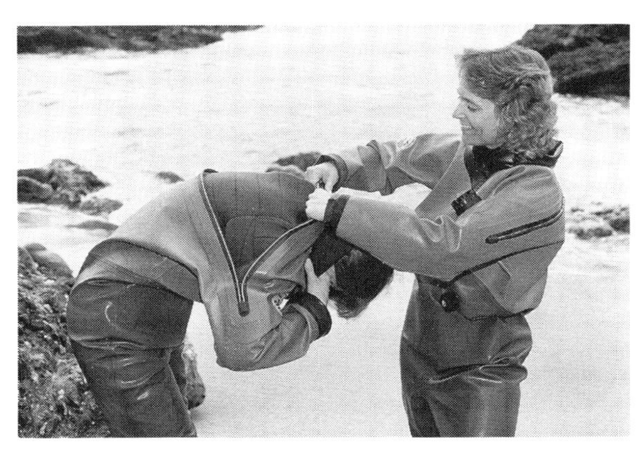

Fig. 2.8 – Teaching private and specialty courses is one of the best ways to be successful as an independent instructor. Scuba instructor Ronnie Damico assists a student during a dry suit specialty course.

Teaching diving in an academic environment, such as a high school or university, can be very rewarding. The caliber of students is usually quite high and most are in excellent physical condition. Due to the extended nature of the academic semester, the courses can be quite complete.

One of the restrictions to teaching in the academic environment is that most schools will require that you have an academic degree, or even a teaching degree, to be employed as full time staff. Some schools do allow scuba instructors to teach diving without academic credentials, particularly for elective or recreation courses, but this is not true in all situations.

For the diving instructor with academic qualifications, the academic environment can be a nice place to teach. Most schools offer excellent benefit packages and many other advantages. Not to be overlooked are the several months of summer vacation available to most teachers in the academic environment.

Although one might imagine that being an instructor at a resort or on a liveaboard dive boat would be very enjoyable, the reality is that like being a dive guide, these jobs can be very stressful. Teaching people to dive in a resort setting places a great deal of pressure on the instructor. First, you must deal with the fact that people who take diving lessons at a resort are on vacation, and are not necessarily in the mood to spend time studying a book. Secondly, since most resort courses are a week or less in length, this means that as an instructor you must be better than average to ensure that your students comprehend all the material you present in a short span of time.

Finally, one of the difficult aspects in teaching in a resort environment can be dealing with the family or friends of the people who are enrolled in your course. These people can make it very difficult for you as an instructor, especially if they want to watch you teach, or accompany their traveling companions during training dives. These situations require a great deal of tact on the part of the instructor so as not to offend the guests of the resort. People who are on vacation expect to be catered to, and rightly so, since they are spending a great deal of money for their enjoyment. As an instructor you must balance giving the customer what they want and making sure that you are not compromising the safety of your students.

Professional Conduct for Diving Instructors

To be a successful instructor it is essential to maintain your professional competence. This means that it is vital for you to continue to develop your knowledge of diving all the time, especially as the technical aspects of diving change. To keep abreast of the changes in diving it is very important for you to read diving magazines and books, attend conferences and symposiums, and meet with fellow instructors in your area to discuss changes in the standards of practice in your area. If you do not maintain professional competence, and one of your students suffers an accident, your career could be on the line and you could suffer serious professional and financial consequences.

As a diving instructor you should project a professional image at all times. You are a public figure and people will be watching you to see how you behave. This means that you must be careful how you behave if you expect people to give you a good recommendation to their friends and other divers. If you do not like this type of scrutiny then teaching may not be the job for you.

Just as punctuality is important in any job, it is particularly important when you are teaching. It is hard to expect your students to be punctual if you are not. Your classes should begin and end on time. If you are teaching for a store or a school they will demand this of you. If you are teaching as an independent you will turn your students "off" if you are habitually late.

When you are teaching, it is also important to dress for the role. This does not mean that you need to wear a business suit to teach scuba, but it does mean that you should be neat and clean. In certain teaching environments, such as the Caribbean, a pair of shorts and a T-shirt may be appropriate dress. However, your shorts and T-shirt should be clean and without holes. Shirts with obscene or suggestive drawings or language is also inappropriate. For teaching in most dive stores, a clean pair of slacks and a polo shirt are the usual attire.

Just as you must dress properly in the classroom, your diving equipment should also be neat and well maintained. Your professional image is at stake.

Your personal conduct, especially while you are in front of the class, must be fitting. It is not acceptable for an instructor to smoke, chew tobacco, drink alcoholic beverages, or indulge in profanity while teaching. You must be fair and impartial when dealing with students and set aside any personal prejudices you might have.

Although you may be personally attracted to members of your class, or they may be emotionally attracted to you, you must not engage in any personal relationships with your students. If you want to date a student after the course is completely over, that's another matter, but don't get involved until the course has ended.

As a diving instructor it is vital that you keep fit. This means that you must be more than fit enough to dive. You must be fit enough to rescue a diver under the most demanding conditions that are possible in your area. If you stop teaching for awhile be sure that you evaluate your personal fitness before you resume.

Working as a Diving Instructor

Every certification agency has developed a set of minimum standards that govern how scuba diving will be taught by their instructors. When you teach scuba diving you must always adhere to the standards of the association that you certify your students through. This is imperative. If you violate your agency's standards you place both yourself and your students at risk. The training standards developed by your association are the result of the experience of many diving instructors. If one of your students should have an accident because you have violated some aspect of the standards it will be very difficult, or impossible, to defend yourself in a court of law.

Depending upon where you teach, your hours and days as a diving instructor may be quite long. If you teach diving through an academic program at a university, your classes may take place any time during the school day or evening. Conversely, if you teach diving through a dive store, many classes are offered at night or on the weekends when people are not working.

Fig. 2.9 – Many diving classes are taught at night. Instructor Curt Wiessner runs his dive store during the day and teaches classes during the evenings and on weekends.

When you teach you not only must carry all your personal dive gear, but you will also need to make sure you have any extra equipment you require for teaching. Specifically, this includes both spares and items like your oxygen system and first aid kit.

As a teacher you are an entertainer. This means that your class must be interesting and enjoyable for people to learn from you. You are "on stage" when you teach diving, and you owe it to your students to make sure that they get their money's worth. You cannot allow your personal life to interfere with your class. When you walk in the door to teach, you must put your personal problems aside and smile, giving your students 100% of your attention and abilities. If you teach a boring, uninspired course you have let your students down. You also will not get too many referrals from past students.

Teaching not only requires classroom time, it also requires preparation time and cleanup time after each class. Prior to going to class you should take the time to review the material for the day's session so that it is fresh in your mind, even if you have taught it before. You also must be sure to arrive early enough so that you can check that the classroom or pool is the way you want it to be. You must allow enough time to set up any audio visual equipment.

When you start a new class there are student record folders that must be set up and administrative paperwork to handle. After class, there are always papers to grade, quizzes to file, and C-card orders to be sent in. Your files should be well kept and orderly, not only to allow you to find the files for students who lose their cards, but also because your files can be subpoenaed if one of your students ever has an accident. Most certification agencies now require their instructors to maintain the files on past students for a minimum of five years for legal purposes. Certain agencies, such as SSI, require that the store maintains the records rather than the instructor.

Many diving instructors do not teach diving full time, but have other jobs that they pursue on the side, or in conjunction with their teaching, such as working in a dive store, or as a dive guide. Part of the reason for this is that teaching diving, historically, has not paid well, particularly if you teach for a dive store.

To make ends meet, many diving instructors must do other things to live a comfortable life style. There are instructors who make a good living teaching diving full time, but they are few. The ones who are successful have carved out unique market niches for themselves and are able to command a good price for their instruction.

Experiences of Diving Instructors

ERIC HANAUER

Eric Hanauer is a well known diving instructor, underwater photographer, and author. He started diving in 1959 after he got out of the army, although he had a hard time choosing between scuba and skydiving. As Eric puts it, "scuba won out because it fit in better with my aquatics background, and it was cheaper!"

Although he became a YMCA scuba instructor in 1961, Eric maintains he wasn't too active in diving for the first seven years that he was certified. He was more concerned with teaching swimming and coaching the swim team at the Chicago high school where he was teaching.

In 1964 Eric moved to Los Angeles to attend graduate school at UCLA. While there he worked under Dr. Glen Egstrom, who did research in diver performance, and met Otto Gasser, another Southern California diver and fellow graduate student. Gasser helped introduce him to the ways of California diving. Egstrom encouraged Eric to take the L.A. County instructor's course, which he passed in 1965. It was during the L.A. County course that he honed his diving skills and became proficient in open water diving techniques.

After completing his master's degree at UCLA, Eric took a job at Newport Harbor High School. While teaching there he introduced the "grab start" for competitive swimming, that has become the standard for swim teams all over the world.

Fig. 2.10 – Instructor Eric Hanauer teaches diving at California State University at Fullerton. (Photo courtesy of Eric Hanauer.)

When California State University at Fullerton opened in 1966, it was his scuba instructor's rating that got Eric his job, although he also taught swimming and coached the water polo and swim teams. Now, more than 26 years later, he is still at Cal State Fullerton.

At first, even at Cal State Fullerton, scuba diving was still secondary to coaching in Eric's life. He was making between 50 and 75 dives a year, with most of his diving taking place during his classes, with a bit of underwater hunting on the side. He also became the school's scientific diving safety officer (see Chapter 7 for more information on this career path).

By 1974 Cal State Fullerton wanted to move on to a higher division in athletics, but Hanauer wanted out of coaching. During this period in his life, he was sharing a house with two other bachelors who were both hard core divers. One of his roommates, a marine biologist named Mike Curtis, persuaded Eric to join him on a trip to Cabo San Lucas, Mexico, along with five other divers. A new highway had just opened, making it possible to drive from Tijuana to the tip of Baja. There were no maps or guidebooks for this new Mexican highway.

While he was in Mexico, Eric had many adventures. When it came time to return home to coach a swim meet, Eric didn't want to leave. He called the school and told them he would be a week late and asked his assistant to coach the meet, staying on in Baja to continue diving. Diving had become the major interest in his life and took up the gap that coaching had left. It was also during this time that Eric became active in underwater photography.

Eric had written numerous articles for swimming journals, so writing about diving came naturally. He combined his writing with his photography and sold his first article to *Skin Diver* magazine in 1977. Initially, he wrote a single article a year, but quickly received assignments from *Skin Diver* for equipment reviews.

Eric met his wife, Dr. Mia Tegner, at a meeting of scientific divers, but it wasn't until they accidentally ended up on a dive trip together that they started dating. They were married within a year. Together, with Mia, they have traveled around the world on diving trips.

For Eric, "Writing is just another way of teaching. Instead of reaching six people in a dive class, you're reaching and influencing thousands of people." Eric's writing and photos have appeared in numerous diving publications including *Discover Diving, Rodale's Scuba Diving*, and *Underwater USA*. He has also written a book on diving in the Red Sea that was published by Watersport Publishing.

Today Eric teaches all forms of aquatic courses at Cal State Fullerton. His diving classes include Open Water I and advanced scuba. He oversees a small group of scientific divers and their activities in the school's biology department.

"Teaching in a university environment is intellectually stimulating," says Eric. "We teach a 15 week Open Water scuba course that lasts 70 hours. The students are motivated and in a course worth three units we can demand a lot. I wouldn't want to teach diving any other way."

Eric averages between 120 and 150 dives a year. Many of his dives are overseas, rather than in the U.S.

As a university instructor, Eric gets a considerable amount of vacation time. During the summer he has three months off, and at Christmas he gets six weeks off. He also recently was awarded a *sabbatical*, a semester off from teaching with pay, to write two new books; one on diving pioneers, and one on diving in Micronesia.

Another positive aspect of teaching in a university environment is that you have instant access to information. If you have a question on oceanography, you can call a professor in that department. You can do the same thing with questions on physics, biology, and physiology.

On the negative side, Eric realizes that his salary is less than he could make if he worked in another type of job. He also dislikes the fact that he and his wife Mia must live apart much of the time, since she lives and works in La Jolla, and Eric lives and works in Fullerton. They have a commuter marriage, with approximately one and a half hours of drive time separating them. "When you work in academia, your job is not usually mobile. You can't always choose where you will work and live," admits Eric.

Eric's advice to anyone who is considering teaching in a college setting is to go all the way and get a doctorate. This will help assure you the possibility of some stability in the university environment.

"In today's uncertain economic environment many schools are dropping programs, like scuba, that are considered "frills." It's not a promising job situation," observes Eric. "Most people who teach in a university setting get hired to teach physical education programs and then build their scuba "empire" once they're inside."

TONY ZARIKOS

Tony Zarikos teaches diving and diving related courses full time, in the Northeastern U.S., between Connecticut and Massachusetts. Besides teaching Open Water courses, Tony also teaches oxygen administration, nitrox diving, dry suit diving, deep diving, wreck diving, and salvage. His only income is from teaching diving.

Tony was born in Greece and started snorkeling and spearfishing there when he was a child. In the suburb of Athens where he lived, the sea was never far away. Diving was part of the family culture, and learning to dive, informally, was considered a rite of passage to manhood. He began using scuba at the age of 12 in 1966. During high school, Tony would go spearfishing with his friends.

Zarikos left Greece to attend college in Germany where he studied engineering. While there he became interested in teaching and began studying how to teach. He lived in various locations in Europe from 1973-1986 and was married during this period.

Fig. 2.11 – Independent diving instructor Tony Zarikos teaches diving full time.

In 1986 Tony came to the U.S. when his wife got a scholarship to attend Harvard University. To help support his wife and himself he taught at the Greek-American school in Boston. He became active in diving in the U.S., became a PADI instructor in 1989, and started teaching diving full time.

Tony teaches between 200 and 250 students a year. Between 60 and 70 of his students are entry level while the remainder take advanced courses of instruction. He trains 20-30 divemasters each year. He teaches through several dive stores and does private instruction as well. He makes 350 to 400 dives in a busy year and 250 dives in what he calls a "dry year."

"If you can market diving and yourself properly, you can survive in this business," says Tony. He enjoys making money teaching, as well as the physical and intellectual challenges in diving.

While the market potential for diving in the U.S. is great, Tony does not enjoy the politics of the diving industry. "Why can't we leave the politics out of diving education?" asks Tony, citing the rivalries between some of the training agencies and manufacturers. "We are talking about the quality of instruction and people's lives when we teach diving. Too many people are only concerned with whether they have covered a subject adequately for legal purposes."

Tony's tips for someone considering a career as a scuba instructor are to know your limitations as a diver, and to ask yourself if you can handle the burden of taking care of other people. You must have the right motivation to teach. You can't teach solely for the glory or the money.

"Your learning doesn't stop when you become a scuba instructor," explains Tony. "Whenever I go to a new area, I always consult the local experts to learn everything I can from them. Someday when I am older, there will be a 20 year old scuba instructor who will take my place and pass on what I have learned."

ED CHRISTINI

Ed Christini is the President of Scuba Schools International (SSI). In less than twenty years he has risen from his initial certification as a diver to being the president of one of the leading certification agencies in the world.

Ed started diving in Ohio in 1974 when he took a NASDS scuba course. At the time he was working in interior design for a specialty furniture store and had a background in sales. With a boat on Lake Erie, Ed began diving with visions of wreck exploration as his motivation to learn scuba.

In a short time Ed became a diving "fanatic." A self-proclaimed "dive store groupie," Ed spent all his free time diving, hanging out at the dive store, and assisting with dive classes. The dive season in Ohio was concentrated between April and November, and Ed went diving almost every weekend during those months.

Fig. 2.12 – Ed Christini is the president of Scuba Schools International. (Photo courtesy of SSI.)

In 1976 Ed attended an SSI instructor course, taught by SSI founder Bob Clark. He began teaching part-time during the evenings and on weekends.

By late 1977 Christini had purchased the dive store where he was teaching and gone into the diving business full time. He moved the store to a new location where he ran it until 1984. The store certified approximately 125 divers each year.

Bob Clark approached Ed in 1982 and asked him if he wanted to represent SSI on a part-time basis in the Great Lakes region. Ed agreed and began recruiting new SSI stores and instructors. He also began working with Dive Rescue International (see Chapter 11 on Search and Rescue diving) and got involved with the local sheriff's dive team.

The following year Clark asked Ed to consider working for SSI on a full time basis.

Ed accepted Clark's offer and moved to Ft. Collins in 1984. He was initially hired as the sales director and was promoted to executive director in 1986.

It was an emotional moment for Ed when Clark announced his promotion to executive director as a surprise at the 1986 DEMA (Diving Equipment Manufacturer's Association) show. He hadn't been told of his promotion prior to its announcement at the annual SSI dealer's meeting held at the DEMA show. Surrounded by SSI dealers from across the country, many of whom are his personal friends, Ed was extremely proud of the trust that Clark had placed in him.

As the executive director Ed ran numerous SSI instructor courses and instructor trainer courses. The position involved extensive diving. In 1992 Ed was promoted to president of SSI. Bob Clark is now the CEO and Chairman of the Board. SSI has over 300 stores in the U.S. and is represented in 11 other countries including Australia, New Zealand, Japan, Singapore, the U.K., and Germany.

Being the president of an international diver training agency places many demands on Ed, who now focuses on the day-to-day operation of SSI. In his present position he makes approximately 50 dives a year.

Ed takes great pleasure in interacting with SSI's retail members and instructors. He enjoys meeting with them to discover their needs and working with his staff to work out ways for SSI to help its members. He finds it very rewarding to have an impact on the diving business at the retail level.

In Ed's position, travel can be an enormous burden, especially when you consider how many countries SSI serves. For example, in 1992 Ed traveled to the DEMA show in Florida, to Japan, to England twice, to Germany, to the Red Sea, to Spain, and to the next year's DEMA show, all as separate trips. Although the travel sounds glamorous and exciting, it is exhausting. After Ed returns from a trip, he still has to go into the SSI office and do his daily job, and maintain his family and personal life as well.

Lawsuits are a fact of life in diving instruction today, and Ed finds dealing with them to be one of the most distasteful parts of his job. Frequently, when a diving accident occurs during instruction, not only is the instructor sued, but the training agency is sued as well. Although an agency may have only one or two lawsuits a year, they involve endless hours of preparation in research and discovery. Even when the instructor and the store have done everything right, if there is an accident, the risk of being sued is always present.

Christini recommends that anyone who wants to work in the organizational end of diving get themselves a good background in diving. It is essential to develop an understanding of the problems of both the instructor and the retail store operator. You must understand the rationale behind training standards before you can make good policy decisions. Get as much leadership and retail experience as possible.

NORM MADISON

Norm Madison started diving in 1974 when he was 28 years old because he was jealous of a friend who went diving for lobster. For Norm, this was a big step, since he didn't know how to swim, and actually took swimming and diving lessons simultaneously. He took his lessons at El Camino College in Southern California. At the time he learned to dive he was working for the telephone company as a lineman.

A few months later Norm enrolled in the Los Angeles County's Advanced Diver Program (ADP). The course opened up diving for him even further, giving him new confidence and knowledge.

Norm started diving actively and put in over 100 hours in the water during his first year. He was diving two or three times a week.

In 1978 Norm enrolled in the L.A. County ADP again so he could meet new people to be his dive buddies. During the program he got talked into taking the L.A. County instructor course and subsequently enrolled. The instructor course improved both his water skills and knowledge even further, and he truly enjoyed the challenge it represented. He completed the course and crossed over to NAUI during a weekend session that was part of the program.

Fig. 2.13 – Norm Madison teaches diving through the L.A. County and NAUI programs.

Norm became heavily involved as a volunteer working with the L.A. County program and was a team leader for ADP programs and the instructor course. In 1981 Norm ran the ADP program and there were over 200 divers enrolled in the course.

During the ADP course, Norm was witness to a traumatic diving accident. A 29 year old diver who was enrolled in ADP had an undiagnosed heart condition. During emergency ascent training in the ocean Norm was working with this student. After completing a successful emergency ascent, the diver, upon surfacing, yelled for help and passed out. Norm immediately began to resuscitate the diver, and took him to the beach, where he administered CPR with the help of another instructor on the staff. A Coast Guard helicopter was summoned and transported Norm and student to the Catalina Island hyperbaric chamber. The young man never recovered. Only after the student was autopsied did it become apparent that he had a serious, previously undiagnosed heart defect, and that he had died of a heart attack.

For some time after the accident Norm was ready to quit teaching. Fortunately, he was able to overcome his feelings of guilt and resume his teaching career.

In 1982 Norm was voted the outstanding instructor of the year by the L.A. County Underwater Instructor's Association. Although he was still working for the phone company, Norm became more heavily involved with diving instruction. He began teaching for several different dive stores, and taught courses at Santa Monica Community College, West L.A. College, and the Beverly Hills YMCA.

Norm began teaching with another instructor, David Moss, through an organization that David had formed called Pacific School of Scuba, Inc. in 1986. By 1990 the business had evolved into a dive shop, and Norm became the Director of Education for the store in 1992. He admits that when times are slow he still must do additional outside work to make ends meet.

Norm teaches approximately ten Open Water I classes each year, two advanced classes, two rescue courses, and one divemaster course a year. He averages 120 open water dives annually. By 1993 Norm had certified more than 700 divers.

Norm Madison finds many positive things to enjoy about teaching. He likes exposing people to a new environment, the sea, that they might never have experienced otherwise. He finds that when he returns from a dive he feels totally rejuvenated.

In most of the teaching that goes on at the Pacific School of Scuba, Norm finds himself frequently handling problem students from the other instructors' courses. He enjoys helping these people overcome their fears. "We alter people's lives,"observes Norm.

Getting into a cold, wet, wetsuit is not always Norm's idea of fun, especially when the weather isn't great. He also does not enjoy dealing with the logistical problems of making arrangements for teaching courses.

For Norm, the most unpleasant aspect of teaching is dealing with that rare person whom he cannot certify. "You know you're doing it for their own safety, but frequently they are still upset with you and want to dive anyway," says Norm.

While you might suppose that it would be difficult to be a black scuba instructor in a sport that has traditionally been dominated by white males, Norm has not found this to be the case. "There are no boundaries of color in diving," he says. "I have found acceptance without prejudice in the industry."

For Additional Information Contact:

Los Angeles County Underwater Unit, 419 E. 192nd St., Carson, CA., 90746. Tel. (310) 327-5311

National Association of Underwater Instructors, 4650 Arrow Hwy., Suite F-1, Montclair, CA., 91763. Tel. (909) 621-5801

National Academy of Scuba Educators, 1728 Kingsley Ave. #6, Orange Park, FL 32073. Tel. (904) 264-4104

Professional Association of Diving Instructors, 1251 E. Dyer Rd. #100, Santa Ana, CA., 92705. Tel. (714) 540-7234

PDIC International, 1554 Gardner Ave., Scranton, PA. 18509. Tel. (717) 342-9434

Scuba Schools International, 2619 Canton Ct., Ft. Collins, CO., 80525. Tel. (303) 482-0883

National Association of Scuba Diving Stores, 8099 Indiana Ave., Riverside, CA., 92504. Tel. (714) 687-8792

National Association of Scuba Educators, 1728 Kingsley Ave., Suite 6, Orange Park, FL. 32073. Tel. (904) 264-4104

YMCA National Scuba Program, 6083-A Oakbrook Pkwy., Norcross, GA. 30093. Tel. (404) 662-5172

Suggested Reading:

All of the training agencies publish their own instructor manuals. We recommend reading them if you are considering becoming an instructor. Contact the agencies listed above to purchase these manuals.

Coren, E. Steven. *The Law and the Diving Professional.* International PADI, Inc. Santa Ana, CA. 1986

Chapter Three

DIVE STORE OWNERSHIP, MANAGEMENT, & EMPLOYMENT

In the early days of sport diving, dive stores were run by divers with little or no business background. Those divers whose stores survived had to learn to become business people the hard way, by doing it.

When the sport was just starting out, it was before the time of the giant discount store. The business atmosphere was more forgiving and many part-time dive stores existed for years.

To run a successful dive store today, you must be at least as much of a business person as a diver. You must be willing to put in long hours, with an understanding of everything from accounting to marketing.

Fig. 3.1 – Smaller dive stores must work very hard to compete with today's retail sporting goods giants.

The Modern Dive Store

The modern dive store is tremendously different from stores in the past. Many use personal computers to automate their businesses, running everything from their rental department to inventory, newsletters, and mailing lists. To run a successful retail diving operation in the current business environment you must be highly organized and competitive.

The retail end of the diving business is all about sales. To make it in the industry, you must like to sell, and be able to "close" (complete) sales. The best salespeople are those who truly believe in the products they sell and don't load customers up with diving equipment they don't need and will never use. Salespeople with a conscience know that it is in their best interests in the long run to be honest with their customers because most business comes from repeat sales.

In the modern dive store, it is essential for you to be computer literate. Whether you are an owner, a manager, or a salesperson, a good understanding of computers will help you go a long way. For owners and managers there are many simple accounting packages that will allow you to keep your business records straight without the need for a full time bookkeeper. These programs can speed up your business so that you spend less time keeping your books straight and more time concentrating on sales.

Fig. 3.2 – Computers are an essential part of the modern retail dive store. Dive store owner and instructor Curt Wiessner uses his to update his mailing list.

Every salesperson in the store needs to know how to access and update the customer database, as well as the inventory. The customer database is one of the most valuable assets of the store. A well designed database should have information on each regular customer, including when they were certified, their instructor, what specialty courses they have completed, and what equipment they own. The database is then used for special and general mailings, such as to notify those customers interested in underwater photography about the next underwater photo course, or to inform everyone when there is a boat trip.

Most successful dive stores publish regular newsletters that are used for marketing tools. With a good understanding of your computer, you can do your entire newsletter in-house, except for the printing.

The newsletter is a way to keep customers involved. It contains a mix of both graphics and news items. The best newsletters contain real news about diving events, as well as instructional information and tips on equipment. Ideally, you'll also want to include articles about your customers and their diving adventures, and if at all possible photographs.

Understanding how to merchandise diving equipment is another key to making your dive store profitable. You must have a good understanding of marketing, as well as a feel for what types of products will sell. Making your store attractive through effective displays takes practice, as well as a good eye for color and artistic layout.

Dive travel is an important profit center for the modern dive store, and selling dive travel is a must for the full service dive center. Today's divers are active travelers and many have been on numerous trips to the tropics. Many people like to travel with a group and want to travel with a knowledgeable diver as their leader. Smart diving retailers know this and provide this service for their customers.

Fig. 3.3 – Sport Chalet is a large chain of sporting goods stores in Southern California. Each store contains a complete dive shop and many have indoor pools. They have been very successful at providing a full service dive operation.

New dive stores concentrate on local travel, while more experienced retailers have the ability to sell overseas travel. Without this important service, you will miss a big piece of potential business.

Last, but certainly not least, is the importance of dealing with liability issues. Diving is an adventure sport and as such it has many risks.

The knowledgeable retailer considers all the risks involved and seeks ways to deal with them. Each area of the store has its own areas of risk and every store owner must be familiar with them.

Product liability is one of the primary risks that you must be concerned with if you work in a dive store. Even though you do not manufacture any products you can still be held liable for manufacturing defects under certain situations.

Rental equipment liability is another key area of concern when it comes to running your store responsibly. It is essential to keep accurate records on each item in rental, when it was last serviced, who performed the service, and what items were replaced. Obviously, any employee who performs maintenance or repairs on a piece of diving equipment should be a factory trained technician.

Training to Work in the Retail Dive Business

If you are just starting out in your career, you may want to attend one of the diving instructional colleges that offers courses in retail store management. This is a good option if you have the money and time to do it. Certainly, you will stand a better chance of getting a job if you have taken training courses relating to dive shop operations than an ordinary diver with no background or training.

Some of the more progressive diving retailers do make long term commitments to their employees and spend substantial money on training them. In fact, some stores will even go so far as to put you through an instructor training program at their expense. They may also pay for other sales or business training as well.

One of the best ways to break into the retail diving business is to get your diving instructor rating. This is a good way to get your foot in the door of most dive shops, since many stores must hire additional instructors during the busy summer months. If you do a good job as an instructor and make yourself available to help around the shop you will probably be offered a job at their first opening. See Chapter 2 on scuba instruction for more information on instructor training.

As an outside instructor, another way to build rapport and trust between yourself and the store owner is to work with the store manager in helping your students select their equipment. This can be an excellent way to establish a good relationship with the store. In essence, what you should do is to meet with the store manager and offer to come in, on your own time, to help your students purchase and select their equipment. It's essential to find out what items the store sells and any special packages the store may offer. You only help the students select their gear and the store negotiates the price and writes up the sale. While not all store managers or owners may want you to do this, those that do will be very appreciative of your assistance. If you do a good job, you will undoubtedly be offered a permanent job should an opening in the store occur.

If you are unable to pay for a course in retail dive store management at one of the instructor colleges, you may want to look into business courses at a local community college or trade school. Most state sponsored community colleges have very low tuition rates and offer some excellent vocational training. Consult your local library for the community colleges in your area.

Courses that will help prepare you for dive store management include computer courses, accounting, retail sales, merchandising, marketing, advertising, inventory control, and graphic design. Each of these subject areas are important if you want to achieve the maximum success in the diving business.

As mentioned previously, computer operation is vital to every small business today, including the retail dive store. Some of the types of computer programs you should be familiar with include spreadsheets, word processing, accounting, page layout, inventory control, database management, and graphics. The more capable you are in these subjects the more valuable you will be. The software programs that we have mentioned are all designed to be used by people with a basic understanding of these topics. This makes it important to understand the fundamentals of these subjects through separate courses in these areas.

Spreadsheet programs are used for a variety of functions in the retail dive store. Most importantly, you should know how to use a spreadsheet to show how well each area of the store is doing from a profit standpoint. This will allow you to make corrections to your management plan and improve those areas that aren't doing well. In addition, if you need to borrow money from a bank, a well prepared spreadsheet will present your business in a way that makes bankers comfortable.

Word processing software is used most commonly for your business correspondence, but you may find it helpful in other ways. For example, if you need to prepare informational hand-outs for your students or customers, a good word processing program is the place to start.

There are many excellent accounting packages available for retail operations today that make keeping the books of a dive store simple.

As mentioned previously, most of them will allow you to do your own bookkeeping without the need for a bookkeeper. You will probably want to have a part-time bookkeeper or bookkeeping service help you, but with the computer, keeping your records straight becomes a relatively easy chore. Come tax time, your accountant will be able to do your taxes more quickly with the reports you can generate with your computer.

With a page layout program and a laser printer you can be your own graphic designer and turn out everything from advertisements, to fliers and newsletters. This can save you hundreds or even thousands of dollars, depending upon your own creativity. A newsletter can be one of your best marketing tools, and most of the more successful dive stores publish one.

Good inventory control is one of the keys to making a dive store profitable. It's essential to keep on top of your inventory so that last year's fins don't end up in a corner while you run out of dive lights at the start of lobster season. Today, there are several excellent dedicated software packages or "solutions" for the diving retailer to manage their inventory and integrate their sales data. Some of these packages even have the manufacturer's prices built right into the software to speed things up for you.

Another valuable software skill is understanding how to use a customer database. The customer database allows the modern dive store owner to effectively track his customers, their purchases, and their interests. Knowing how to set up a database is not an essential talent, but it is certainly useful. Understanding how databases work and how to use them is imperative.

The last piece of software you should be able to use is a basic graphics package for creating simple illustrations. While you can buy inexpensive computer generated art to liven up your newsletter or fliers, there will be times when you will want to create your own illustrations, such as maps to dive sites, handouts for courses, and sales fliers. You don't need to be an artist to use these programs, and the illustrations you create will spark interest in your printed pieces.

If you have no sales experience, enroll in a sales training course through a vocational school. If there are no courses in your area there are many excellent books on the art of selling that are available. Remember, that when you are selling something you are not just selling the product, you are also selling yourself. People must trust you before they are willing to buy from you.

People purchase products as solutions to their problems. They buy an item such as an underwater camera for what it will do for them, not for the item itself. Nobody buys a Nikonos to put on the shelf and look at; they acquire it for the pictures it will produce. The same thing is true for any other piece of diving gear, whether it is a regulator or a pair of fins. Good salespeople understand this and seek to help customers find the answers to their problems.

Fig. 3.4 – Attractive displays are essential to enticing customers to buy. Curt Wiessner sets up a display at his California store.

Before you can sell someone a set of dive gear, you must first get them into your store. That's what marketing is all about; getting people to come into your store. Through marketing, you make people aware of the equipment, classes, and other services that your dive shop provides. Advertising is just one form of marketing, but there are many others. Anything that you can do to gain publicity for your store is marketing.

Where your store is located can have a big influence on what you do to market your operation. For example, if you are located near a harbor or marina, your shop might sponsor an underwater cleanup. Such an event is newsworthy, and if you handle things right you can get excellent free publicity through your local newspaper and television stations. Conversely, if you're located in a "landlocked" state, you might gain local attention through sponsoring some type of underwater competition to raise money for charity at your store pool.

Another aspect of marketing includes developing a distinctive store logo for use on baseball caps and other clothing. This logo becomes part of your store identity. Ideally, your logo should be registered as a trademark to prevent unauthorized persons from stealing or using it. You should have an attorney register your logo as a trademark to ensure the paperwork is done properly.

You can also market your store effectively by providing lectures on diving and marine life to local schools and civic groups, sponsoring underwater film festivals, and other similar activities. Many of these events can be done at little or no cost and can generate thousands of dollars of promotion that you could never afford to buy.

Understanding advertising is essential to the successful diving retailer. You can waste thousands of dollars on advertising that is not effective, or you can spend very little on advertising that pays for itself.

One of the keys to a successful diving operation is to remember that it is far more expensive to solicit new customers than it is to nurture and keep the ones you already have. This is one of the reasons why a newsletter is such an effective marketing and advertising tool. With a newsletter you reach your target market of customers who are already divers. These are the people who are most likely to buy high ticket items such as scooters, dive computers, cameras, and dry suits. Your cost for reaching these people is relatively low, compared to the cost of attracting and training new diving students.

If you are able to repair a wide variety of diving equipment this can make you extremely valuable to a dive store owner. Equipment repairs are an important profit center, and the ability to turn equipment around rapidly is critical. Most of the diving manufacturers offer service and repair schools for their equipment, either in-house or in conjunction with trade and consumer diving shows. To attend these courses you usually need to be affiliated with a shop or be an instructor. The more brands of equipment you know how to repair, the more valuable you will make yourself.

Fig. 3.5 – Equipment repair is an important part of a service oriented dive store.

Dive Store Management and Employment

Although many divers have opened dive stores with no prior retail experience, it's a good idea to get a job working in a dive store before investing the time and money in opening a store of your own. You may decide it's not for you!

Working in a dive store is not always fun. The hours are normally long and the pay is usually not great. Most smaller retail stores are not large enough to have retirement packages or good health benefits. However, on the positive side you will usually receive good discounts on equipment, or even free equipment, free air fills, and the opportunity to participate in dive travel at reduced prices or for free.

Most young people who work in diving stores do not make a career of employment in the retail industry. If they stay in the diving business, they usually either go on to work for a manufacturer or eventually may open their own store. Working in a retail store as an employee gives you a good opportunity to learn the business while making a living.

Unless you are an instructor, or have other special training, you will generally start out on the bottom rung at any dive store that will hire you. You will probably end up doing many of the more mundane tasks such as sweeping the floor, filling tanks, cleaning rental equipment, sweeping the pool, and similar jobs.

With time, as you demonstrate your capabilities, you will be given the opportunity to work in positions of greater responsibility. The best way to get promoted, and earn more pay, is to willingly take on tasks of greater responsibility and show that you can do them. It may take some time for your pay to catch up with your abilities, but any good employer will quickly be aware of what you are doing and reward your efforts.

Fig. 3.6 – When you work in a small business there are many mundane tasks that must be done. Dive store manager and instructor Robert Camenzind also vacuums the dive shop where he works on a regular basis.

As a store employee you are expected to know all the technical information regarding the products your store sells, as well as competing products. You should be able to state the features and benefits for each product and explain these in a way that any person can understand, even if they are not technically oriented.

Dive store employees with a professional attitude never say bad things about competing dive shops, they only accentuate the positive. Negative remarks about a competitor or his products are not healthy for the industry and should be avoided.

Managers of retail dive businesses have tremendous responsibilities and must usually work long hours in salaried, not hourly positions. As a manager you may be asked to both open and close the store, work weekends, work evenings, and even work certain holidays. Managers may also find themselves both hiring and firing, and being responsible for the performance evaluations of employees.

Retail Dive Store Ownership

Owning a retail dive store is like any other small business, yet it is very different. There are numerous demands made on the owner of a dive store that are unlike the typical small business operation. In addition to the normal demands of operating the store, the diving retailer must contend with operating a swimming pool, running classes, boat operation or charter, travel, rentals, and numerous other details. There is probably no other recreational activity that makes the kinds of demands that diving does on the retail operator.

To thrive in the retail diving market today, the dive store owner must provide a high level of service to compete with the larger sporting goods stores, such as the Sport Chalet chain in Southern California. These large chains have tremendous buying power and the typical diving section in their stores is comparable to most independent retailers' operations.

In order to compete with the buying power of the large store, the independent diving retailer must find a "niche" or specialty area, because you can't compete on prices with these larger stores. For example, you may offer courses in underwater photography or underwater hunting; or, you may specialize in training divers for leadership levels all the way through the instructor level. The key to survival is to find some type of service that the larger retailer can't or won't provide.

Perhaps the most difficult part of running your own operation is the long hours that you must put in to make your store a success. It is not unusual during the first several years of operation for a store owner to put in 70 hours a week or more. These long hours can take their toll on your health, your sanity, and your personal relationships. Of course, there is also a great deal of satisfaction to be gained in making a success of your own business, as well as the potential for financial gain.

The initial investment to open a retail diving store is usually substantial. In addition to the store lease you must also provide decorations, fixtures, cash registers, and other office equipment. A minimum air compressor installation can easily run $10,000.00, with more sophisticated fill stations running as high as $25,000.00 or more. On top of your initial sales inventory, you must also add in the cost of rental equipment, and for even the smallest store, you'll probably need at least 20 complete sets of gear.

If you have the cash to purchase your own store facility, you'll undoubtedly want to consider putting in a pool. This will probably be your other single largest expenditure aside from the property itself. Most stores with pools have custom designed installations and they work to keep them in use with swimming lessons or other activities so the pool pays for itself.

Fig. 3.7 – Every dive store must have an air compressor and be able to fill tanks quickly.

Experiences of Dive Store Owners and Managers

SALLY SANTMYER

Sally Santmyer owns one of the most successful group of dive stores in Southern California, Laguna Sea Sports. The store was originally started in 1952, and was purchased by Sally and her late husband Al in 1963 for $4000.00.

Sally was originally certified as a diver in San Diego by Jim Stewart, the retired diving officer from Scripps Institution of Oceanography. Shortly after buying Laguna Sea Sports, the Santmyers purchased the Duchess, which was the first charter dive boat in San Diego.

During the first year of operation of Laguna Sea Sports, Al operated the store by himself and commuted on a daily basis from San Diego up the coast to Laguna. After a year, the business had grown to a point where Sally quit her job in San Diego and joined her husband at the Laguna store.

"Most of the male divers who came into the store wouldn't even talk to me," remembers Sally. Diving was such a male dominated sport then that a woman working in a dive store was considered a novelty.

To keep herself busy, Sally concentrated on keeping their rental gear in shape, and repairing the pile of wetsuits that accumulated after each busy weekend. She also began to make custom suits and would make miniature wetsuits to serve as gift certificates at Christmas for those divers whose spouses had bought them new suits.

In 1970, Laguna Sea Sports opened their Costa Mesa store, and also purchased Bay Travel, becoming one of the first dive stores to specialize in dive travel. In 1971 they opened yet another store in Van Nuys, in Los Angeles County, followed by two more stores in 1973. To complete their travel business, Laguna Sea Sports purchased the Current Club on North Eleuthra in the Bahamas, but the drug trade there made them decide to close that operation. Sally estimates that today, there are probably 10,000 customers who know her on a first name basis.

Fig. 3.8 – Sally Santmyer is the owner of Laguna Sea Sports and has been in the diving business since 1963.

Sally notes that women can do very well as dive store employees, managers, and operators, provided they know what they are doing. Today, there are many male customers who come into her store and tell Sally they were instructed to deal with no one but her. That's quite a change from when the Santmyers first purchased Laguna Sea Sports!

CURT WIESSNER

Curt Wiessner is another dive store owner who never originally intended to own a dive shop. A graduate of the University of California at Santa Barbara (UCSB) with a degree in marine biology, Curt planned to teach diving and tend bar to work his way around the world. Instead, he got caught up in teaching recreational diving classes at UCSB and opened his dive store, Aquatics of Santa Barbara, in the summer of 1980. His was the fourth dive store in a highly competitive local market.

Curt opened Aquatics with a loan of $48,000.00. He spent $12,000.00 on his compressor, $10,000.00 on rental equipment, and held $10,000.00 in reserve in the bank. This left him only $8000.00 to stock the store with merchandise and fixtures.

Aquatics of Santa Barbara opened with 750 square feet of space, including office, repairs, and rentals. There was a single employee, Curt, and for the first year he worked seven days a week. He did everything himself, from teaching classes to repairs, rentals, and sales. His first year in business he paid himself $3500.00.

The initial inventory of the store consisted of three sets of fins, five masks, and three snorkels. Curt hung the buoyancy compensators on a circular rack and inflated them to make them take up more room. He spread multiple copies of the same book on the counter to make them take up space. During his first year if he did $150.00 worth of business on a Sunday that was a good day...

Curt's philosophy for opening the store was to only carry products that he believed in, because he didn't truly enjoy selling. He felt that if he educated his students properly they would be able to pick the equipment they needed to enjoy diving. He sticks by that same principle today and Aquatics has grown accordingly. Today the store occupies over 2000 square feet and employs ten people including Curt and his wife Patty (who is also an instructor).

Wiessner's instructions to his salesmen further reflect his own beliefs on how customers should be treated. First and foremost, he instructs his salespeople to never lie to a customer. All customers must be treated properly and with respect. "Our only goal is to make customers happy," says Curt.

Fig. 3.9 – "Be prepared to work ungodly hours when you first start out," warns Curt Wiessner, dive store owner and instructor.

"Be prepared to work ungodly hours when you first start out," warns Curt. He also notes the importance of having sufficient capital to invest in the business.

Curt cites his lack of having a good certified public accountant to help him manage his finances as costing him "thousands of dollars." "If you can, find an accountant who knows the diving business," advises Wiessner.

"Today you need expert consultation to be successful in a retail dive store," says Curt. "You need people who can advise you in diverse areas such as marketing and business management. If you can't afford that, then you must at least read books on these topics. That's how I trained myself."

ROBERT CAMENZIND

Robert Camenzind is the manager of Underwater Sports, also located in Santa Barbara, California and has been diving since 1975. He learned to dive in the San Francisco Bay area and completed his open water dives in Monterey when he was 14 years old. Robert first started working part-time in a dive store in 1985 and became an instructor in 1986. He has worked full-time in dive stores since 1987.

For Robert, the positive aspects of working in a dive store are the opportunity to meet new people, the flexibility of his schedule, and the diving associated with working in the store and instruction. On the negative side, he dislikes the long hours required during the summer months and the seasonal nature of the business. He also notes that when you work with the public you must put your personal problems aside when you deal with customers.

Fig. 3.10 – Robert Camenzind writes up a sale for a customer.

Suggested Reading

Cohen, William. *Developing a Winning Marketing Plan.* John Wiley & Sons, New York, 1987.

Hawken, Paul. *Growing a Business. Simon & Schuster*, Inc. New York, 1987.

Holtz, Herman. *The Secrets of Practical Marketing for Small Business.* Prentice-Hall Inc., Englewood Cliffs, NJ, 1982.

Smith, Roger. *Entrepreneur's Marketing Guide.* Reston Publishing, Inc. Reston, Virginia, 1984.

Chapter Four

RESORT DIVE GUIDES & CHARTER BOAT OPERATIONS

If there is a job that almost everyone in diving has dreamed about, it's probably working as a dive guide in a tropical resort. The mythical image of this job is that it's almost always fun, it's glamorous, and there are tremendous romantic opportunities. Just picture yourself on a tropical island somewhere, soaking in the rays of the hot sun, sipping a pina colada, diving only in beautiful, crystal clear waters, and mingling with all those gorgeous bronze bodies. Ahhhhh, what a life! The reality of this job is that it is hard work, it's rarely glamorous, and the lifestyle is frequently lonely.

Training to be a Dive Guide

Although you can work as a dive guide with only a dive master rating, most resorts prefer to hire scuba instructors who can serve as both a guide and an instructor. In addition, as an instructor you can usually command a higher level of pay. To ensure yourself the best chance of getting a job as a dive guide you should obtain your diving instructor's rating. See chapter 2 of this book for more information on becoming a diving instructor.

Some of the schools that train diving instructors also specialize in preparing instructors for working in dive resorts. This is especially true of several facilities that are located in Florida.

As an instructor you will gain experience leading groups of divers on underwater tours, and in many ways, working as a dive guide is very similar. However, working as a guide in a resort situation requires even a higher level of ability and insight. You must be able to size people up very quickly and evaluate and predict their abilities. You must be very much in tune with what the divers you are responsible for are feeling.

A good dive guide should be capable of handling minor equipment repairs at the dive site. The more types of equipment you can repair, the better equipped you will be to keep your customers happy and diving. You should try to attend as many different manufacturers' repair schools as possible. These schools are usually held at industry trade shows such as the DEMA (Diving Equipment Manufacturer's Association) show as well as regional consumer shows, such as the Boston Sea Rovers annual show.

Fig. 4.1 – As a dive guide it is essential that you have the ability to operate small boats. Inflatables are very common in diving operations.

Another important aspect of working in a resort is the ability to operate, and navigate small boats. If you work on a liveaboard dive boat the responsibility for the operation of the vessel will normally fall to the captain and crew. In land based resorts, instructors will frequently be expected to take out groups of tourists in an open cockpit boat, such as a Boston Whaler or inflatable. If you want to operate small boats carrying six passengers or less in the U.S. you must have a Coast Guard "six pack" operators license. To operate larger vessels, carrying more divers, you need an ocean operators license to carry passengers for hire.

As a land based dive guide you must be capable of running a boat, navigating to the dive site, anchoring, conducting the dive, and successfully navigating back to port. This is as big a responsibility as being a dive master. If you don't have these skills you should acquire them to make yourself more versatile and attractive to a wider variety of resorts. Take a course in small boat handling and seamanship from your local community college or power squadron.

If you intend to work in a dive resort, it is also extremely handy to have the ability to maintain and repair small engines and compressors. There are few things more embarrassing than having a boat full of tourists and being unable to start the outboard on your boat. This is especially unpleasant if the weather has turned bad or the boat is dragging anchor towards a reef.

Getting a Job as a Resort Guide

While diving resorts and liveaboard dive boats are constantly advertising positions they have available, it's important to be discriminating when you are in search of a job. You shouldn't necessarily take the first offer that comes along without fully investigating the facility. While you may be anxious to get hired, and excited to be offered employment as a guide, remember that the resort needs you as much as you need the job.

If at all possible, you should make every effort to visit the resort before you agree to work for them. If you decide to accept employment based solely upon pictures of the resort or a magazine article you may not be getting the entire story. It is not uncommon for resorts to show their best rooms and dive sites in a brochure or video. Sometimes, when you actually arrive, the resort's brochure does not match the current appearance and condition of the resort. This is why it is essential to visit the facility to see for yourself.

In most cases, your initial contact will probably occur on the phone, when you respond to their advertisement for employees in an instructor journal or other diving magazine. If you are a recent graduate of an instructor college you may be contacted by the school's placement office.

Even if a particular resort isn't hiring, if you really want to work there you should make every effort to visit them. Most of the better resorts will not hire someone over the phone. By making the effort to visit the resort you stand a much better chance of getting hired, if not initially, later down the road.

Be sure to make an appointment to meet with the owner or manager before you visit any resort where you are trying to get a job. If they say they aren't hiring, ask them if they could at least meet with you to discuss their operation. Most people are willing to do this.

Remember that your initial telephone contact with a potential employer is part of the interview process. You should prepare a list of questions that will help you decide whether you want to spend the time and money to visit any resort that makes you a tentative offer. Usually, any offer made over the phone will be "tentative" until the employer interviews you in person.

Some of the questions that you will want answered might be as follows:

1) What is the size of the resort in terms of guest capacity? This will give you some idea of the work load, as well as how important your position will be in the operation.

2) What is the daily schedule of dives at the resort? This will give you some idea of the hours you are expected to work. Are you expected to guide night dives?

3) How many days a week are you expected to work?

4) What is your exact job description?

5) How old is the resort? How old are the boats, compressors, and dive gear?

6) What type of safety standards does the resort maintain? Are divers allowed to dive solo? Can buddy teams dive without direct supervision? What is the resort's policy regarding deep diving, nitrox, and decompression diving?

Fig. 4.2 – Before you go to work for a resort be sure to check it out in person. Take a good look at all the equipment, particularly boats and compressors, and see how well they are maintained.

7) What type of vacation schedule can you expect?

8) How much authority will be vested in you as a dive guide? Can you forbid someone from diving if they are hungover, drunk, or otherwise unsafe?

9) Will you be expected to teach and serve as a guide, too? Will you be paid at different rates for teaching compared to guiding?

10) What is the policy of the resort in regard to tips to employees from customers?

11) Will the resort provide you with living quarters, or must you secure your own? What are the usual expenses for someone who lives and works at the resort, including housing, food, electricity, and water?

12) How much will you be paid? How often will you be paid? Will you be paid in U.S. dollars or foreign currency? Does the country tax your earnings?

13) What happens if you become sick while working at the resort? Is there paid medical care? Will you be paid for a certain number of sick days?

14) Is there any limit to how long you can work in the country where the resort is located? Will your work permit expire?

When you visit the resort you should try to inspect everything there. Talk to the guests to find out how they are enjoying their stay and how the resort compares with other places they have been. Try to talk to the employees separately to find out how they enjoy working there. Many resorts will reimburse you for the airfare you spent to interview if you work for the resort for at least a year.

Be sure to have a brief, one page resume with you when you go to visit the resort. It is also helpful if you have letters of recommendation from past employers. Don't pressure the owner or manager to take these if they are not hiring, but bring them out last, as if they were almost an afterthought.

If after visiting a resort you don't get hired it pays to be persistent. Follow up your visit with a "thank you" note to the owner or manager for taking the time to talk with you. Call them every few months while you are looking for a job to see if the situation there has changed.

Not all dive resorts have retirement plans or other benefits such as health care. When you negotiate for a job at a resort or on a live-aboard dive boat it is important to inquire what benefits are provided. At the very least, the resort should provide you with Divers Alert Network (DAN) insurance in the event you should have a diving accident requiring hyperbaric treatment. Since the typical resort guide may make 400 to 800 dives a year, the potential for a case of decompression sickness is quite high. Coverage for diving accidents is essential.

At places outside the United States, anyone wishing to work must usually first obtain a work visa and work permit. In most cases, this is absolutely necessary, and will not be waived. The employer is usually responsible for getting a work permit for the potential employee, which means you will have met with and negotiated employment before this step is taken. The employer is also normally responsible for the cost of the employee work permit. This means that in order for your employment to be "worth" the cost and effort required of the employer, you must be a highly qualified and desirable candidate. You need to make yourself highly marketable by attaining as many skills and as much training and experience as possible before looking for work.

Of course, if you are going to work outside of the U.S.A., you will need to get a current passport. Next, you will need to find out what the requirements are for hiring people from outside that particular country. For example, in Cozumel, dive guides are never hired from the U.S., as there is a law which requires the hiring of local workers whenever possible, if they can do the work. For this reason, local people will usually be hired as dive guides in Cozumel. It is also a lot less expensive and less hassle for the employer not to have to deal with visas, work permits, etc. However, someone holding special experience and expertise, with certifications to match, has a much better chance of being hired, due to their "unique qualifications." In this way, the employer can satisfy the local law, and make possible the hiring of a person from outside the country.

Working as a Resort Dive Guide

Working in a diving resort is pleasant, although the hours are usually long. The work is not especially difficult or physically demanding most of the time, but there are those times when you may have to haul 20 or 30 tanks to the boat from the dive shop and back at the end of the dive.

One of the most important skills you must develop to be successful as a dive guide is the ability to size up the diving experience of new visitors as they arrive at your resort. Most dive masters use a combination of reviewing a diver's logbook and a skills evaluation dive to determine each diver's skill level. In addition, experienced dive guides can tell a great deal about a new diver just by watching them get dressed. If they get dressed quickly, can hook up their tank properly, and show no hesitation in preparation, they are probably a good diver. Another good clue to a person's ability is if they know how much weight they will need to be neutrally buoyant at any depth.

There is always a certain amount of stress whenever you are responsible for other peoples' safety. This is natural, and helps to keep you on your toes. As a resort dive guide you must be continually aware of what is happening during each dive. You must anticipate problems and think about how you will handle each situation. You must be one step ahead of every situation.

As a resort dive guide or a charter boat operator you must always be courteous to your customer. You cannot let your personal life interfere with your job. You must be cheerful and pleasant even when you are unhappy or upset. Your guests are on vacation and they expect to enjoy themselves, and be entertained.

Fig. 4.3 – Whether you work on a charter boat or at a resort you must always be courteous to the customer. These dive boat skippers work aboard the Truth Aquatics' boats in Santa Barbara, California, an operation that is noted for its exceptional service.

If a guest makes a special request, you must do everything in your power to accommodate them, as long as their request is within reason. You must not do anything that would jeopardize their safety, or the safety or enjoyment of your other guests. The attitude of most people who are on vacation is that they have paid a great deal of money for their vacation and they want to do everything possible to enjoy themselves.

At some resorts, all the dives are strictly chaperoned by the dive guides. Other locations allow the guests to explore on their own, as long as they stay within sight of the guide. Yet other operations allow guests to freely roam at will, on their own and out of sight of the guides. You must adapt to the demands of the resort's management and follow their directions for handling diving operations. The only exception to this would be in a situation where the management asks you to do something that is unsafe, or violates the standards established by your instructor association.

When there is more than one dive guide on a boat, the divemaster is the one who calls the shots. The divemaster will choose the dive site(s), and when present will be the one to give the pre-dive briefing. In a way, the divemaster is the "supervisor" or "foreman" for the staff on a dive boat.

Most resorts prefer to hire instructors as dive guides or divemasters so that they can do "double-duty" and teach dive classes as well. Resort instructors frequently teach "crash" courses to certify divers in a week, as well as resort or introductory courses. The resort course is designed to allow the visiting non-diver to gain experience scuba diving under the direct supervision of an instructor. The typical introductory resort course lasts three hours.

Many resorts have a single person who has overall responsibility for all dive operations including instruction, boat charters, guided underwater tours, retail sales, and rentals. This person is usually called the "*dive operations manager.*"

Generally, the person who fills this position is someone who knows the operation well, which means they have probably worked at the resort for some time in at least one, if not several different positions.

The dive operations manager must be highly responsible, friendly, courteous, good with people, good at solving problems, and very organized. This person can be worth their weight in gold to a resort who recognizes their value and potential.

The dive operations manager should expect to have to roll up their sleeves and do whatever needs doing when they're in charge. While usually functioning in more of a supervisory role, "whatever needs doing" is the ultimate responsibility of this person. This means that they may find themselves sweeping the floor at the end of the day, emptying the trash, filling tanks, or "whatever needs doing." These may also be daily tasks for the dive operations manager at a very small resort.

People who work in dive resorts have the opportunity to meet countless people from all walks of life. The opportunity to make lifelong friends from all over the world is one of those things that can't really be measured, but is one of the benefits of the job that most people cherish.

Fig. 4.4 – Although Glen Fritzler is one of the owners of Truth Aquatics in Santa Barbara, he pitches in and does whatever needs to be done aboard his boats. Filling tanks is not something that he has to do, but he doesn't consider it below him.

The typical dive resort is chronically understaffed. This means that most dive guides end up working long stretches of time without any time off or vacation. This situation is especially common for guides who work on live-aboard dive boats. It is not unusual for a dive guide to work for 60 or 90 days straight with no time off.

Working as a resort dive guide usually means that you will be working outside the United States, unless you work in the Florida Keys or Hawaii. While there are many positive aspects to living and working abroad, there are also some negative aspects.

Living on a remote tropical island does have some disadvantages. When you live on a small island you are always somewhat isolated, even on islands that have as many conveniences as the Caymans or Puerto Rico. Many of the things that you take for granted on the mainland are not always available on islands.

Living on an island, unless you live someplace like Hawaii, also means that you live with a limited number of people. While you will continually meet new people who visit your resort, you must live and work with the same people day after day. There is no escape and very little privacy. On an island, everyone knows everyone else's business.

If you are the type of person who likes cultural stimulation, there is very little of this type of entertainment on most small islands. There are usually no live theaters, art museums, or libraries on most small islands. If you're a television addict, you may find your viewing choices extremely limited. If you like to read, you may find yourself dependent on the generosity of the tourists you serve to give you their discarded novels and magazines when they leave.

Working in a foreign country can be difficult, since many countries take a hostile attitude towards outsiders entering their land to work. In most situations, you will be required to possess a work permit for that country. The conditions of these permits can be quite restrictive and are usually revocable for any violation of the laws of that country. You may also find yourself subject to the hostility of the local people who believe that you are taking work away from them.

Living and working on a liveaboard dive boat is even more confining than working on an island. Aside from the normal limitations of living on an island, you live in even closer quarters when you live on a ship. There is usually little or no room for you to store any personal possessions. While you are on the boat, the only way you can communicate with friends or family in the outside world is by mail, radio, or cellular phone. Radio calls and cellular calls are expensive.

Frequently, the crew's quarters on a liveaboard vessel are not as nice as the passenger's accommodations. You will undoubtedly have to share a room and a bath, and you may not have a say as to who will be your roommate.

Be careful not to spend all your earnings at the bar! Many people who find work in a dive resort get themselves into trouble because you can usually "sign" for drinks and food in the restaurant/bar of your employer, and this adds up fast. Keep track of what you are spending, and pay cash whenever you can.

It's also a very good idea to make arrangements for a way back home (airline ticket, money in the bank, etc.) *before* you leave for paradise. Some people find that because of the high cost of living, relative to what they earn in a dive resort, they have trouble getting back home when they are ready to leave.

The average length of time a person works at a dive resort is between 12 - 18 months. Some stay for three months, six months, one year, two years, and others never leave. The average, however, is around one year. Most people find out that it's initially great fun, but after awhile they "burn out" and return home.

Working on a Dive Charter Vessel

There are many dive charter vessels operating in U.S. waters that employ divers in various capacities. These range from small, one man "six pack" dive boats, to full size charter vessels that may carry as many as 40 passengers and a crew of five or more.

Fig. 4.5 – Charter dive vessels are big business in Southern California. The Conception, one of the three Truth Aquatics' boats is shown here, returning from a multiday trip to Santa Barbara's Channel Islands.

Six pack dive boats are normally operated by a single skipper/divemaster. It is not uncommon in these operations for the owner of the vessel to be the operator as well. On a six pack dive boat the skipper is also responsible for loading the boat, provisioning it, navigating the boat, leading the dive, and cleaning up the boat at the end of the day. The day is long in this type of operation.

Charter dive vessels are more sophisticated operations and have become big business in many locations, especially Southern California. The boats there frequently run multiday trips, up to five days long. The better boats feature televisions and VCR's for playing back your underwater videos, darkrooms for developing film, live game holds, showers, dressing rooms, large bunks, and full galleys.

The crew on a liveaboard dive boat or charter vessel must often share many of the responsibilities of the operation of the ship. This means that you may be expected to help wash dishes, stand an anchor watch at 2:00 o'clock in the morning, pick up the groceries when the boat is in port, clean bathrooms, and help maintain the engines. Being a diver, a dive guide, or even an instructor is generally not enough in a liveaboard dive boat situation. To be accepted as a member of the crew, you will be expected to pitch in and help out. Even in those rare operations where you are expected to do nothing but function as a dive instructor, the more you do to help the rest of the crew, the better you will be accepted.

Most of the deckhands who work aboard larger charter dive boats work towards getting their Coast Guard license for operating passenger vessels for hire in ocean waters. Coast Guard licenses are based upon the size of the vessel and its operating area. In the U.S. you must have a Coast Guard license for legal and insurance reasons.

Fig. 4.6 – On a charter boat, everyone in the crew must pitch in. Proper engine maintenance is critical to the success of Truth Aquatics' operation, and owner Glen Fritzler regularly inspects the engines on his boats.

The usual path of promotion on a large charter dive boat is to start out as a deckhand and earn your license or "ticket" by accumulating sea time and passing the Coast Guard exam. While you accumulate sea time, the captain you work under will allow you to operate the boat from time to time, under their direct supervision. Once you have your license you will work as the "second ticket," or relief skipper. Eventually, if you demonstrate the right attitude and capability, you will get the chance to skipper your own boat, and train new deckhands.

A Day in the Life of a Dive Guide

A typical day for a dive guide might start at 6:30 A.M. when she must start the day by filling all the tanks that were used on the night dive the previous evening. Depending upon the compressor system in use and the number of tanks that require filling, this job could easily take an hour or more. Once the tanks are filled, they must be loaded aboard the boat for the morning dive.

On the morning dive, the boat must also be fueled and the cooler loaded with soft drinks or perhaps fruit. There should also be fresh water aboard for drinking and rinsing cameras. The dive guide carries the gear for each of the guests down to the boat.

The boat leaves the dock at 9:00 A.M. with our dive guide at the helm. It is a 25 minute run to the dive site. The dive guide anchors the boat in a sandy area just outside the reef and helps her guests suit up if they need assistance. Once she is sure that all the guests have what they need to dive, she enters the water to check the anchor to be sure it is hooked up correctly. She waits on the bottom for the other divers to make their way to the bottom. The policy of her operation is to allow guests to roam freely on the bottom, as long as they stay within sight of the dive guide.

The divers enjoy the dive, and with their buddies, they make their way back up to the surface. It is the responsibility of the dive guide to remain underwater until the last diver is aboard the boat. The guide cannot afford to surface before her guests or she has lost control of the dive. Once the last diver is back aboard the boat, the dive guide picks up the anchor and wraps up enough line to ensure it will not foul on the reef. She then surfaces, removes her gear, pulls the anchor, and pilots the boat to the second dive site. The second dive goes smoothly and she pilots the boat back to the resort.

Back at the dock, the divemaster must unload the boat, fill tanks for the afternoon dive, and grab a quick lunch. Since she is an instructor, she has a 1:00 o'clock private diving course to teach for a husband and wife team who are vacationing from Chicago. Her class session will last for three hours including lecture and pool work.

At 4:00 P.M. the divemaster is finished with her class and hurries down to the dock to help fill tanks from the afternoon dive. She fills cylinders until 5:30 P.M. and then grabs dinner before she loads the boat for the night dive that leaves the dock at 7:00 P.M.

At 7:00 o'clock sharp the boat leaves the dock with ten divers for the night dive. There are two guides aboard. It takes 30 minutes to reach the wreck where the night dive will be made and it is a calm, clear night. Due to the shallow depth, the dive lasts for over an hour and it is almost 9:00 P.M. before everyone is back aboard the boat with their gear stowed and ready to get underway.

When they return to the dock, both dive guides unload the boat, clean it up, and fill all the tanks. This takes another hour and it is almost 11:00 P.M. before the guides are through for the night.

Owning and Operating a Dive Resort

Starting your own resort diving business is a difficult and expensive proposition in today's financial climate. Even if you only provide the diving services for a group of hotels, at a minimum you need a reliable boat, a compressor, and enough dive gear to outfit at least six people, plus spares. This represents a sizable investment. If you want to operate in a foreign country you also must obtain all the necessary permits and licenses required to operate a business there.

In some cases it may be preferable to buy an existing dive operation rather than try to set up your own business. If you elect to go this route, you should have a qualified business consultant help you review the books of the operation. However, no ordinary business consultant can advise you on the working condition of the boats and other equipment owned by the resort. You can only evaluate this by visiting the facility, talking to the employees, and interviewing current and past visitors.

As the owner/operator of a dive resort you will make more money than a dive guide, but you will do less diving. Like the retail end of sport diving, the operation of a dive resort has characteristics that are typical of any small business, as well as details that are peculiar to the diving industry.

One of the more challenging parts of running a resort diving operation is keeping your equipment up and running in a tropical environment. Diving equipment that is used in a resort operation normally spends more time in the water than equipment used in the busiest mainland dive store. The wear and tear on boats that are subjected to the sea, humidity, and divers on a daily basis is tremendous.

Part of keeping your equipment running includes the difficulty of getting parts and supplies when you are in a remote location. Depending upon where your operation is located, it can be extremely frustrating waiting for shipments to arrive and clear customs. You must also have trained staff members who can do the repair work, since you cannot depend upon a repairman being available when you need him.

Finding and hiring good people is the most difficult task that faces any small business owner, and this is especially true for tropical dive resorts. While there is usually no end to applicants for your available dive guide positions, truly competent and dedicated professional guides can be difficult to find. Many people who go to work as guides "burn out" after a year.

Fig. 4.7 – Good dive guides are hard to find! Part of being a good guide is being able to show visiting divers where the interesting marine life is on the reef. Instructor and guide Nick Craig knows where to find the sea turtles in the clear waters of Hawaii. (Photo © Jeff McConnel)

Since hiring and training new people is an expensive proposition, it is especially important to find the best people possible. Some resorts offer special incentives to employees who stay for extended periods of time, such as paid airfare back to the U.S. on an annual basis.

Your tax situation as a U.S. citizen living and operating a business abroad is more complex than for a small business owner in the U.S. The Internal Revenue Service gives careful scrutiny to citizens who hold bank accounts in foreign countries. If your diving operation is located in a foreign country, you will probably be obligated to pay taxes in that country as well. You may need to have a tax accountant in both the U.S. and the country where you operate your business to keep your records in proper shape and advise you on tax laws.

Experiences of Dive Guides, Resort and Liveaboard Operators

NICK CRAIG

Nick Craig is the director of training at Ocean Sports Waikoloa in Hawaii. His entire life has revolved around diving. Nick started snorkeling at the age of eight, to earn money cleaning boat bottoms and recovering lost articles in Newport Harbor. When he started scuba diving at the age of 12, his initial incentive was to earn more money cleaning boats.

Nick learned to dive, as he puts it, "by osmosis." He visited a local dive store after school each day and eavesdropped on classes whenever he could. The store owner, who was also an instructor, finally certified him. He subsequently took a complete formal course in instruction at the age of 14 from veteran spearfisherman and instructor Ron Merker.

When Nick graduated from high school he attended Orange Coast College and got involved with the scuba program there. He became an assistant instructor and helped teach seven classes each semester. In 1973, when he turned 21, he attended a NAUI instructor's course in Monterey, California.

Nick continued teaching at Orange Coast after completing his instructor training, but also began to teach private classes and dive store courses. In 1975 he met Bob Widmann, who runs the recreational diving program at the University of California at Santa Cruz (UCSC). Widmann hired Craig to help teach diving classes at the school.

At UCSC Nick taught sport diving courses, but also became involved with the school's research diving program. By the end of 1976, Nick had also become involved with the diving program at O'Neill's Dive Shop, and eventually became the store's manager. He stayed there until the end of 1979, building up the business. He also maintained his friendship with Bob Widmann, and participated as a staff member in several NAUI instructor training courses (ITC's). He pioneered much of the early work in diver rescue techniques and helped develop the NAUI Rescue Diver course.

Fig. 4.8 – Nick Craig is the Director of Training at Ocean Sports Waikoloa in Hawaii. (Photo © Jeff McConnel)

In late 1979 Nick visited Hawaii for the first time. He liked what he saw so much that he moved there in 1980. Nick landed a job at American Dive Hawaii and became the store manager. At that time they were the busiest dive shop in Honolulu. Nick worked teaching diving and guiding dive trips. On an average day, the store taught introductory scuba lessons, followed by an open water dive, to between 30 and 40 people.

Nick's next job was with Ocean Sports Hawaii (which subsequently became Ocean Sports Waikoloa). The facility conducted activities and training in all watersports, although snorkeling and diving were their main attractions. Nick was employed there until 1984 when he had a back operation, and it didn't appear he would be able to sling large numbers of scuba tanks on a daily basis. He subsequently took a job with NAUI Headquarters as Member Services Coordinator.

While he was at NAUI, Nick helped create many new programs, including their Dream Resort and Professional Educator. He also expanded their Pro Facility membership, and hired their first regional sales representatives.

By 1986 Nick's back had recovered, and he got an offer to work on a liveaboard dive boat in Grand Cayman. After less than four months the operation fell apart and Nick took a job with the Cayman Diving Lodge. Nick's position there lasted for nine months until the business was sold and he was offered the job of divemaster aboard the Peter Hughes boat, *Sea Dancer*.

Aboard the *Sea Dancer,* Nick worked anywhere from 16-18 hours a day. Each employee was expected to work for a period of five months before they were eligible for any vacation. During the five month period the employees worked, they got three hours off the boat, to conduct their personal business, between each group of tourists! In addition to working as divemaster, Nick also served as the photo professional, ran the darkroom aboard the boat, and shot video.

With no room for advancement, and burned out from the long hours, Nick left the *Sea Dancer* in 1989 and started a photo business he called Wet Images. He shot images for brochures and made promotional videos.

Nick returned to Hawaii in 1990 to work for Ocean Sports Waikoloa, initially as the manager of diving operations. Today he is responsible for the training of the entire staff, both new personnel and those employees who are promoting. Nick also teaches tourists and guides dive trips. He dives 3-4 days each week, depending on his training schedule. He also captains the numerous boats owned by the center including their 26 foot sail boat, a 36 foot power boat, and a 42 foot and a 58 foot catamaran.

Ocean Sports Waikoloa encourages their employees to get "cross-training" so that they can teach other watersports, such as windsurfing. "This makes each person valuable to the company," explains Nick.

"Our typical customer is the novice diver," says Nick, "and it is lots of fun to see their enthusiasm. Of course, we get our share of experienced divers, too, but 2/3 of our visitors are novices. We get to work with a broad cross-section of people and in the type of work we do we get to know people very quickly."

Nick enjoys the responsibility of entertaining people and making sure that everyone has a good time. He sees guiding dive trips as an open-ended learning experience, where you must contend with boats, the weather, the ocean, and all the other factors that contribute to a dive.

"Working as a dive guide is a lot more work and a lot less glamorous than you think," observes Nick. "The job includes long hours, hard work, lots of sunburn, and low pay." Although Nick works 40 hours a week at Ocean Sports Waikoloa, he has to work an additional 20-40 hours each week outside his job to make ends meet in Hawaii. On the side he shoots photos of luaus and other activities to bolster his income.

Nick points out that there are lots of stressful situations that you must cope with when your guiding. "You have to be able to think quickly," warns Nick. He also notes that you must be a good salesman. "You must sell yourself to your guests so that they want to come back tomorrow. You also want them to tell their friends about you."

"When you're looking for a job as a dive guide you need to research where you want to go," stresses Nick. "Find out if the people who run the operation share your philosophy regarding safety and how dive operations should be run. The single biggest thing that sells me on hiring someone for our operation is when a person makes the effort to come to our operation and pays their own way to dive with us. We get the opportunity to see how they dive and whether they truly enjoy it. It's expensive to do this, but in the long run it pays off."

NEAL WATSON

Neal Watson is the owner of Neal Watson's Undersea Adventures. Although he isn't strictly a dive guide any longer, he is an important resort operator and diving is part of his job.

Neal started diving in 1953 in Florida, his home state. He was with his friends on a camping trip to Blue Springs when one of his brother's friends brought out a set of scuba gear from the trunk of his car. It was an old steel tank with electrical tape holding the regulator together. When the friend asked who wanted to try the gear, someone in the crowd volunteered Neal.

Neal swam down to the bottom of the spring and at 60 feet, turned over on his back and looked back up at the surface. As he did so, the old, two hose regulator quit giving him air and he shot to the surface. Back on the bank of the spring, when one of the boys asked him what it was like, Neal answered, "Going down is great, but coming up is a bitch!"

Fig. 4.9 – Neal Watson is one of the most successful dive resort operators in the Caribbean. (Photo courtesy Neal Watson)

By the time he was 14, Neal was a self-taught scuba diver who regularly broke into golf courses at night to dive in the water hazards and recover golf balls. When he was 18 he enlisted in the Marines and joined the Recon teams (see chapter 12 on military diving) where, as he puts it, he finally learned to "do it (diving) right."

In the 1960's there wasn't much opportunity for someone who wanted to be in the diving business, so Neal joined the police force in Daytona Beach, where he stayed from 1963-1965. While he was on the force he regularly made dives to recover bodies and evidence.

In late 1965 Neal moved to Freeport, in the Bahamas, to work in security for the casinos there. With a friend, he bought a glass bottom boat in 1966, and took divers out on the side, but there weren't enough people diving for the business to be successful. Neal taught introductory scuba lessons as well, but the glass bottom boat trips are what kept the business alive.

To stimulate their diving business, Neal and his friend would go to the hotel pools to drum up work. Each week, one of them would play the instructor while the other would pretend he was a tourist. The "instructor" would dive in the pool and come up and ask in a loud voice if anyone wanted to learn to dive. If there were no takers, the partner, who played the "tourist," would eagerly sign up for diving lessons, go to the bottom of the pool, and surface to tell everyone at poolside how much fun it was to dive.

Neal helped train his partner's girlfriend to set a woman's underwater depth record. In 1968 Neal set the men's underwater depth record of 437 feet on scuba, which stood for many years.

To move more aggressively into diving, Neal started the Xanadu Beach Dive Resort in Freeport and bought a 36 foot long Chris Craft cabin cruiser. To make ends meet he continued developing other businesses, including a karate school and a security operation. He commuted back and forth from West Palm Beach to the islands. He also spent some time treasure hunting with Bob Marx on the wreck of the *Maravilla*.

When the government in the Bahamas changed from British rule to local rule, Neal became disillusioned and sold his diving operation. He got into the night club business, but on the side he trained to set an underwater distance record. In 1975 he swam 66 miles underwater, nonstop.

With diving in his blood, Neal again set up a resort operation in Bimini. He decided he wanted to be a "dive bum," work weekends, and lie on the beach during the week. The only problem was that the business was successful, although Neal soon realized that its growth would be limited. Originally, he had the misconception that if you treated your customers great they would come back. He quickly realized that the most you could hope for was that satisfied customers would tell their friends.

"People want to see different things," says Neal, "and they're unlikely to return to a resort for another trip. I saw that the best way to expand my business was to open another operation."

Watson went in on a joint venture operation at the Andros Beach Hotel, and the following year took over another operation at Chubb Cay. When he recognized that he had a problem with air transportation, he quickly started an air charter business. As the business grew, he saw that he couldn't stay on top of everything, there was just too much to do. He developed the idea of a franchise diving operation and sold his Bimini assets, but kept control of the name. It was this formula that proved to be a success.

"Nobody runs a business like the owners. You have more incentive to take care of it when you own it," explains Neal. "I didn't have a new formula, but I was the first to apply it to diving."

Neal sold his operation on Andros as another affiliate resort as well as his operation on Chubb Cay. He was careful to make sure that each of the people he sold to were the type of people he wanted to run an operation with his name on it. To keep the type of people he wanted in a management position he saw that it was essential to give them a piece of the "action." He has been approached by numerous people with start-up operations and existing operations.

Today Neal is associated with ten land based operations and one liveaboard dive boat. He estimates that he turns down ten requests for affiliation for every one operation that he accepts. He turns down operations for a variety of reasons including inferior diving, unmotivated people, or a poor hotel. Neal realizes that he must be selective, because his name goes on the operation, and that's what he is selling. People come back to dive at Neal Watson resorts because they like the way they are run.

"As soon as our logo goes on a resort it has instant name recognition," says Neal. "We are plugged into 1500 dive stores, and have a mailing list of 15,000 customers."

Watson loves the diving industry and the people associated with it. He sees a tremendous future here.

"I have my cake and can eat it, too," observes Neal, "I regularly dive at all our resorts and make about 100 dives a year to ensure that our quality levels are maintained. We are in a position to make the industry grow."

If there is a weak link in the resort business, Neal believes it is the people without a business background who get into the resort business because they love diving. "Fifteen years ago you could get into this business with an 18 foot boat, a compressor, a bunch of tanks, and some weights. Today, it takes half a million dollars, and you're up against Hyatt resorts. This is a real business, not a hobby anymore," remarks Neal.

Neal feels that his biggest job is to educate the consumer about his product, and that this is the advantage of multiple resorts. He has a product for everyone, and his staff screens customers to match them up with the right resort.

"When I have an irate customer, 99% of the time it's because they didn't research the type of vacation they wanted," says Neal. "This is a weak link with travel agents. Of course, when the weather is great, we can do no wrong, but when the weather is bad, we can do no right. Even though people know you can't control the weather they are still disappointed when it's bad, and rightly so."

There are many things to consider if you're thinking about going into resort work. Perhaps the most important thing is to realize that you're probably not going to get rich doing this type of work.

He explains the criteria he looks for when hiring diving instructors. "When I interview someone for a dive instructor position, the last question I ask them is about their instructor qualifications. I look for people who can run a boat and know how to fix a compressor. We go through thousands of resumes to select a handful of people."

Neal also looks for people who are entertainers. He wants people who realize that their job is to make sure that the customer who works for 51 weeks a year has the vacation of a lifetime.

"Everybody wants to feel like people care about them. When the weather is bad, as long as people go home feeling like you have done everything possible for them, you've done your job. The real joy of this business is to see customers come back from a dive, glowing with enthusiasm," says Neal. "When the visibility is down to 60 feet it's easy to become jaded and say that it's not worth going out. What you have to remember that the worst day of the year in the Caribbean is the best day that 90% of our visitors will ever experience diving at home."

Watson's office is located in Ft. Lauderdale and his staff continuously tracks the reactions of his customers to the resorts. Following their trip each visitor receives a "thank you" card, along with a "Report Card," that they may return anonymously. Guests are asked to rate every aspect of the business from the office to the boats, guides, dive sites, and hotel. Watson personally screens every card and tracks the trends. He looks for suggestions from the guests and implements them whenever possible.

GLEN FRITZLER

Glen Fritzler is co-owner with Roy Hauser of Truth Aquatics, one of the most successful charter dive boat operations in the United States. Their operation is located in Santa Barbara, California and their boats dive the Channel Islands almost daily. They own three large boats that were built for diving from the hull up, the *Truth, the Conception,* and the *Vision.*

Glen started diving at the age of 11 in 1971, in Laguna Beach, where he went diving with his father. They first met Roy Hauser on a dive trip on the original *Truth,* that Roy operated before the current boat was built. Through a navigational error, the original *Truth* ran aground and was lost on San Clemente Island.

Through a coincidence, Glen and his father went on a dive trip on the boat, *Mr. C,* that Roy was running after the original *Truth* was lost. Roy was so impressed with Glen's enthusiasm for diving that he asked Glen if he wanted to help him build the new *Truth.* Hauser saw lots of himself in the young Fritzler.

Glen spent the summer of 1973 helping Hauser build the new *Truth* in a shipyard at Marina Del Rey. This was one of the first large charter vessels to be built specifically for diving. The new *Truth* is 65 feet long and carries up to 40 divers. When school started again, Glen continued to spend his weekends in the shipyard. Once the boat was launched, Glen worked on the boat every weekend and during his summers.

Fig. 4.10 – Glen Fritzler has been involved in the construction of every one of Truth Aquatics' boats. Glen checks out a dive site at the helm of the "Vision."

In 1977 Hauser suffered a serious case of the "*bends*" (decompression sickness) that left him paralyzed from the waist down. He continued to run the boat and quickly got back in the water. The following year he moved the *Truth* from San Pedro to Santa Barbara.

Glen followed the boat to Santa Barbara and enrolled in college there. After earning his captain's license at the young age of 19, he decided to go into the charter business full time. He became a partner with Roy in 1979.

By this time Roy and Glen were discussing the construction of a second boat, and the work actually began in 1980. Glen moved back to Long Beach to supervise the construction of the *Conception* and spent a year helping build the new boat. He played a major role in producing the beautiful woodwork that decorates the boat. The *Conception* is 75 feet long and carries 40 divers.

When the *Conception* was launched in 1981, Glen served as its first captain. He ran the boat until 1984, when the two partners started construction of yet a third boat that would be named the *Vision*. This time the new boat was built in Oxnard, a small town that is a 30 minute commute from Santa Barbara. Of the three boats, the *Vision* is the largest at 80 feet, and also carries 40 divers.

Glen supervised the construction of the *Vision*. In addition, he did all the design work and drawings, as well as the mechanical and engine installation. The *Vision* was completed and launched in July of 1985.

Glen ran the *Vision* for two years, and estimates that during that time he was averaging 250 dives a year. He married his wife Dana in 1986, and had a son in 1990. Today, he shares in the management of the business with Roy, but still runs a minimum of at least one 3-day trip each month. In more recent years he has averaged approximately 100 dives a year.

Truth Aquatics runs single and multiday dive trips aboard the three vessels on a year-round basis. Glen credits much of their success to the outstanding crews who work on the boats, and the personal customer service they provide. They have a staff of 18 who work on the boats full time, plus another 18 who work part time. In the office it takes eight people to man the phones and cash register during the seven day work week.

Glen gets the most enjoyment from his work when he takes out a group of new divers to the islands, and they have a special experience. For most people, their first boat trip is something they never forget. He also derives great pleasure from having someone take the time to find him when he is cleaning the boat at the end of a trip to say "thank you." He takes pride in ensuring their boats meet the highest standards of convenience, cleanliness, and service.

Like all the other resort and charter operators, Glen admits that you can't meet people's expectations on every trip. "We can't control the weather, but sometimes it's as though people hold us responsible for it," laments Glen.

The days at sea are long, especially when a compressor breaks down in the middle of a trip, or a pump fails in the middle of the night. A typical day for a captain may last up to 18 hours.

During the recession of 1992, Roy and Glen made the tough decision of putting some employees on part-time status. Business was frequently slow since many people did not have the money to go diving. Unfortunately, as government fees have risen, Truth Aquatics has had to fight to keep its costs down. New FCC taxes (on radio licenses) and Coast Guard fees have all increased operating costs. Eventually, those costs must be passed along to the consumer.

In an operation as large as Truth Aquatics, that has served as many divers as they have over 20 years, some diving fatalities have occurred aboard their boats. The emotional stress caused by these tragedies has led some captains to leave the operation. "In every diving accident we've seen, with the exception of one heart attack, it's always been a case of diver error," says Glen. "It's something that can always happen, even if we do everything right."

Glen's advice for someone considering going into the charter business is to carefully consider where you will locate your business. "You've got to ask yourself where you can take people to dive when the weather turns bad," explains Glen. "We're fortunate here with the islands, because there is almost always someplace to dive."

Start small, watch you investment, and build your business up slowly, is Glen's suggestion for starting a new business. He advises against buying a large boat with big payments before you know what you are doing.

JON HARDY

Jon Hardy owns and operates Argo Diving Services on Catalina Island off the coast of California. In addition to leading guided tours, Jon also does "light" commercial diving, underwater instruction, movie and television stunt work, expert witness work in diving accident cases, and writing for *Rodale's Scuba Diving* magazine. Jon is a career professional in the diving industry with more than 30 years of diving experience.

Jon started scuba diving in 1956 when a high school friend purchased a set of scuba gear. Jon tried the gear in his buddy's girlfriend's swimming pool. The only instruction Jon got was a

Fig. 4.11 – Jon Hardy runs Argo Diving Service on Catalina Island in California. (Photo courtesy of Jon Hardy.)

warning from his friend not to hold his breath, but his friend couldn't tell him why.

After reading Cousteau's book, *The Silent World*, Jon understood a bit more about diving and went to buy his first set of diving equipment. He purchased his gear from Mel Fisher, salvor of the *Atocha,* who at the time owned a store called Mel's Aqua Shop in Redondo Beach.

By 1958 Jon was a self-proclaimed diving instructor who issued his own brand of certification card. To support himself after high school, he took a job at Camp Fox on Catalina Island as a maintenance man. He quickly found himself diving to service the camp's moorings and floats, recovering lost items, and repairing the camp's seawater intake.

Jon attended the first YMCA scuba instructor's program held in Sacramento in 1960. In 1961 he went through the L.A. County Underwater Instructor's Program. He started working in a dive shop known as Sea Hunter in Eagle Rock, a suburb of Los Angeles, and taught diving at the local YMCA. During this same period he attended L.A. State College and got a degree in Recreation Education. During this time Jon was making about 200 dives a year. He also subsequently became a NAUI, PADI, and SSI scuba instructor.

With the start of the Vietnam war, Jon enlisted in the Naval Reserve, and in 1964 went on active duty. He challenged the officer exam, passed, and was sent to OCS (Officer Candidate School). While he was in the Navy he worked aboard submarines, but due to a slight imperfection in his eyesight was denied acceptance for Navy diver training. When he left the Navy he held the rank of Lieutenant Commander.

Still intent in learning more about advanced diving techniques and systems, Jon enrolled in the first commercial diving course held at Santa Barbara City College. Although he really enjoyed the technology and the work, he didn't enjoy the commercial diving lifestyle. Instead of pursuing a career in commercial diving, Jon left Santa Barbara and went to work for NAUI (National Association of Underwater Instructors) as the Director of Special Projects. During the time he worked for NAUI, Hardy developed many teaching materials for them. He left NAUI in 1973 to return to Catalina Island as the business manager and diving officer of a private school on the island.

By chance, Jon started doing expert witness work in diving accident cases in 1971. As an expert witness, Jon investigates diving accidents and gives testimony during trials dealing with diving instruction, diving equipment, and diving procedures.

Jon returned to NAUI Headquarters at the request of NAUI's Board of Directors in 1974 and served as the Executive Director of NAUI from 1974-1978. During that time he pulled NAUI out of the financial problems caused by their rapid growth and traveled extensively to fight against restrictive diving legislation.

By 1978 Jon had decided that he wanted to stop writing and talking about diving, and make the opportunity for himself to dive on a daily basis. During his transition period he worked on dive boats out of Los Angeles, and did writing and legal consulting on the side.

In 1980 Jon moved back to Catalina and opened Argo Diving Services. He purchased a boat and started running guided diving tours, gradually building the business up to what it is today. He is a licensed six pack operator, and provides a very high level of service and individualized attention to his clientele. Jon emphasizes that while Argo Diving offers guided tours, divers who use Jon's services are not forced to dive under supervision. He specializes in making adventurous experiences available for those divers who want them.

Most of Jon's charters today are groups of friends who want to dive together, rather than individual divers who come aboard and dive with people they don't personally know. One of the highlights of his operation are shark dives in open water, something that he considers "high-end adventure." Jon has run dozens of shark trips without mishap or injury. "These are peak experiences for people," notes Jon.

Argo Diving occupies 80% of Hardy's time, while the other 20% of his time is spent consulting. Working in an outdoor environment doing physical things provides him with tremendous enjoyment. He takes pleasure in providing divers with an enjoyable underwater experience and enhancing their lives.

For Jon, another advantage to working as a dive guide is the opportunity to make better money that the average instructor working in a dive store. "Personal service is "tippable," explains Jon. "Some of the tips my crew makes exceeds their daily salary."

There are negative aspects to working as a dive guide that range from diving when you're not necessarily in the mood, to dealing with unpleasant people. As a dive guide you have to be "up," interesting, and helpful, whether you feel like it or not. A big part of the job is based on your ability to handle personal relations with your guests.

Not every day at sea is pleasant, and even in the best operation there are the days when the boat breaks down or the equipment doesn't work. "This is a dynamic activity done out in the open ocean," says Jon. "You can't expect everything to go right all the time."

Of all the stressful things that happen to a dive guide one of the most terrifying is losing a diver underwater, even if it is only for a few moments. The ultimate negative aspect of this type of work is having a diver die in the water. Even if you do everything right, this is always a possibility, since diving is an adventure sport.

Jon's advice to anyone considering becoming a dive guide is to get as qualified as possible. Get your instructor's rating, take first aid courses, learn CPR and oxygen administration, as well as diver rescue. Not only should you take the basic courses, you should also keep all your certifications current.

You need as much boating experience as possible, in addition to your operator's license. Take power squadron courses and Coast Guard Auxillary courses.

To be a good dive guide you need hundreds of hours in the water. "It's unrealistic to think that you can be an effective guide if your clients have more water time than you do," observes Hardy. "The ultimate test of a professional guide is to rescue them from a life threatening situation. You've got to be a strong water person to handle these situations, and you must have excellent rescue skills. Hopefully, if you do your job right, you'll never have to go through this."

CHAPTER FIVE

MARINE BIOLOLOGY

The career of marine biologist has been, and continues to be, very popular. Yet it probably is one of the most misunderstood and romanticized careers of the past decade. Jacques Cousteau's television specials on the oceans and their inhabitants have popularized the study of living organisms in the sea. Say the words "marine biologist," and people think of divers on a vessel pursuing whales, sharks, and other large creatures with their cameras and video equipment.

The reality is that most marine biologists spend very little time at sea. When they do go to sea it's frequently in bad weather under less than comfortable circumstances, with a very limited amount of time to do their research. If you're not an instructor at the college level, the majority of marine biology jobs are with state or federal agencies. Because these agencies generally manage resources that are being utilized, most positions are involved with sport or commercial fisheries. Consulting firms also hire some marine biologists.

Education Required to Work as a Marine Biologist

The minimum requirement for a job in marine biology is a bachelor's degree in a biological science. Very few schools offer an undergraduate degree in marine biology. If you have a broad background in natural resources and solid base in biology it will serve you better than a narrowly focused degree. Any degree in the biological sciences will require several courses each in chemistry, physics, and calculus.

Although not always required, courses in botany, computer science, and statistics are highly recommended. A general course in ichthyology (the study of fishes), invertebrate zoology (the study of animals without backbones), mammalogy (the study of mammals), and oceanography will also prove useful.

Fig. 5.1 – It's essential for a marine biologist to be computer literate.

A marine biologist is always identifying creatures from the sea. It's not always easy to determine whether it's plant or animal. Did that jaw bone come from a fish or a marine mammal, or was it a land animal lost at sea? The more general background courses you've taken the easier it will be to make your initial choices.

Collection of data is an integral part of any marine biologist position. You may not be expected to design a computer database for the type of information you're collecting, but you have to know enough about the subject to explain to a programmer what you need. A "*biostatistician,*" a person knowledgeable in statistics and their application to biological data, may be available to assist you in designing a sampling program. The decision on which collection technique to use and the information required is the biologist's. The biostatistician will suggest what statistical analysis can be used based on the initial decisions you have made.

Courses in writing and oral presentations will also prove helpful. To be useful, your data must be written up for a variety of audiences and purposes. You have to be able to respond to questions from the media, and general public, without preparation.

Currently, many applicants for government jobs have master's degrees. Graduate school is where most students specialize in marine biology. A master's degree also gives you the option of going into the teaching profession. Unless you've selected the academic route, a Ph.D. (doctoral degree) will not necessarily increase your chances of employment with an agency. In fact, in some cases it may be a liability. Many employers assume that a person with a Ph.D. will continue to look for a better position, and will leave as soon as they find one.

Fig. 5.2 – Marine biologists are employed by schools, government agencies, and private research organizations, like the Hubbs Center that is part of Sea World.

Getting Hired as a Marine Biologist

To be hired for a permanent position by a state or federal agency you have to be on a hiring list for the specific job classification you are applying for. For example, the state of California has several agencies that hire biologists. Each agency within the state government has its own lists. Generally, for state government there is some sort of written examination for the job classification. A passing score qualifies the applicant for an oral interview. The applicant receives a ranking or score based on their performance at this interview. Personnel Board policy requires that a list then be compiled based on these scores.

When a supervisor has a position open they must go to this list and send out inquiries to individuals in the top three ranks at that time. An interview is then arranged for the specific position. This is a much more comprehensive interview process than the initial screening. Generally the list is maintained for 2-3 years. Then the whole announcement and testing process is repeated. Frequently you may have to make the list more than once to get hired.

The state of California requires that you apply for any job classification exam by submitting Form STD 678, the standard Examination Application. A resume is not acceptable in lieu of this form. The form may not be submitted until an exam is scheduled and filling dates are announced. It's a good idea to keep a xerox of this form, since most seasonal positions with state agencies also require it to apply. Most other states have similar procedures.

Be aware that many states will not accept applications from people who are not residents. You usually have to reside in a state for a year to establish residency. Although Hawaii and Alaska might not welcome nonresident applications, states like Florida and California do. State agencies like Fish and Game, Parks and Recreation, Forestry, Food and Agriculture, and Health Services hire biologists.

When seeking to get employment with a federal agency you have to contact the Office of Personnel Management (OPM). You'll only be able to apply for a particular job classification if it's open. Federal agencies that hire marine biologists include the National Park Service, National Marine Fisheries Service (NMFS), U.S. Fish and Wildlife Service, and the National Oceanic and Atmospheric Administration. The U.S. Fish and Wildlife Service has jurisdiction over all marine mammals and endangered species.

U.S. government job classifications combine a title with a salary range. Many seasonal and entry level biologist jobs are hired off the biologist range 5-7 list. The OPM requires the submittal of a Personal Qualifications Statement, Form SF-171. This form is very comprehensive because you're being placed on a hiring list based on the qualifications you submit in writing.

When asked what equipment you know how to operate don't be modest. Also, don't assume that it's too trivial to mention. Knowing how to operate a pH meter, that measures the acidity of a solution, may seem like no big deal to you, but it could put you higher on the particular list you're applying for. Avoid the temptation of overstating your abilities. When an agency has a specific job to fill they'll send out inquiry letters to people on the hiring list and request a comprehensive interview of the candidates that look promising.

It's important to get your foot in the door before you try to specialize. If you can get employed as an inland fisheries biologist or water quality biologist, take it. You can always transfer within an organization, but you might not get another job offer from the agency you're interested in.

Abilities and Duties of a Marine Biologist

A solid foundation in biological or environmental sciences is necessary to perform the duties of a marine biologist. Math is also a requirement. You're constantly working with numbers, measurements, percentages, and so on.

Being computer literate is imperative. Given the volume and complexity of data that you work with, the computer is an essential tool. There is a tremendous amount of paperwork associated with any government job. Word processing is a skill that you should master, too. You must be able to write letters, memos, and a wide range of reports. You might need to prepare a summary report of 1-2 pages or you could be assigned an environmental impact report of 100-200 pages.

Charts, graphs, and plots are all done on computer today. Statistical packages and modeling programs are regularly employed. Most biologists have a PC terminal at their desk, and DOS is the operating system most frequently encountered on their computers. Many agencies have remote terminals for mainframe systems that house large databases. You're not expected to have experience with all the software and systems, but you have to be able to acquire it on the job. Many agencies do not provide much training. So you must have the initiative to train yourself or seek courses from local community colleges and universities.

Fig. 5.3 – Marine biologists must be able to work as part of a team. Here, Kristine Barsky leads a research cruise off the California coast.

You must have people skills as a marine biologist. You have to be able to communicate with your colleagues, the general public, politicians, and other agencies and organizations. You may be a brilliant scientist, but if you can't share information verbally or in written form at the appropriate level for your audience you will never be successful.

To be successful as a marine biologist you must be a team player. Frequently you have no say in what research project you're assigned to, or who your dive partner (s) will be. Most marine science involves long term monitoring or studies, where you work with scientists from other agencies. As a marine biologist, you will frequently find yourself supervising or directing people with education or skills that are comparable or even superior to your own. You can't let this intimidate you.

One of the best things about being a marine biologist is that you have the opportunity to learn something new each day. The ocean is always yielding the unexpected. New behaviors or natural history information is gained every time you go to sea. New scientific literature is literally coming out on a daily basis. If you don't want to be continually learning this is not the field for you.

Marine biologists frequently work long hours at odd times of the day and night. Split shifts are not unusual. If you're on a cruise where time is limited, you'll work long days in frequently uncomfortable or unpleasant conditions.

Surprisingly, many marine biologists get seasick. It doesn't preclude you from the occupation, especially since some effective medications are now available. However, you are expected to work even if you don't feel good. The researcher in charge is not going to cancel or disrupt their research cruise to take you back to shore.

Government cruises are on charter vessels or the agency's own research vessel. Conditions vary widely. You could be on a small vessel where everyone sleeps in the same cabin, and there aren't enough bunks to go around. Larger vessels will frequently have two bunks to a cabin. Some vessels have fully equipped galleys, and others have limited food preparation equipment. There will usually be at least one "head" (toilet), but a shower is not always available. Besides science

Fig. 5.4 – A significant amount of research at sea is done using small vessels like this inflatable boat.

you may be expected to cook, clean, stand anchor watch and perform other duties as required to get the job done.

A great deal of work is done on one day trips aboard small (15-30 foot) vessels. These can be inflatables or open whalers, or vessels with some sort of cabin. They're generally lacking in the social amenities. That means no toilet, running water, or shelter from the weather. You have to be able to function in cramped quarters with people whom you might not normally choose to associate.

If you have moral objections to killing any type of creature this is not the field for you. Marine biologists as a group love life. In fact, it sometimes seems that as a group they live their lives with gusto. Yet, research frequently involves sacrificing a few creatures for the good of many. Many scientists will use photography or video when possible, instead of physically collecting. However, to sex a fish you have to cut it open (unless it's a shark), so marine biologists must frequently kill fish. Marine biologists often work at fish processing plants to collect data. There they can identify an animal's sex and take samples from fish that are already dead and being used to feed people.

Fig. 5.5 – If you have moral objections to killing any type of creature then marine biology is not the field for you. (Photo by Kristine Barsky)

Small boat handling is certainly a worthwhile skill for a marine biologist. Mechanical skills are also highly desirable. A great deal of sampling equipment is custom designed on a shoestring budget. Tie wraps and duct tape are popular tools of the trade, and adaptability and ingenuity are valued skills. Obviously, photography skills are of great value. You may be asked to take pictures under a microscope, in a poorly lit lab, outside, at night, at sea, from altitude, and underwater. Video is becoming more accessible and editing and titling skills are very useful.

Fig. 5.6 – Photography is an important skill for any marine biologist. In this photo, scientists from Channel Islands National Park are shooting a series of photos of the bottom using a grid system to align the camera.

Marine biologists are expected to put slide talks together for a wide range of audiences. In most cases, shooting your own slides may be your only option. Lettering machines are widely available, so you're no longer expected to do the lettering by hand. There are also computer programs that generate graphics for title slides, and icons and illustrations for diagrams.

Specifically, a marine biologist is usually a problem solver. The problem is usually resource allocation in some form. Take the red abalone, *Haliotis rufescens*, for example. This single shelled mollusk lives along the entire coast of California. It is taken both recreationally and commercially. In Southern California its populations are dwindling.

To devise good management policy for the abalone, which means regulations to govern its harvest, the natural history of the animal has to be understood. If you're going to protect the animal when it's reproducing, you have to know specifically what months of the year it does that. Since California's coast encompasses more that one temperature zone, it turns out that abalones on the north end of the state are doing different things at different times then those at the southern end.

Since abalones live on rock bottom in shallow, nearshore waters, diving biologists have been studying and counting them for years. A standard technique for surveying invertebrate animals that live on the bottom is to set up a "*transect line*." Normally that involves just laying out a measuring tape along the bottom. Then all the animals in selected squares along the line are counted to get population density figures. Variations in the density figures are expected, even along the same line, but you're looking for trends. If a trend of decreasing numbers emerges you know there is a change taking place. If management doesn't respond to changes in the abalone populations there will eventually be a problem.

Sometimes you're lucky enough to study a species, or a community of species before there is a problem. Frequently you don't become involved until after a problem emerges. Solutions in the marine environment aren't simple. Not only are they complex, but they're usually a compromise. If you say, "Don't harvest the abalone at all!," then people might seek another species to harvest, like limpets. That animal may not be able to tolerate any harvest either.

Fig. 5.7 – Marine biologist Kristine Barsky measures a snail along a transect line at Santa Cruz Island off California. Note the tape used for determining position and the slate with waterproof paper.

Biologists studying abalone learned that their blood lacked clotting agents. They did surveys and discovered that when abalone were pried off the rocks with a sharp instrument their foot was usually being cut. If they were too small to harvest (below the legal size) people would put them back on the rock and they would bleed to death. By getting this information out to the people in California who harvest the abalone, state biologists were able to prevent the needless death of many abalone. The managers also specified that a blunt, iron bar had to be used for prying, rather than a sharp instrument.

Frustrations of Being a Marine Biologist

Marine biologists must be problem solvers with limited budgets and tools. If you like a routine and lots of stability, marine biology probably isn't a good career choice. Most people don't enjoy dealing with government agencies. That means they have an attitude or preconception before you even start trying to help them. Getting things done inside an agency can be equally frustrating. There are rules that can't be broken that don't cover all the situations you encounter. You can't take your frustrations out on people you work with, or the public.

Many marine biology positions are headquartered in large cities. Cities are frequently not considered desirable places to live. Costs in most large cities are high, and the salaries agency biologists receive are usually standardized for the whole system. Generally, biologists in the public sector make less than their counterparts in the private sector. It used to be that benefits and the job security compensated for the smaller salary. However, many government agencies cut salaries, benefits, and even jobs, when the economy is bad.

Most state and federal employees get a paycheck once a month. Travel and other miscellaneous expenses are fronted by the employee and reimbursed at a later date when an expense claim has been submitted and processed. You must keep track of your own expenses, and prepare all the required paperwork.

Some organizations require a uniform, but it's usually not extensive. Marine biologists frequently have the luxury of wearing casual clothes to work. However, they have to dress appropriately for meetings, conferences, and other public appearances. A suit and tie, or dress and nylons, are not things of the past.

Fig. 5.8 – Some marine biologists are required to wear uniforms.

People and politics are an integral part of resource management. You have to be willing to negotiate and compromise to achieve your goals. You have to be determined and persistent. A project that should take six months could take years in a political situation. Although agencies these days are trying to be "proactive," most continue to be reactive. Budget and manpower limitations are a given. If you can't function in this kind of framework this line of work isn't for you.

Very few agency marine biologists have the luxury of researching a species that interests them. Species that are being harvested or exploited are generally the ones you'll be assigned to research. A sea cucumber might not excite you, but its role in the nearshore ecosystem may be critical if large numbers are being removed. All of a sudden you may find yourself working with a slimy creature that very little is known about. Challenging? Yes! Frustrating? Most likely! You'll also have other responsibilities and duties as well.

Fig. 5.9 – You might be personally repulsed by an animal like a hagfish (also known as a slime eel), but as a marine biologist you could be assigned to study them. These animals were caught by a commercial fisherman and were exported to Korea to make eel skin wallets and purses. (Photo by Kristine Barsky)

Every biologist wants to do great science. However, when money and time are limited, you're frequently forced to do less than great science. If legislation has been proposed that requires a response in two months, then you're going to have to use existing data and not go out and do your own "study."

Diving as a Marine Biologist

The most important thing to remember is that you're a scientist first and diver second. Very few marine biologists dive as a regular part of their job. When they do, it's because scuba diving is the best tool to study the species or habitat they're interested in. Consequently, to be effective, you must be a comfortable, experienced diver so you can concentrate most of your attention on your research. You have to be able to adapt to less than state of the art equipment and frequently abysmal conditions. If you have a shipment of abalone to transplant into the ocean, you can't let them expire on land because the ocean is rough, the water is "freezing," it's raining, or there's no visibility.

You never are expected to dive if it's unsafe. However, you may be asked to do something that is beyond your capabilities or potentially hazardous. You should have the knowledge of your diving abilities to evaluate such situations, and the courage to say no if need be.

Most agencies and institutions have diving safety boards or officers (see chapter 7) that manage their dive programs. Regular physicals and training are just some of the requirements to maintain certification with the organization.

Fig. 5.10 – A research diver uses an "electro-shocking grid" to stun and capture fish so they can be tagged and released without harm. (Photo by Steve Barsky. © Diving Systems International. All rights reserved.)

To become a diver with a scientific organization you will already have to have a certification card from a nationally recognized training agency. You'll be required to have a physical and written approval from a physician to dive. Next you'll have to past a swim test. Then you'll have to take a research diving course that's sponsored or sanctioned by the organization. CPR and first aid training, and sometimes life saving are also required. A minimum number of dives per quarter are usually required to maintain your certification with the organization once you've attained it.

Wetsuits were originally the standard issue by most agencies, but now many organizations provide their divers with dry suits. Dive computers are now commonly used. Alternate air sources are now considered standard equipment. Although many agencies allow their divers to select their dive equipment based on their own preferences, sometimes you're forced to use what the specific project or agency already owns. Some projects may require something besides the standard scuba unit. For example, full face masks with surface supplied air have allowed biologists to do better surveys of bottom dwellers in less time.

Seasonal employees or technicians frequently get to do more of the diving and other hands on work than the biologist in charge. Since their salaries are much less costly than a biologist's, your agency will want you back at the office, on the computer, analyzing the data that's already been collected.

Experiences of Marine Biologists

KRISTINE BARSKY

Kristine Barsky is a marine biologist with the California Dept. of Fish and Game. She graduated from Humboldt State University with a B.A. in Zoology. She also has an A.A. degree in Wildlife Law and Conservation and has taken graduate courses.

Kristine learned to dive one summer while still in college. She'd always loved the water, but she specifically learned to dive because her goal was to be a marine biologist. The marine biologist position she was offered by the Department in 1979 required diving certification, and was partially responsible for her getting the job.

Kristine graduated from Humboldt in 1973. She found employment with a variety of organizations and companies in biology until she achieved her goal. She sampled sewage for the Water Quality Control Board, prepared study skins for the Los Angeles County Museum of Natural History, and cloned ferns for a private firm. She fed lobsters at the Bodega Marine Lab, sold hardware, surveyed the range for the Bureau of Land Management (BLM), and assisted a game warden for the California Department of Fish and Game.

Kristine was working for BLM in northern Nevada when she interviewed for a marine biologist position in Santa Barbara, California. The movie "Jaws" had been playing for a week at the only theater in town when she announced she'd taken the diving biologist position with the California Department of Fish and Game (CDFG). People gave her their condolences and told her she was crazy to leave the safety of the desert.

Kristine's first job with CDFG was doing an environmental survey of a bay where a Liquefied Natural Gas terminal was proposed for construction. The survey involved doing baseline studies of all the invertebrates and fishes in the area, and documenting the recreational and commercial fisheries in the area that would be impacted. After two years she transferred to an invertebrate research project based out of Long Beach.

For eight years Kristine made dives off a variety of boats counting and surveying sea urchins and abalone. She was also involved in an abalone enhancement effort for most of those years. That project involved tagging abalone, transplanting adults to different areas, and outplanting thousands of hatchery reared juveniles (1/4-3" long) on the bottom.

In 1988 she took a management position in Santa Barbara. She became responsible for all marine activities in two coastal counties. In this position, she supervises seasonal fish samplers who monitor sport and commercial catches, and spends lots of time on the phone responding to questions and information requests. Writing status reports on a variety of fisheries and resources are among her regular duties.

Kristine interacts with mariculturists who lease acreage on the ocean floor to grow abalone, mussels, scallops and other invertebrates. She also acts as a liaison for the Department with a variety of city, county, state, and federal agencies. She is learning about several species that are harvested locally on a small scale so that other biologists can use her as a resource on those species when questions or problems arise. Presently she is an associate marine biologist. If she were to promote to the senior level it would be necessary to return to the regional headquarters in Long Beach. Her job would then primarily be that of an administrator.

Kristine loves her job because "there's still mystery in the sea, and a constant opportunity to learn and grow." Fishermen bring her specimens she's never seen or heard of before and together they go about determining what it is. When you're underwater time, weight, and what you see are all altered by the medium you're immersed in. It truly is one of the last frontiers. You can plan and have a ship full of electronic equipment and the sea is still in charge. She also enjoys the independence her position offers her. Her work hours may change, and her office may be a boat, a dock, or the beach. She likes people. That's important because most biologists have to be able to relate to the general public and their colleagues.

Kristine was making 250 dives a year when she was doing abalone enhancement work. Now she makes a total of 50-75 dives a year, including recreational and scientific dives.

WALTER JAAP

Walter Jaap is a biologist with the Florida Department of Natural Resources (DNR). Walt is with a unit of that organization called the Florida Marine Research Institute. Specifically, Jaap directs all the coral research being done by DNR.

When Walt returned from the army in the 1960's he had a friend who taught him how to dive. He went back to school on the G.I. Bill at the University of Miami, to study coral reefs and major in biology. When Walt decided to take a formal scuba course, marine science was not an established field yet. Walt was only able to take one dull course on marine oriented science at the University's marine lab. At that time scuba diving was not looked upon favorably by the academic world.

Jaap received his bachelors degree in 1970, and took several graduate courses He continues to take courses and attend workshops today, although he has never gotten a master's degree. After graduation he spent the summer in Europe to "see the world." When he returned to the U.S., he had the opportunity to work for DNR for 7-8 months as a ship's biologist. That was where he was indoctrinated and had to make the grade with a "crusty" captain. When that assignment was completed Walt was able to pursue his interest in coral reefs.

Walt has been studying changes in reef communities since the early 70's and has published numerous papers on the subject. He has also testified before the U.S. Senate on coral bleaching in the Florida Keys. In the 1950's reef communities were characterized as stable. Walt's work and that of other researchers has shown that the various species that compose a reef may change significantly over time.

In the past decade coral bleaching incidents have increased significantly. Walt is now studying the relationship of coral bleaching with climate (primarily temperature), ultraviolet light, and ozone depletion. Walt estimates that he makes 45-50 research dives a year. His diving is usually in concentrated blocks, sometimes in exotic locations.

Fig. 5.11 – Marine biologist Walt Jaap inspects a coral head for signs of bleaching off the coast of Florida. (Photo courtesy Walt Jaap)

Fifteen years ago a DNR employee had a serious diving accident. A female researcher was diving off a vessel and was fatigued and dehydrated. She passed out underwater and Walt was able to get her to the Navy chamber in Panama City (which doesn't normally treat civilians). Despite serious injuries she did fully recover, but Walt realized that DNR's diving program could be eliminated if another accident were to occur. To prevent an end to his research, Walt took on the responsibility of Diving Safety Officer for the 30 divers at DNR.

"When it comes to diving, you have to pay attention to what everybody in your organization is doing. One person's mistake could impact everyone," says Walt.

Walt loves the variety of things he does for DNR. He has opportunities to travel and present papers all over the world. Walt felt that his academic credentials are more heavily scrutinized because he works for the government, and that respect and acceptance of your research is harder to get.

DNR has been involved in a program to assist foreign countries with the management of their marine resources. For example, Walt recently returned from a diving research trip to Nicaragua. During his career he has found that diving in third world countries is potentially dangerous. The Nicaraguan boatman was competent, but had no experience or knowledge of diving activities. Walt and his colleagues' time in the country was short, so they chose to dive despite huge swells and generally undesirable water conditions. In this line of work, you have to constantly weigh the risks and make choices. Walt has a family at home that he wanted to return to as a healthy person.

Walt recommends that people interested in marine biology get a broad background in the sciences. To study the coral reefs he not only needed a strong biology background, but he also had to have knowledge of geology and oceanography. Diving he listed last, but stressed that with the weakness of today's sport diving courses you should pursue a research diver course. He feels that many students he encounters today lack general physical fitness. They're not involved in some regular form of exercise, like swimming, jogging, or bicycling. Without this fitness, a field biologist position shouldn't be considered.

Walt does primarily observational work underwater. He uses video and still photography as his main tools. He does hydraulic drilling to take cores of the corals for analysis of their skeletons. Walt uses ordinary scuba since most of his diving is in shallow water, but also uses nitrox at depths of 60 to 120 feet. In addition, his department uses surface supplied equipment when communications are needed. When the water gets cold, some of their divers have needed to use dry suits to get the job done.

In 1975 Walt had the opportunity to participate in SCORE, a Hydrolab project in the Bahamas. He lived underwater in Hydrolab, a research habitat, at 60 feet under marginal conditions. For six days he studied a coral reef that extended from depths of 35 to 250 feet. He rode a submersible to 250 feet and recalls being "blasted" with a movie camera light by another diver when he exited the sub. Since it's normally dark at that depth and he was breathing air, he really didn't comprehend what was happening immediately. Today the technology is much improved, and given the opportunity he would do it again.

DR. MIA TEGNER

Dr. Mia Tegner is a marine biologist on the permanent research faculty of Scripps Institution of Oceanography. She's been with Scripps since she received her Ph.D. from that Institution in 1974.

Mia started snorkeling during high school when she spent her summers as a camper and a counselor at a Girl Scout Camp on Catalina Island. She'd known back in elementary school that she wanted a career in science. What type of science she wanted to do she didn't decide until college. She received a Bachelor's in Biology from the University of California San Diego, but there was no money for scuba diving until she was in graduate school.

Scripps pays 1/4 of Mia's salary. She is expected to get grant money to support her research and provide the other 3/4 of her salary. Mia already had a sea urchin research program underway at Scripps (she had received a post doctoral research position right after completing her Ph.D.) when she received her research appointment in 1975.

In her early years of research Mia was making as many as 250 dives a year. Now it's on the order of 100 dives a year. She now has three staff members doing the diving for her research program. It's typical that the further along you get in your career the more time you spend in front of a computer and attending meetings.

Fig. 5.12 – You must be completely at home in the water to be able to do research in the ocean. Dr. Mia Tegner demonstrates a high comfort level as she prepares to dive near Scripps Institution of Oceanography. (Photo courtesy Scripps Institution of Oceanography)

The tools Mia has used underwater have been primarily scientific, coming under the category of measuring and sampling devices. She also had to learn how to analyze the data, and recognize all the plants and animals she encountered underwater. Mia feels her "special skill" was being able to see lots of things underwater and remember those observations. That ability gave her a feeling for the whole kelp forest community, not just individual species. Mia has made over 2900 dives, so her bottom time is significant.

Mia enjoys the freedom, variety, and challenge associated with her work. When asked about negatives she immediately responded that "she would like to retire to a 40 hour week." Fifty to sixty hour work weeks are normal for Mia.

"You would best look elsewhere if you're looking for a 9 to 5 job, or one that only requires eight hours a day," advises Dr. Tegner.

Mia's advice to someone seeking a career in marine biology is to "study diving last." You need a very solid grounding in the basic sciences. What is more important is a love of the ocean, curiosity, observing and wanting to know how things work.

Mia maintains that the most "ferocious" creature in the ocean is the sea urchin. She's had numerous spines surgically removed from several parts of her body.

Twenty-one years later Mia still recalls the awe of seeing a gray whale underwater. She was a newly certified diver poking around in the rocks off La Jolla. She looked up into the eye of a gray whale 15-20 feet away. It circled her and then swam off. Since then she's jumped in and swam with whales. But the memory of a whale "finding her" is something she'll never forget.

At Scripps, Mia hires technicians who have bachelor's and master's degrees. If you're interested in designing your own research program, asking your own questions, or being the boss, you'll need a doctorate.

Mia initially worked on sea urchin ecology and fisheries biology in Southern California. One of her contributions to that field is her work demonstrating that sea urchins were controlled by predators like sheephead and spiny lobster long after the disappearance of sea otters. Because of her reputation, the California Dept. of Fish and Game and California Sea Grant Program approached Mia about leading an experimental abalone enhancement project. She spent years exploring the natural history of abalone and four different approaches to increasing abalone numbers in Southern California. From there she went on to study kelp forest ecology, where she actually focused on the kelp plants themselves. Specifically, she studied the effects of natural disturbances, such as El Niño and storms on the kelps.

For the last two years Mia has been looking at the effects of sewage on kelp forest communities. This work has gotten her more active in the community. She testified at the trial of the City of San Diego when sued by the Environmental Protection Agency for not having the proper level of treatment for their sewage. She's also now on the San Diego City Wetlands Advisory Board, whose goal is to preserve the remaining wetlands in the area. Mia is also on the Interagency Water Quality Panel on San Diego Bay.

Suggested Reading:

Carson, Rachael. *Silent Spring.* Fawcett Crest Book. New York, NY.1962.

Clark, Eugenie. *Lady with a Spear.* Harper and Brothers. New York, NY. 1953.

Steinbeck, John. *The Log From the Sea of Cortez.* The Viking Press, New York, NY. 1971.

Chapter Six

MARINE ARCHAEOLOGY

Marine archaeology is the study of various people and their cultures based upon artifacts and other remains found underwater. The study of marine archaeology is extremely varied, ranging from the excavation of the submerged city of Port Royal in Jamaica, to the recovery of prehistoric human artifacts from Warm Mineral Springs in Florida, to the mapping of the wreck of the destroyer *U.S.S. Arizona* in Pearl Harbor, Hawaii. While marine archaeology is not treasure hunting, many treasure hunting expeditions now employ archaeologists to help locate wreck sites and artifacts, and to help preserve submerged objects when they are raised to the surface. The work of preserving these artifacts is known as "*conserving*", and people who do this work are known as "*conservators.*"

The father of underwater archaeology is Dr. George Bass. Dr. Bass started diving in 1959 when he enrolled in a YMCA scuba course, so he could excavate a bronze age shipwreck in Turkey. He conducted the first complete excavation of a shipwreck on the sea bed, and has been responsible for many of the innovations in underwater archaeology. In 1973 Bass founded the Institute of Nautical Archaeology (INA), which in 1976 became affiliated with Texas A & M University. This was the first academic program in the U.S. devoted to the archaeology of seafaring.

Training Required to Work as a Marine Archaeologist

To start training as a marine archaeologist you must begin your education with a basic program in archaeology or anthropology, the study of man. At the time of this writing there are no undergraduate, or "bachelor's" degree programs, in marine archaeology. Any degree you might earn would be in general archaeology rather than underwater archaeology. Most bachelor's programs take four years to complete.

Florida State University is an example of a university that offers both undergraduate and graduate degrees in anthropology. These undergraduate courses in anthropology include a *Basic Introduction to Archaeology, Physical Anthropology, Introduction to Folklore,* and *Language and Culture.* They offer three undergraduate courses in underwater archaeology including *Techniques in Underwater Site Research, Underwater Archaeology,* and *Anthropological Fieldwork in Underwater Archaeology.*

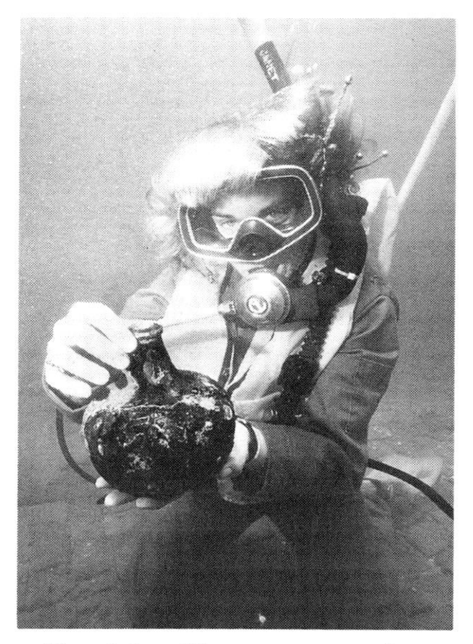

Fig. 6.1 – The recovery of an "onion" jar from the sunken city of Port Royal in Jamaica. Artifacts such as these tell us a great deal about the past. (© Doug Kesling)

To take the fieldwork courses you must be certified to dive under the university's diving program which is administered by the campus diving officer (see chapter 7 on diving safety officers). As a university research diver you will be expected to follow all university diving regulations and to log all your dives with the diving safety officer. This is required of both faculty and students. The diving officer only ensures that you are a competent diver. It is up to your professor to teach you the underwater research techniques required to be a competent marine archaeologist.

To work as a marine archaeologist in most places requires a master's degree at a minimum, and preferably a doctorate (Ph.D.). This represents an extensive amount of education, since most Ph.D. programs demand roughly seven years to complete a dissertation, in addition to the course work required. This process is pretty much the same for any academically oriented field you might choose, whether you are working to complete a doctorate in marine archaeology, marine biology, chemistry, physics, or any other subject.

Most course work at the graduate level is in the form of seminars and independent study, rather than the traditional lecture courses you attend as an undergraduate. Graduate courses are far less structured than undergraduate classes. Most of your time will be spent in researching and writing your dissertation.

A dissertation is basically a written scientific report on some type of original research that you have conducted under the direction of a professor at a university. The dissertation process starts when you and your supervising professor identify some topic that you would like to study in detail.

Fig. 6.2 – A doctoral student working on a dissertation on ship's weapons might need to dive a number of wreck sites to compare weapons from different cultures. In this photo a marine archaeologist marks a canon for further study. (Photo by Steven M. Barsky. © Diving Systems International. All rights reserved.)

The next step is for you to find two other professors at the university who are willing to serve on your dissertation committee. You must then write a proposal for your dissertation topic. The topic must be approved by your department and your committee.

In most cases, you will probably be working on some specialized topic that is part of a larger project that your supervising or "major professor" is conducting. For example, if your *major professor* is excavating a series of wrecks from the Spanish ships that explored the Americas, you might specialize in a topic such as the weapons that were carried aboard those ships, or the construction methods used to build the ships.

To write your dissertation you may need to dive on the wreck site, study the artifacts in place, photograph them, and help recover them. Your research may take you to museums in other states or countries to compare similar weapons from different cultures.

Once you complete your dissertation it is reviewed by the other members of your dissertation committee. They may request you to make any changes they feel are appropriate to ensure the accuracy of your paper. Depending upon the care you have taken in writing your paper, these changes can be either minor or extensive.

The final hurdle in obtaining your doctorate is the defense of your dissertation. Your defense is a formal session that is open to all members of the faculty. They are free during this time to ask you any questions they may have about your dissertation. You must be able to defend your work and explain why you used particular methods and how you came to the conclusions that you presented. Upon successful defense of your dissertation you will be awarded the degree of Doctor of Philosophy, or "Ph.D." This is the highest academic achievement you can reach.

As a Ph.D., you are considered a professor or "doctor." In the academic world this title carries a variety of privileges. As a professor you can supervise graduate students who are working on their doctorates, you can teach graduate level courses, and you are generally considered qualified to obtain research grants (money), and conduct your own research.

There is an alternate degree known as the Ed.D., or Doctor of Education. This degree is more oriented towards teaching. The process of earning a Ed.D. is similar to the Ph.D., but the Ph.D. degree is far more popular.

Working as a Marine Archaeologist

Most marine archaeologists are either employed as faculty at a university, or as researchers for either government agencies or private foundations. For example, the National Geographic Society funds many archaeological research projects. These projects often appear in the form of articles or television specials funded by the society.

In many cases, marine archaeologists, like marine biologists, are funded by what is known as "*soft money.*" Soft money is a grant that is funded on an annual basis. The grant must be applied for, and won, for each successive year. The researcher who works on soft money is out of a job if they fail to win a grant that particular year.

University professors who teach and have regular faculty positions are on "*hard money.*" Usually, these people are still expected to do research and apply for outside grants, but their positions are not

Fig. 6.3 – Marine archaeologists specialize in many different areas. This scientist is recovering a stone Indian bowl off the coast of California. How these bowls came to be in the ocean is an unsolved mystery. (Photo by Steve Barsky. © Diving Systems International. All rights reserved.)

Fig. 6.4 – A magnetometer would easily locate a steel hulled ship like this one. This wreck is in the waters of the Channel Islands National Park off the coast of California. (Photo by Steve Barsky. © Diving Systems International. All rights reserved.)

dependent upon outside funds. The grant money that they secure is used to help fund graduate students while they are doing research for their advanced degrees. Grant money also pays for research expeditions and the purchase of specialized equipment needed for research. In addition, the university takes 50% of the grant, or more, directly off the top to pay for "administrative costs."

A marine archaeological research project may begin in several ways. For example, a fisherman or sport diver may accidentally find a wreck or archaeological site and share the information with friends. Eventually the researcher may hear about it. A researcher may read about a lost ship and begin research by reading through all available historical accounts on the subject. Whatever form a project takes, most marine archaeologists have some sort of specialty area that is their main interest. They strive to become specialists in particular areas of submerged history.

Marine archaeologists use many tools to do their research. If they are searching for a shipwreck that contains any iron or steel, one of the most likely tools to be used will be a "*magnetometer.*" A magnetometer is a metal detector that can be towed behind a research ship to help locate metal items on the bottom.

Another commonly used device is "*side scan sonar.*" Side scan, depending upon the experience of the operator, can give a very accurate picture of the profile of the bottom and any objects that lie exposed upon it. Side scan, in the hands of the right operator, can pick up detail as small as the image of a two inch cable lying along the bottom.

A more specialized electronic device that is increasingly used today is the "*sub-bottom profiler.*" This device uses low frequency sound to examine bottom sediments and create an image of any items that are buried beneath it.

To accurately determine the location of each "target" on the bottom, scientists use navigational devices such as "*Loran*" and "*GPS*" (Global Positioning Systems). These systems are essential to allow the scientists to return to the site easily. Loran systems rely upon land based transmitters that send out timed radio signals. A Loran receiver aboard the research vessel receives the signals from a minimum of three stations and electronically calculates the position of the vessel.

Fig. 6.5 – Hand-held metal detectors are sometimes used to locate buried artifacts.

Global Positioning Systems (GPS) receive radio signals from satellites high above the earth's surface. GPS is far more accurate than Loran and can allow a vessel to return within 50 feet of the original location.

Once the site is located the scientist uses a wide variety of other tools. Hand held metal detectors may be used to locate metal objects that are buried on the bottom. Underwater cameras are used to document the location, condition, and position of individual objects on the bottom. If the water is clear enough still photography is also frequently used to create what is known as a "*photo mosaic,*" or a composite image of the entire site, pieced together from a series of individual photographs.

Another tool that may be used is an "*airlift*" or "*dredge.*" Airlifts are constructed from pipes, tubing, and hose. The lift itself is a simple tube or section of pipe with a valve attached to it at the bottom end. An air hose is attached to the valve, usually supplied with air from a low pressure air compressor on the surface. When the air is turned on, it enters the pipe through the valve. Of course, underwater, air always rises to the surface. As the air rises through the tube it expands and fills the pipe. This rising air creates a vacuum or lift inside the pipe. When the scientist holds the airlift against the bottom it removes whatever sand or mud may be covering an artifact. This is a very rapid method of excavating an archaeological site.

Many tools used by marine archaeologists are very simple, common items. For example, ping-pong paddles have been used to gently fan sand away from delicate objects that are too fragile to be uncovered by a dredge.

One of the more common techniques for surveying a site is to establish what's known as a "*baseline*" or "*transect line*" down the middle of the site. For example, if you were surveying a shipwreck the transect line would probably be laid along the keel line of the most intact section of the wreck. Plastic tags with identifying numbers can be attached to each significant feature on the site. From there measurements can be made to other sections of the wreck. By using triangulation and taking several measurements to the same point from locations on the baseline, it is possible to draw an extremely accurate picture of both the size and location of each section of wreckage. This is particularly effective for wrecks that are not intact.

The use of a transect line is just one technique used to survey an underwater site. It is also possible to map the site by laying down an underwater grid to divide the area into hundreds of numbered squares. These grid systems may be made from a variety of commonly available materials, such as plastic pipe. Each square is usually individually photographed as it is excavated to contribute to the photo mosaic, and to show the relative position of all artifacts in different layers on the site.

Hundreds, or thousands of measurements are made while the objects are still underwater. In some cases certain artifacts may never be raised to the surface. This is either due to the cost of conserving them, or because it may not be possible to conserve them after submersion, particularly in salt water. Items that are recovered must be tagged and cataloged to identify where they were located on the wreck so their placement will be in context for further study.

Once a site has been completely mapped it is relatively easy to compile a detailed map of the site by plugging all of the coordinates and measurements into a computer mapping system. In addition, each artifact recovered from the site can be placed into a computer database for rapid retrieval of information.

Marine archaeologists are excited by their work for many reasons. George Bass points to the role that ships and shipping have played in man's culture and history. Until the development of the airplane and the automobile, ships were used to transport virtually all manufactured goods and raw materials, and to spread cultures to the ends of the earth.

For other archaeologists, like Duncan Mathewson, who supervised the work on the Spanish galleon *Atocha,* the importance of a shipwreck lies in the fact that each shipwreck is like a time capsule. It contains a "snapshot" of the history and culture of that period.

Fig. 6.6 – Marine archaeologists use the diving gear most appropriate to the job at hand. In the case of a shallow wreck off the Florida coast, Duncan Mathewson chooses scuba gear for his work. (Photo © Peter Ellegard)

One of the continuing arguments among archaeologists are the relative merits of excavating a shipwreck, or other underwater site, compared to leaving the material undisturbed on the bottom. According to Mathewson, in his book, *Treasure of the Atocha,...*

"Archaeology is a destructive science. Once a site is excavated, it can never be put back together. The contextual data, the spatial relationships that are so critical to proper interpretation of a site, are destroyed. Yet, historical sites are part of our common heritage, and the information they contain belongs to everyone. In the process of excavating a site, the archaeologist assumes a responsibility to the public, to

proceed carefully, extracting every morsel of data from the site as it is dismantled. Because so much is unknown about everyday life aboard ship, every artifact, no matter how small or seemingly insignificant, might be important. Each must be mapped as it is removed, then cleaned, preserved, studied, and currated."

Like all scientists who work underwater, marine archaeologists use a wide variety of diving equipment, and select the gear that is most appropriate for the job. In very shallow water, a set of mask, fins, and snorkel may be suitable. In deeper water they may use scuba gear, or surface supplied equipment consisting of a full face mask, or helmet, with an umbilical and topside air supply.

Fig. 6.7 – Exhibits of marine artifacts recovered from shipwrecks are very popular with visitors.

As in all the professions we have discussed in this book, the diving techniques employed by these scientists are merely a means of transportation to go underwater and do their job. For them, diving is not an end to itself. It is just another tool that they use to get the job done. It is understood that if you do this type of work you must be an extremely competent diver.

As previously mentioned, some marine archaeologists work for universities, while others, like Mathewson, work for commercial salvors. There are also a number of archaeologists who are associated with museums or government agencies. For example, the U.S. National Park Service operates the National Maritime Museum in Golden Gate Park in San Francisco. This museum is visited by thousands of tourists and school groups each year. Marine archaeologists have played an important role in preserving and interpreting the artifacts on display in the museum. In addition, archaeologists have participated in the reconstruction of several historic ships that are on display at the museum's wharf. Other marine museums around the country have similar exhibits.

Fig. 6.8 – Ships like the "C.A. Thayer" have been restored with the help and supervision of marine archaeologists. The Thayer is at the wharf at the National Maritime Museum in San Francisco.

Experiences of Marine Archaeologists

DUNCAN MATHEWSON

R. Duncan Mathewson III is the Executive Director of the non-profit National Center for Shipwreck Research, Ltd. Mathewson is especially noted for having been the chief archaeologist in the discovery and salvage of Mel Fisher's *Atocha*, off Florida's Marquesas Keys.

Duncan has been involved with anthropological research for over 25 years. Since 1973 he has been specializing in marine archaeology and cultural resource management in the Florida Keys. He has extensive teaching experience, and for the past several years has concentrated on developing educational programs for the public schools in the Keys. He has taught marine archaeology courses to over 1500 divers in 20 different states. He has written and edited five books and over 50 articles on historic shipwrecks and environmental education.

Mathewson completed his undergraduate work at Dartmouth College, and has done graduate work at the University of London, the University of Edinburgh in Scotland, and Florida Atlantic University. He has also worked as the director of excavations for the Institute of Jamaica. He is currently working on his Ph.D. in environmental education.

Mathewson did not learn to dive until he went to work for Mel Fisher in 1973. During his time with Fisher, Duncan taught many young salvage divers to use proper archaeological techniques, so they would not destroy the valuable information that was part of the shipwreck site. At the same time, he used his work on the *Atocha* to complete his master's thesis (similar to a dissertation) at Florida Atlantic University.

Despite over 12 years of continuous work on the wreck, and the discovery of many artifacts, it was not until July 20, 1985 that the main cargo of the *Atocha* was located. It was Mathewson's job to direct the cataloging and recording of 1,041 silver ingots, over 115 gold bars, 60 gold coins, 100,000 silver coins, and thousands of everyday personal items that had been carried aboard the ship by the Spaniards.

For years Mathewson took a lot of criticism from the academic community for working with a treasure hunter like Fisher. In 1973 when Mathewson started consulting with Mel Fisher as a professional archaeologist, he was the only academic in the country willing to work for a commercial salvage company. Today there are over a dozen marine archaeologists consulting with private sector shipwreck salvors. Now some of the best known names in marine archaeology agree with Mathewson's approach. Professional marine archaeologists have a major role to play with commercial salvors to assure that reliable archaeological data is recorded and preserved in salvage projects.

Mathewson has been awarded major grants from the National Endowment for the Humanities, the Kidder Peabody Foundation, and the U.S. Department of the Interior, as well as many other organizations. He started the National Center for Shipwreck Research in 1988. One of Mathewson's goals is to help train sport divers to be "paraprofessionals" in the field of underwater archaeology.

Duncan enjoys teaching shipwreck archaeology and meeting the diving public. He doesn't enjoy the adversarial nature of relations between professional archaeologists and the diving community at large. Duncan feels that most professional researchers want to keep the diving community unaware of findings from shipwreck research. He believes that the more recreational divers know about historic shipwrecks, the more they will assist in protecting them.

Duncan's advice to anyone considering marine archaeology as a career is to learn the language of archaeology. Additionally, you must learn the interdisciplinary nature of shipwreck research, which not only involves archaeology, but also aspects of marine biology and naval architecture, as well as other disciplines.

Fig. 6.9 – Duncan Mathewson teaches shipwreck archaeology to the diving public.

Working as an archaeologist also means that you must learn to work as part of a team, since nobody can excavate an archaeological site single-handedly. You must also learn to appreciate shipwrecks as nonrenewable resources. In 20 years of doing shipwreck research, Mathewson notes that he has only learned one thing about shipwrecks; "the more we learn, the less we understand." According to him, "The best wrecks are yet to be found!"

Mathewson's current project is the Ship of Discovery Artificial Reef. The "reef" is a full size replica of a sixteenth century Spanish galleon made of ferrocement. The ship will be built in several pieces, and the plan is to anchor it on the bottom in the Florida Keys National Marine Sanctuary. This "wreck" will be used to teach scuba divers about marine archaeology. Divers interested in getting a taste of what marine archaeology is all about have an excellent opportunity to do that each summer during the two week field school that Mathewson holds each year in the Florida Keys.

DAN LENIHAN

Dan Lenihan was working as a school teacher when he started diving in 1970 in the Virgin Islands. In 1971 he moved to Florida, where he took an advanced diving course, and subsequently completed a Master's degree in Anthropology at Florida State University. While in Florida he became involved in cave diving. This interest would eventually serve him well in his exploration of shipwrecks for the National Park Service.

Lenihan first worked for the National Park Service in a temporary position in Florida in 1974. It was a temporary position with the Southeast Archaeological Center in underwater archaeology. He also worked for the North Carolina Division of Cultural Resources as an underwater archaeologist in 1975.

In 1976 Dan landed a full time job with the National Park Service with the agency's Submerged Cultural Resources Unit (SCRU). As

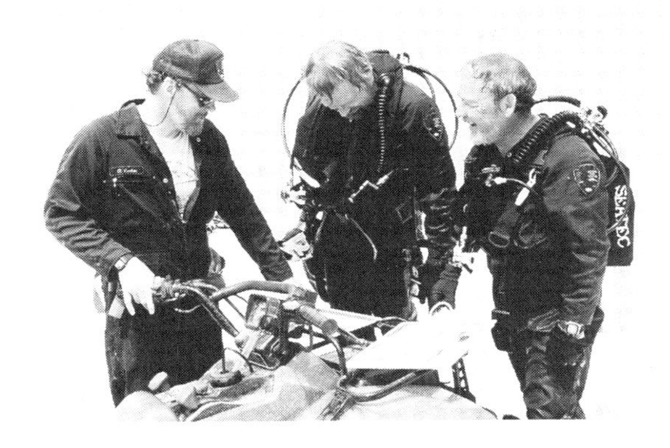

Fig. 6.10 – Dan Lenihan is the Chief of the Submerged Cultural Resources Unit for the National Park Service. Their complex projects illustrate the importance of teamwork. Here, Lenihan (in the hat) briefs fellow team members Larry Nordby and Jerry Livingston prior to a dive on the ships sunk during the atomic tests at Bikini Atoll in the south Pacific. (National Park Service photo by Larry Murphy.)

Chief of this unit, Dan has directed a wide variety of shipwreck research around the world. Dan has completed a major study of ten shipwrecks in Lake Superior at Isle Royale National Park, a study of the *USS Arizona* in Pearl Harbor, and a survey of the sunken fleet in the Bikini Atoll of the Marshall Islands in the South Pacific. His diving projects have taken him to the Aleutian Islands of Alaska, Guam, Palau, and Kosrae.

The findings from Lenihan's research are shared with the general public in many ways. For example, his team has produced a detailed drawing of the *Arizona* as it currently rests on the bottom, so that people can understand the condition of the wreck.

Lenihan and his divers use a wide variety of diving equipment, including full face masks, dry suits, surface supplied gear, communications systems, underwater cameras, and underwater video systems. They also use surveying equipment, side scan sonar, and magnetometers on a regular basis.

As an employee of the federal government Lenihan enjoys many excellent benefits including health care and retirement. The job has provided good security for many years, although budget cuts and funding are a continuous source of concern for all federal employees.

While travel is one of the benefits of Dan's job, it also is one of its liabilities. Oddly enough the home base for the Submerged Cultural Resources Unit is Santa Fe, New Mexico. Since Lenihan and his team serve the entire National Park Service, and also consult with foreign governments under a variety of international agreements, the SCRU team members spend a great deal of time away from home. This is not unusual for an archaeologist, since many excavations often take months, or even years, to complete.

DELLA SCOTT

Della Scott works for the Florida State Department of Underwater Archaeology. Della started diving in 1986. Her scuba lessons were a gift from her parents when she graduated from high school.

Della became interested in archaeology as a child when her father read her the *How and Why Wonder Book of Lost Civilizations*. To fulfill her dream she attended the University of West Florida in Pensacola, where she majored in anthropology and also studied archaeology. She completed her degree in 1990.

While she was in college Della took courses in terrestrial (land based) archaeology. However, in the spring of her junior year she attended a lecture by Dr. Roger Smith of the Florida State Department of Underwater Archaeology and realized marine archaeology was the field she wanted to pursue. That summer she participated in a field school where she studied a British warship that was eroding in the surf on Florida's Dead Man's Island. The opportunity confirmed her desire to become an underwater archaeologist.

Fig. 6.11 – Della Scott works for the Florida State Department of Underwater Archaeology. (Photo courtesy of Della Scott.)

Upon graduation from college Della traveled to Israel to take part in an underwater archaeological survey in the Mediterranean. The project was the excavation of Caesarea Maritima, a seaport city built by Herod the Great. Della spent a month on the project before returning home.

While in college Della earned her divemaster rating and continued to work on her skills. In the summer of 1991 she became a NAUI scuba instructor.

Della's next involvement in underwater archaeology was as a volunteer on a shipwreck survey conducted by the state of Florida off Pensacola. She looked for ways to assist the project and made herself indispensable. In March of 1992 she was hired on full-time by the state as a Field Supervisor.

In her present job she locates wrecks in Pensacola Bay using a magnetometer and side scan sonar. To date her project has located 33 wrecks, with the majority dating from the turn of this century.

One of Della's goals is to earn her doctorate degree. She hopes to study with Dr. George Bass.

Della finds tremendous excitement in her job, especially when she discovers a wreck that nobody knew existed. She particularly enjoys figuring out what a wreck has to tell her about the past. Although she likes the diving, she is quick to point out that your first love must be for archaeology. She looks forward to getting up and going to work each morning.

"If you're not prepared to put your time in at school, then underwater archaeology isn't for you," says Della. "You also have to be prepared to deal with water conditions that aren't always pleasant. Even in Pensacola, the water can get down to 58 degrees during the winter months."

The most distasteful part of Della's job is dealing with people who don't understand the value of archaeology, specifically, treasure hunters and vandals. This makes her very upset.

Della's advice for the prospective marine archaeologist is to plan on earning a master's degree, at the very least. Work on your diving skills to take them to an advanced level. She makes between 200 and 300 dives a year, between her full-time job and teaching diving on the side.

For More Information on Underwater Archaeology:

National Center for Shipwreck Research Ltd.
P.O. Box 1123
Islamorada, FL 33036
Tel. (305) 852-1960
FAX (305) 852-8617

Underwater Sciences and Education Resources
Indiana University, Smith Research Bldg. #190
Bloomington, IN 47405
Tel. (812) 855-5053
FAX (812) 855-8545

Suggested Reading:

Mathewson, R. Duncan III. *Treasure of the Atocha,* Pisces Books, New York, 1986

Gould, Richard A. *Shipwreck Anthropology.* University of New Mexico Press, Albuquerque, New Mexico, 1983

Rule, M. The Mary Rose: *The Excavation and Raising of Henry VIII's Flagship.* Conway Maritime Press, London, England, 1983.

Chapter Seven

DIVING SAFETY OFFICERS

Diving safety officers are diving instructors who work for a university, or other scientific organization, to supervise the diving of the people who dive under the jurisdiction of that organization. Students and scientists that use compressed air diving include those in the fields of physical oceanography, engineering, marine biology, biochemistry, human physiology and performance, and archaeology. The job of the diving safety officer typically includes many duties, from instructing new divers to on-site visits to ensure the safety of the divers on individual research projects.

The position of diving safety officer exists for two principle reasons. First, diving safety officers act on behalf of the organization to ensure safety and to help avoid situations that could create liability problems and put the organization at risk. Secondly, when the scientific divers entered a court battle with the Federal Government over OSHA (Occupational Safety and Health Act) Regulations, diving safety officers and their authority within the research diving community, were identified as one of the key elements in differentiating scientific divers from commercial diving organizations. There are no recognized scientific diving organizations that do not have a diving safety officer. The diving officer has a position of extreme responsibility that requires knowledge, experience, education, and diplomacy.

History of Diving Officers

The first diving officer in the United States was Conrad Limbaugh at Scripps Institution of Oceanography in La Jolla, California. Limbaugh was one of the earliest scuba divers in the United States and provided the training that was the start of many diving programs in this country.

After Conrad Limbaugh died, Jim Stewart replaced him at Scripps and became the most widely recognized diving officer in the U.S. Stewart and the Scripps diving program became the models that other diving officers, universities, and research organizations strove to emulate. Stewart freely shared his knowledge and experience with other diving officers across the country as scuba became a common research tool for many types of scientific exploration.

In the early 1980's, an organization was formed known as the American Academy of Underwater Sciences (AAUS). AAUS grew out of the battle between the scientific diving community and OSHA. Basically, OSHA wanted to place research divers under the same system of organization and constraints as commercial divers. The government argued that since scientific divers were working, they should be subject to all the regulations that working (commercial) divers faced. The scientific divers successfully argued that the nature of their work, research, as well as their diving methods, organizations, and procedures were totally different from the commercial diving industry. The scientific divers realized that if they did not put up a united front it would become very difficult, if not impossible, for them to do their jobs. By uniting the way they did, they were able to effectively present their case before the government and the proposed restrictions on scientific diving were dissolved.

One of the outgrowths of AAUS' battle was the formal recognition of a policy known as "*reciprocity*" that had already existed for many years in the scientific diving community. Reciprocity deals with the acceptance and recognition of the equality between various research diving programs. The idea behind reciprocity is that if a scientific diver is certified to dive under a particular organization's diving program, he need not be recertified when he transfers to another organization, provided their training and annual recertification programs are the same. Reciprocity is one of the keys to the tremendous safety record of the scientific diving community. Everyone that works in scientific diving tries to maintain a certain uniform level of training and ability. The diving officers in the U.S. meet regularly to cooperatively determine and enforce these standards.

Qualifications for Diving Safety Officers

Diving safety officers hold positions of tremendous responsibility, since they are held accountable for everyone who dives under the auspices of their program. If they work at a university, they are responsible for both the students and faculty who dive to support their research projects. Even if the students and faculty travel to remote locations, such as Antarctica, the diving safety officer is still held accountable for the safety of their diving operation.

The most basic qualification for a diving safety officer is they must be a certified diving instructor with a nationally recognized certifying organization. However, beyond this, most organizations will require any job applicant to have a reasonable amount of diving experience under varied conditions. For example, if you are a diving instructor from the midwest, and all your diving experience is in the Great Lakes, it would be unreasonable to expect that you would be considered well qualified for a diving officer position on Catalina Island, off Los Angeles.

The more specialized training you have in a wide variety of diving situations, the more qualified you are considered for a safety diving officer position. Specialties that would enhance your chances of landing a job in this field would include ice diving, cave diving, surface supplied diving, deep diving, and blue water diving. Blue water diving is a specialty that involves diving far out in the open ocean, in mid water, in water depths where for all practical purposes, there is no bottom. Blue water diving is commonly done to collect tiny biological organisms that drift with the ocean currents.

Fig. 7.1 – Diving safety officer John Heine is knowledgeable in many different areas, including ice diving, cave diving, surface supplied diving, and blue water diving. John has made several trips to Antarctica, where this photo was taken. (Photo courtesy John Heine)

Most scientific diving programs now require their divers to maintain current certification in CPR throughout the time they are active in the program. Part of the job of the diving safety officer will include testing their organization's divers' CPR skills. For this reason, it is highly recommended (and sometimes mandatory) that a diving safety officer be certified as a CPR instructor. This additional training will allow you to provide training and periodic review for your divers.

Usually, a diving instructor is only required to complete certification in first aid at the time they are first certified. Because of the nature of training you will be providing as a diving safety officer, it will be important to maintain and increase your knowledge and skills in this area This can be accomplished by renewing your certification in general first aid periodically, or, better yet, by becoming trained as a First Aid Instructor or Emergency Medical Technician. While this may not be a requirement of the job, it will make you a much more desirable candidate, and provide you invaluable insight, knowledge and skill as an educator, and as a potential rescuer.

One area of emergency medical training that is becoming more accessible is hyperbaric chamber operations. This specialized kind of training is usually only required for diving safety officers who work at a site where a hyperbaric chamber is located (usually remote research stations). Beyond this, the training and experience by itself is invaluable for anyone charged with providing training in all areas of dive rescue and accident management.

One of the most important areas of training in the area of dive accident management, is oxygen administration. This is a must for any diving safety officer. The use of oxygen at the scene of a diving accident has been documented many times over as probably the single most important step in field care (other than life support) of an injured diver. There are training programs available all over the United States through the Diver's Alert Network (DAN) and some of the diver training agencies that specifically address the role of oxygen in dive accident management. It is incumbent upon any diving safety officer to provide adequate training in the use of oxygen to the divers in their program.

While not all university diving officer positions require an academic degree, in most cases you stand a better chance of landing one of these jobs if you have graduated from a four year college. Even if your academic degree is in a nonscientific area such as art or music, you will have greater success in these positions if you hold a degree. The higher the academic degree that you hold, the easier you will find dealing with people who hold advanced degrees. Unfortunately, there is quite a bit of intellectual snobbery in certain academic circles that can make it difficult to do your job if you do not hold an academic degree.

The best preparation for a diving officer position, aside from a scuba instructor's certification, is prior participation as a diver in a research diving program. This will give you the best insight into the type of work that research divers do, and the demands placed upon people in an academic diving program. If you do not have a scientific background, it may be possible to volunteer to serve as a buddy for research divers at an institution in your area. This is an excellent way to gain experience and knowledge about scientific diving.

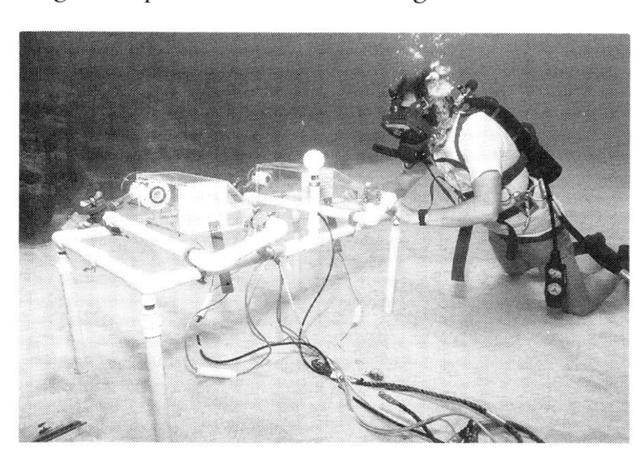

Fig. 7.2 – The best preparation for a diving officer position, aside from a scuba instructor's certification, is prior participation as a diver in a research diving program. (Photo © Doug Kesling)

Working as a Diving Safety Officer

Diving safety officers have many responsibilities and must be capable of juggling multiple priorities. Given the tight funding on university campuses today, it is not uncommon for diving safety officers to be asked to fulfill multiple roles in addition to their diving tasks.

One of the key roles of the diving safety officer is to interface with the "*diving safety board*" or "*dive control board.*" The diving safety board is a committee of people, within the larger organization where the diving officer works, who set the policies for diving within that organization. At a university, the diving safety board might be made up of professors from several departments, representatives from the student body, representatives from the school administration, and the diving safety officer. Both the faculty and student body representatives on the diving safety board will normally be divers. The chairman of the diving safety board will usually be a faculty member, not the diving safety officer.

In a government agency, the diving safety board will normally be made up of divers from various offices throughout the department. At the California Department of Fish and Game, the diving safety board is made up of marine biologists and wardens from across the state of California. You must be a highly experienced diver to be considered as a member of the board. New members are selected from the Department's divers by the existing members of the board. To be a member of the diving safety board, you must be a scuba instructor, although you may be provisionally appointed to the board, contingent upon your satisfactory completion of a scuba instructors course. In this situation, the chairman of the diving safety board is considered to be the Department's diving safety officer.

Diving safety boards meet a minimum of once a year, although most meet at least quarterly. The purpose of the board is to review diving practices within the organization, and set policy. The diving officer makes recommendations to the diving safety board. In particular, the board will deal with situations that are unique to the organization's requirements, make rulings on exceptional situations, and will pass judgment on divers who have violated the organization's policies and procedures. In rare instances, the board will suspend the diving privileges of an individual if there is sufficient cause, such as deliberate unsafe diving practices. Divers who willfully ignore the organization's diving regulations place the entire scientific diving community at risk. Entire diving programs have been shut down by universities and other organizations as the result of a single accident.

The diving safety officer needs to have an excellent working relationship with the diving safety board. Although the diving safety board does not usually have the final say in the hiring or dismissal of a diving officer, the board usually has serious input into these decisions. It is almost impossible for a diving officer to do their job effectively if they do not have the cooperation and support of the diving safety board.

Each scientific diving organization has a "*diving safety manual*" that outlines the policies and procedures for that particular group. The diving safety manual is not an instructional manual, but serves as a reference guide whenever there is a question about policy. Every diver in the program is given a copy of the manual to ensure that there is no question regarding procedures. It is normally the responsibility of the diving safety officer to ensure that the manual is up-to-date, and that revisions are made as technology and policies change. The diving manual includes all information related to a diving program, from defining its scope, responsible persons in the system, structure of the regulating body within the program, to a set of guidelines for equipment, procedures, training, etc.

Diving safety officers are responsible for the training of all research divers in their organization. The standard research diving course is 100 hours long and includes 12 open water dives. This standard was established by Jim Stewart at Scripps and is considered the optimum program for training scientific divers. Even if a student is a certified sport diver, they are required to attend and satisfactorily complete the "100 hour course." The only exception, of course, would be a diver who transfers in from another diving program that has reciprocity with that scientific diving program.

In the University of California system, when a student or faculty member completes the research diving course he is certified to dive to 33 feet. To be certified to dive deeper, the diver must log 12 dives between 33 feet and the next certification depth of 66 feet. This procedure is followed for diving certifications down to 132 feet. To dive any deeper than this requires special permission from the diving safety officer and the diving safety board.

Fig. 7.3 – Diving safety officers are responsible for the training of all research divers in their organization. In this capacity, John Heine trains divers in dry suit diving techniques at Moss Landing Marine Laboratory.

The standard research diver training course is designed to bring all the divers in the program up to the same level of competency. It is roughly equivalent to an advanced diving course, only there are more dives and a high level of knowledge is expected. In addition, many research diving courses will include the use of specialized diving equipment, such as dry suits or surface supplied gear. The course may also include the basics of scientific diving techniques.

The diving safety officer is responsible to make sure that any diving activities that are conducted are of a safe nature, and that the most appropriate approach is being taken to accomplish the work required underwater. This usually means that the diving safety officer will dive with each diver in their organization to see first hand what is being done, and to offer any assistance that may be needed. Many programs also require a dive plan proposal which gives a detailed report of the type of diving anticipated on a given project (depths, times, frequency of dives), the time frame of the project, the faculty advisor (if applicable), other divers on the project, and what the project is attempting to accomplish.

Every scientific diver must file his diving logs with the diving safety officer on a regular basis. Some organizations require this monthly, while other agencies require logs only quarterly. It is the duty of the diving officer to review each diver's logs as they are submitted. In examining the logs, the diving officer checks to ensure that the diver is logging the proper number of dives per quarter, that the diver is not exceeding allowable dive depths, and that the dives follow the dive tables or recommended dive computer profiles. Any diver who is not following the diving regulations of the organization will receive an inquiry from the diving safety officer.

One of the most difficult parts of the diving officer's job is dealing with people who violate the diving regulations of the organization. In the urgency to complete a research project, some scientific divers will look for ways to bend the rules or get around the diving regulations as outlined in the diving safety manual. It requires great tact to deal with a professor who is in a rush to complete a research project, to get him to comply with regulations, without alienating him. While it is rare for a diving officer to be placed in a position where they must forbid someone from diving, it does happen. While a diving officer must be strong enough to maintain their position, they must also be diplomatic enough to try to get along and get an uncooperative diver to modify their stance.

Another responsibility that is common to all diving officers is the maintenance of records of divers' physicals and equipment. All scientific diving organizations require a physical examination on a regular basis, although some programs require them annually while other programs demand them only every other year. While the diving officer will not normally see the diver's physical exam papers, he will keep a record of the dates of each diver's physical as well as the physician's summary on each diver.

Fig. 7.4 – Nicole Crane, diving officer at Hopkins Marine Station in Monterey, California, reviews dive logs with Jim Coyer, a diving scientist, in his lab.

Since many students obtain their scuba physicals through their campus Student Health Center, there is usually a working relationship between the diving safety officer and the Director of the Health Center. It is the responsibility of the diving safety officer to work with the medical staff, and offer any assistance available to be sure that they have the information they need in evaluating a person's fitness to dive. There are times when a physician will consult with the diving safety officer in making decisions regarding divers who have a medical history or condition that may be "questionable." The diving safety officer is a tremendous resource for the physician in these kinds of instances.

Most research diving programs will allow a diver to use his own equipment, as long as the gear meets the standards established by the program. However, some agencies will require divers to use equipment supplied by their program. Regardless of whose equipment is used, every diver's gear must be inspected and serviced on an annual basis. The diving officer must notify each diver when his equipment must be serviced and must maintain copies of receipts for equipment serviced by dive stores or manufacturers.

In some organizations it may be the diving officer's responsibility to maintain some or all the equipment. When this is the case, the diving safety officer must be trained to perform equipment repairs by the manufacturer.

As a research diving safety officer, one of the most important things you can do is to get out and dive with the divers in your organization on a regular basis. This is essential for several reasons. First, and foremost, this builds rapport with the other divers in your organization. This is the only way you can develop a good understanding of the problems facing the research projects your divers are working on.

Secondly, by diving with your researchers on a regular basis you can identify any potential problems in diving techniques that may lead to accidents within your organization. Finally, by keeping abreast of the demands of each project in your organization you will be able to better prepare new divers who join your team to meet the demands of the diving that your people engage in.

Fig. 7.5 – As a diving safety officer it is important to get out and dive with the people in your organization. Nicole Crane dives frequently with the scientists at Hopkins Marine Station.

One of the things that frequently happens with most diving organizations, is that divers from other agencies will visit to assist with the research being conducted by the people in your organization. Even though there is reciprocity between most research diving programs, most diving officers will conduct a check-out dive with visiting scientists. This is a normal procedure and does not convey any lack of confidence in another group's diving program, but recognizes that there are differences in individuals and their abilities. In this way, the diving safety officer ensures that he understands the capabilities of any visiting diver so that they do not engage in diving that is beyond their capacity.

All scientific diving programs have annual recertification programs, to check to see that skills are maintained and upgraded. The typical recertification program lasts for one or two days, and includes a series of watermanship tests, cardiopulmonary resuscitation (CPR) recertification, and training in some new aspect of diving. The watermanship tests usually include a swim test and a review of basic diving emergency skills, such as emergency swimming ascents and buddy breathing. This annual recertification ensures a very high level of skill, knowledge, and fitness among scientific divers.

Diving safety officers are expected to keep abreast of the latest changes in diving technology and in research diving techniques. It is essential for a diving officer to be more than just familiar with the latest dive computers, procedures such as nitrox diving, and the latest navigational equipment.

Resources available to the diving safety officer varies from program to program, usually dependent upon available funding. For example, a diving safety officer in one program may have their own secretary and/or an assistant, whereas another may be a "one-man show." Some diving programs own all their own diving equipment including masks, fins, snorkels, regulators, cylinders, and even a fill station, where another might "own" no equipment at all. One campus program may have a Student Health Center that will conduct diving physicals for students and employees of the university, where another may have no funding available to offer that service, and divers must go to a private physician. Some programs have the ability to conduct their own testing of dive gear, where others may have to require divers to bring a written report from an authorized repair station, to meet the requirements of the program. Whenever possible, it is in the diving program's best interest to keep as much support inside the program, for consistency and assured quality standards in the care, maintenance and inspection of equipment. Also, this allows for much more thorough record-keeping for all work done.

Fig. 7.6 – Diving safety officers need to understand the equipment their scientists are using in order to ensure they are using safe techniques. These scientists are taking a sample with a coring device that drills into the bottom. (Photo © Doug Kesling)

The kinds of resources that are almost always available to a diving safety officer are liability insurance, health and safety consultants, and legal counsel. Just about all diving programs are housed in the kind of institution that has departments to handle these kinds of issues, and the diving safety officer can call on them whenever necessary for advice.

There are many fringe benefits that make the job of a diving safety officer quite appealing. For example, if working for a college or university, almost always there will be a fee waiver program, which allows the employees of that institution to attend classes for credit, often on "company time," for free. Another benefit is the opportunity to be involved with exciting, "state of the art" research projects that will provide unique opportunities and experience for the person involved. There is also an endless amount of knowledge and experience that can be gained by the individual truly interested in learning.

Whether working as a diving safety officer for a very small, tropical marine research station somewhere, or for one of the largest research institutions in the world, the job of a diving safety officer is an exciting, challenging and rewarding diving profession.

Experiences of Diving Safety Officers

JACK NICHOLS

Jack Nichols is the diving safety officer at the University of Miami at the Rosenstiel School of Marine and Atmospheric Science. He started diving in 1978 in Panama City, Florida and worked in a dive shop there for several years.

Jack became an instructor in 1980 when he took a NASDS instructor course in Panama City. He moved to Miami the same year to work for the Dade Marine Institute, a private, non-profit organization that uses diving as a method to rehabilitate juvenile delinquents. He taught there for four years.

In 1983 Nichols "crossed over" as a NAUI instructor. He applied for the position of diving officer at the University of Miami in June of

Fig. 7.7 – Jack Nichols is the diving officer at the University of Miami. (Photo courtesy Jack Nichols)

1984, when he heard that their existing diving officer was retiring. He was both surprised and happy when he got the job.

Nichols oversees approximately 60 divers at the university (the number varies from year to year) and makes between 100 to 150 dives each year himself. He also supervises student boat operations.

Jack enjoys his job thoroughly, especially the opportunity to get out and dive almost whenever he chooses. He also enjoys meeting students and visiting professors from different parts of the country. As the diving officer he sets his own schedule, and has the opportunity to regularly participate in research cruises to the Bahamas, and Turks and Caicos Islands.

The stressful parts of Jack's job include having to screen new divers, dealing with minor accidents, and responding to the demands of the University's administration. In addition, there is the self-imposed stress that Jack generates when he encounters a diver whose diving abilities are borderline.

In those situations where he questions whether he is being too picky in judging whether a diver is truly qualified to participate in the university program, Jack finds a great deal of pressure. As Jack puts it, "Rejecting someone from a university diving program is a serious decision since these people need to dive for their education, or as part of their career. It's not just a decision affecting someone's recreation; it may affect their entire life."

At the University of Miami, Jack's benefits include 24 days of vacation each year, health care, and sick leave. There is no dental coverage or vision plan.

NICOLE CRANE

Nicole Crane is the diving officer for Stanford University's Hopkins Marine Station in Monterey, California. She also works as a research diver for the California Dept. of Fish and Game.

Nicole started diving in the Mediterranean when she was 12 years old in 1976, although she was not formally certified until 1980. She became a diving instructor in 1980 at Ft. Ord, California. Nicole holds both Bachelor's and Master's degrees in Marine Biology.

Nicole finds that there are many positive aspects to being a diving safety officer, although she thinks the job title is a misnomer. "Saying that you're a diving officer implies that you're a diving policeman. I prefer to think of myself as a research diving coordinator or facilitator," she remarks. Among the things that she likes about her job are the diving, the interaction with interesting people, and being able to continue her own research.

JOHN HEINE

John Heine is the diving safety officer and a research associate at Moss Landing Marine Laboratories in California. The lab acts as a field facility for training scientists from several state universities in California. John has been the diving officer at the lab since 1980.

John first started diving in 1976 while he was an undergraduate student in marine biology at the University of California at Irvine. Upon graduation he worked for a year on a research grant at the Channel Islands off the California coast.

In 1979, John enrolled in graduate school at Moss Landing, where he completed his master's thesis on photosynthesis in subtidal marine plants. While he was enrolled at school, the lab approached him to see if he would be interested in working as a part-time diving safety officer. They offered to pay for him to attend NAUI instructor's training, provided he passed the course. He attended a NAUI program at San Diego State University and was certified to teach diving in June of 1980. Since then, John has taught a research diver's course at Moss Landing every semester.

Fig. 7.8 – John Heine relaxes between dives during a research expedition to Antarctica. (Photo courtesy of John Heine)

When John graduated from school, Moss Landing offered him a 3/4 time position as diving officer at the lab. The job became full time in 1985.

Some of the highlights of John's job include travel to Alaska and Antarctica to participate in diving research projects. He has also participated in operations with Russian scientists, making deep submersible dives to 10,000 feet in the Monterey Canyon, off the central California coast.

On a day-to-day basis, John spends his time doing lots of paperwork, reviewing dive logs and physical exam forms, and conducting check-out dives for visiting scientists and students from other institutions. He spends one full day a week teaching a research diving course for students and scientists. He is responsible for maintaining and repairing many pieces of diving equipment for the university program including a scuba compressor, cameras, regulators, and scientific collecting gear.

John finds the things he enjoys most about his work include teaching, working for the university system, going diving, the flexible hours, and being around college students. The only truly negative factor is dealing with increasingly tighter budget constraints.

If you're interested in working as a diving safety officer, John's advice is to learn as much about research diving techniques as possible. A scientific background is helpful, but not necessarily essential.

DOUG KESLING

Doug Kesling is a diving safety officer for NOAA (National Oceanic and Atmospheric Administration). He works out of the National Undersea Research Center (NURC) at the University of North Carolina (UNC) at Wilmington.

Doug started diving in 1977 at Wright State University in Ohio where he attended college. He took his Open Water I course from Dan Orr, a well known diving instructor who has gone on to work in education for the Diver's Alert Network (DAN). Based upon his experience in Orr's course, Doug decided to become as active as possible in diving.

Fig. 7.9 – Doug Kesling, diving safety officer for NOAA, with the Johnson Sea-Link research submersible. (Photo courtesy Doug Kesling)

Through Wright State, Doug got a work-study job to help teach diving and maintain the school's gear. He worked 20 hours a week while he went to school assisting with scuba classes. Doug also got to spend a summer working as a field supervisor at a marine archaeological project in Jamaica. This helped to solidify his career decision that he wanted to follow a path that would keep him involved in diving.

In May of 1983, Doug won the *Our World Underwater Scholarship*. This unique program sponsors a young person each year to travel throughout the U.S. and meet the leaders in diving. The scholarship winner typically will spend several weeks each month in different parts of the U.S. during the course of the scholarship year. Typically, the young divers work with marine scientists, diving equipment manufacturers, and other diving specialists as part of the program.

Doug took a year off from college to complete the Our World scholarship. With a college major in nursing, he was very interested in diving physiology and hyperbaric medicine, particularly saturation diving. As part of the scholarship, he went to the West Indies Lab at St. Croix in the U.S. Virgin Islands, to the site of Hydrolab, the only active scientific saturation diving habitat in the U.S. at that time. At Hydrolab, divers lived and worked in the habitat on the bottom of the ocean. Doug worked topside support during a saturation mission.

Doug also spent several months in California, with time at the U.S.C. chamber on Catalina, and traveled to the Sea of Cortez. By the end of that year, he had reaffirmed that doing what you love to do could be your career. He realized that if you want to do something seriously enough you can do it, although you may have to make sacrifices. He returned to college to complete his degree and looked for a job working with hyperbaric systems.

It was not a coincidence that Doug got hired a year later by the West Indies Lab to serve as a diving supervisor and diving safety officer for Hydrolab. Upon graduation, he moved to the Virgin Islands for what he describes as a "dream come true opportunity."

While at Hydrolab Doug learned the importance of training and preparation. The topside support team trained continuously to handle every conceivable emergency to ensure the safety of the divers living underwater. One of the most serious potential accidents they prepared for was the possibility of a diver accidentally surfacing, without decompression, from a saturation dive. When this actually did happen, because a team of scientists became disoriented on the bottom, Doug's team actually rescued the divers and got them back under pressure in less than eight minutes. Fortunately, the divers suffered no ill effects.

Doug spent over two years at the lab, working with numerous scientists who used the lab and its saturation diving capability to conduct extended underwater research. As the Hydrolab program began to wind down, NOAA was readying a new habitat known as the George F. Bond Saturation Facility. The late George Bond was the Navy diving medical officer who developed the concept of saturation diving, and supervised the early Navy diving experiments in saturation diving. As the program changed, the habitat was renamed the Aquarius habitat and Doug was transferred to that program as a diver/technician.

When hurricane Hugo devastated St. Croix in 1988, it put the new habitat program on hold. As a result of changes at the West Indies Lab, NOAA withdrew their funding and support for the program there. By 1990, Doug, and the new habitat, had been transferred to NOAA's program at University of North Carolina at Wilmington.

At UNC Wilmington, Doug is responsible for the training and safety of scientific divers who participate in the program there. The NOAA program makes their equipment and personnel available to assist scientists from throughout the country who come there to work on NOAA funded research. UNC Wilmington's diving operations extend from Virginia to the Florida Keys and the Gulf of Mexico. UNC Wilmington has established a satellite facility at Conch Reef in the Florida Keys where the Aquarius Habitat will be located.

Doug's responsibilities include the safety of the 30 NOAA staff members at UNC Wilmington, as well as that of the 60 to 120 divers who visit their facilities annually. The divers use scuba, nitrox, and surface supplied diving equipment.

Doug finds living and working in and on the ocean to be a thoroughly enjoyable career. He likes the teamwork that comes from participating in a mission and making it a success. He finds that he constantly learns new things from the visiting scientists, and feels fortunate to have a job that is as good as his.

Working as a diving safety officer is a serious commitment that frequently involves long days, that frequently stretch into weeks and months. In addition, Doug finds the amount of time that he spends away from home can be significant. The politics of academia, along with the continual battle for funding, is stressful.

Doug recommends that anyone who is considering a career as a diving safety officer get some education beyond high school. Even an A.S. degree (associate of science) in Marine Technology is helpful. He suggests you get as much varied experience in diving as possible.

"What amazes me most," says Doug, "is that there is no one proven career track in diving. If you look at people who are successful in the field they have taken a variety of routes to get to where they are today. It's difficult to tell somebody how to do it; you just have to find the path that works for you."

For More Information on Scientific Diving Contact:

National Undersea Research Program, 6010 Executive Blvd. Suite 805, WSC-5, R/OR2, Rockville, MD 20852 Tel. (301) 443-8391

Suggested Reading:

National Oceanic and Atmospheric Administration. *NOAA Diving Manual: Diving for Science and Technology.* Best Publishing, Flagstaff, AZ. 1991.

Chapter Eight

COMMERCIAL DIVING

Commercial diving is one of the most physically demanding diving careers. When most people think of commercial diving they think of treasure hunting or ship salvage. In reality, most commercial diving is devoted to much more ordinary, but challenging work. In fact, most of the commercial diving done today is either in support of the offshore oil industry or as part of inland maintenance or construction of docks, piers, or dams. While inland diving usually pays reasonably well, the best money is normally made offshore, especially in deep water jobs.

Training to Be a Commercial Diver

Training to be a commercial diver can be a lengthy process. While the diving itself is not particularly complex, there are many support skills that you need to be a successful commercial diver. If you have a strong mechanical and technical background you are an ideal candidate to be a commercial diver. If your mechanical know-how is weak, you will need to develop at least a few mechanical skills if you expect to be employed as a commercial diver. There's an old saying in commercial diving that goes, "Nobody will pay you (just) to make bubbles." As a commercial diver you must be able to do productive work.

Some of the skills that are especially valued by commercial diving companies include mechanical drawing and blueprint reading, the ability to repair and maintain engines and compressors, welding, rig-

Fig. 8.1a – Most commercial diving today is done in support of the offshore oil industry or...

Fig. 8.1b – as part of inland construction or maintenance.

ging, technical report writing, photography, and electronics knowledge. Other skills that are helpful are small boat handling, plumbing, and a background in emergency medicine.

At commercial diving school you will learn to dive with specialized diving equipment, but it will be the skills that we have previously mentioned that get you a good job. Mechanical drawing and blueprint reading are important skills because you will be frequently asked to dive on structures you may never have previously seen. Some structures, such as offshore oil rigs, are very complex. Frequently, the only way to find the portion you are asked to work on is to be able to read and interpret any existing drawings and use them as your road map to find your way around. Quite often, the customer will ask you to make drawings of damage or other features on a particular structure. The ability to make simple sketches or do computer drawings is invaluable in this situation.

Almost every diving job will require the use of a compressor and a variety of other diesel driven equipment. Machinery powered by diesel engines found on diving jobs includes welding machines, water blasters for stripping paint, winches, davits, and hydraulic pumps for hydraulic power tools. A diver with a good background in diesel mechanics is considered priceless on any diving job.

If you are talented in welding and cutting you will find ready employment in the diving industry. Topside, welding skills are in demand in the diving field for fabrication of equipment and maintenance. On diving jobs where you are based on a large ship or barge, the equipment is normally welded to the deck of the vessel for the duration of the job. Of course, at the end of the job, it must be cut off without damaging the vessel, or the equipment.

Rigging is the ability to tie knots, splice various types of rope, and secure heavy objects for lifting. Good rigging is an art, but there is also a science to it. A competent rigger will know the safe lifting capacity of various types of rope, slings, and shackles. All commercial divers must be familiar with rigging to get the job done safely. At its simplest, you need to know how to rig your equipment to get it safely from the dock to your vessel and back. More complex rigging jobs may require sophisticated rigging skills to lift heavy objects that are underwater.

Technical report writing is a skill that you might not associate with diving, but it is essential to many underwater operations. Technical reports are a vital part of any underwater inspection job. With the aging of offshore oil platforms, insurance companies and many governments now require these structures be inspected on a regular basis. At the end of a lengthy platform inspection job, what the client is really paying for is not the diving, but the report he receives when the work is over. The ability to write and put together technical reports with illustrations and drawings is a valuable skill that will place you much in demand. The capability to use a computer to write and illustrate your report should be part of your technical report writing talents.

Fig. 8.2 – Underwater photography is a part of most underwater inspection jobs.

Photography, both topside and underwater, is part of most inspection projects, and may be required on some construction projects to verify that the work has been completed. If you want to sell your skills as an underwater photographer, it's not only important to be able to shoot the photos, it also helps to be able to process the film. It's not uncommon in the Gulf of Mexico for a diver to fly out to the job, make the dive, shoot the photos, and process the film in a bathroom aboard a drill rig. The more skills you have like this, the more likely you are to be employed and successful.

With the increasing use of electronics, the skill to fix this equipment will make you a hero in most commercial diving companies. Electronics equipment abounds in the commercial diving field, in everything from oxygen analyzers to underwater video systems.

Divers who are competent machinists make a valuable addition to a diving crew. Quite frequently there is the need for unique equipment to be fabricated on-site, or for parts to be made to repair equipment that has failed. A diver/machinist can save the day when problems come up.

Since so many of the skills we have listed are topside skills you might wonder how they will relate to your employment as a diver. Experience has shown that these skills are the ones that get you out on a job. Once you're on the job, you'll get the opportunity to dive, but you must have the skills that get you hired and offshore. Essentially, most divers find that if they are truly skilled they can barter their skills against the jobs they want.

Fig. 8.3 – This commercial diving student is performing a repair on an underwater oil well or "Christmas tree" as it's more commonly known.

Most commercial diving schools do not have the time to fully train you in the skills that we've previously mentioned. There are barely enough hours to teach you the skills you will need to handle surface supplied diving, chamber operations, and mixed gas diving. At best, you will only be given an introduction to the skills we have listed above. If you're serious about a career in commercial diving, and don't have the skills we've mentioned, then you should seek additional training in these areas through your local community college.

At diving school they will train you to use a variety of commercial diving masks, helmets, and other equipment. Your training will be devoted almost exclusively to surface supplied diving gear, where your breathing gas is supplied from topside via a hose rather than using sport scuba gear. The advantages of surface supplied gear include an unlimited air supply, communications with topside, and redundant backup systems. In addition to learning to dive with the gear itself you will also learn how to run the topside equipment that supports the diver, such as the air manifold control box, the communications system, and the tending of the diver's hose.

Most of your dives at diving school will be devoted to performing simulated underwater work tasks. These exercises may include such diverse jobs as pipeline connections, rigging objects for lifting, welding steel plates, and using a wide variety of underwater hand and power tools.

Decompression chamber operations are another skill you must master. You will be expected to know how to handle routine decompression as well as how to treat decompression sickness.

Working as an Apprentice

Upon graduation from diving school you are eligible to be hired as a "*tender*" or apprentice diver. Very few diving school graduates get hired as divers straight out of school by the more reputable diving companies. Even the best diving schools cannot fully train you for the realities of offshore work. You can only learn the fundamentals in school. The "real world" is where you learn what the job is about.

Fig. 8.4 – As a tender, you will work topside and "tend" the hose or "umbilical" that supplies the breathing gas to the diver. You will also help the diver to dress into his gear.

If you decide you want to work as an inland or inshore diver you may need to join a union. In certain parts of the country, particularly New York and San Francisco, many of the divers belong to the Dock Workers' and Pile Drivers' unions. At times, it can be difficult to join the unions unless you have the right connections.

If you decide to work in the offshore oil patch, your initial employment will be dependent upon the state of the oil industry. Since the oil industry is a "boom" or "bust" business, the demand for oil will directly affect your chances for employment. If the price of oil is high, your chances of getting hired are better than when the price of oil is low. Similarly, if you choose to work inland construction, you may find jobs are scarce when there is no new construction or repair work in your area.

Getting hired by a diving company as a tender is not always easy. Very few companies are willing to hire tenders without meeting you first. This means that if you want to work in the oil patch, but you've attended a diving school on the east or west coast, you must be prepared to travel to Louisiana without a commitment from anyone for a job. Don't bother to send your resume in advance; it's better to carry it with you and hand deliver it during your interview.

Sometimes the hardest part of getting hired by an offshore diving company is just getting your foot in the door to get an interview. In cases like this it pays to be persistent, yet polite. Even if you get an initial "no" and are turned away, you should go back repeatedly to each company that interests you until you are hired.

When you do get an interview, be sure to go prepared. You should be neatly dressed, but don't overdo it. A clean pair of slacks and a nice shirt are appropriate. A suit and tie is probably overkill, but blue jeans don't make a good impression either.

Your resume should stress both your prior job experience and any skills that you may possess. Any skill that you have that could be valuable on a diving job should be stressed, even if you have never used it on a job. For example, if you've done amateur film developing and printing, be sure to mention this in your resume.

If and when you are offered a job you should be prepared to go offshore immediately. It is not uncommon for a tender to be offered a job one day and be sent offshore the same day. Be sure to indicate that you are willing to go offshore immediately.

Although there is no set age limit for commercial divers, most diving companies will be hesitant to hire an apprentice who is over 40 years of age. Since most commercial diving work is somewhat strenuous, most companies will have a natural tendency to lean towards younger divers who are in good health. Also, the majority of diving companies will hesitate when it comes to hiring an older apprentice due to family considerations. Since the nature of the job requires long periods away from home, many older divers will have families and be less tolerant of these working conditions. A mature apprentice may be less adaptable and more apt to spend a shorter time with the company. Finally, you should keep in mind that as an older diver you may very well find yourself taking direction from a diver who is many years your junior.

Women divers are starting to become more common in the commercial diving field, although the industry is still dominated by men. As a woman diver, you may find yourself on older drill rigs that do not have separate facilities for women. This is not uncommon and in these situations you will receive your best acceptance if you are flexible and willing to compromise, rather than being demanding and militant. In addition, as with any diving, you should not dive if you are pregnant or suspect you are pregnant. This is particularly true of commercial diving since so much of this type of diving involves decompression. Decompression sickness could be especially harmful to a developing fetus.

As a tender you should plan on the fact that there may be long periods where there is little or no diving work. If you have planned in advance, you should have a sufficient bankroll to see you through the initial lean periods. If you don't have enough money put away to do this, then you should be prepared to take other employment until you get hired full time by a diving company. This is another reason why it pays to have some sort of trade skills prior to attending diving school.

If you go to work in the Gulf of Mexico it is essential for you to have a reliable car to get to job sites all along the Gulf. Even though you may be based out of New Orleans, it is not unusual to be sent to Texas or Mississippi in the middle of the night to catch a crew boat that will take you out to the job site.

Your time as a tender is the time for you to learn as much as you can about your profession and the politics of employment as a diver. In the commercial diving field, as is true in much of life, your success will be more dependent upon how well you get along with people rather than your actual working skills. We have seen many divers who were not especially talented but who have been very successful because they had pleasant personalities. This type of situation is especially true in the offshore environment where you may be stuck aboard a drill rig or barge for weeks at a time.

How long you serve as an apprentice depends upon many factors, but the most important one is usually the level of demand for new divers. For example, in 1976, at the height of the North Sea oil boom, SubSea International, a major diving contractor, went from 50 divers in one year to almost 300 the next. Many apprentices who started at that time were promoted from tender to diver in less than a year's time. Conversely, in the 1980's when the oil glut was at its worst, many tenders had to wait three to four years before they were able to "*break out*," the term used to describe a person who has just been promoted to diver status.

Fig. 8.5 – Offshore construction work involves massive amounts of equipment and materials. This North Sea barge supported several hundred workers and heavy construction.

Following hurricane Andrew in 1992 there were many opportunities for divers and tenders due to the immense destruction of oil platforms in the Gulf of Mexico. More than 2,000 platforms were damaged, and many were totally destroyed. Despite the fact that the oil industry was not healthy then, the demand for divers was suddenly very high.

Other factors that will affect your time as a tender are your trade skills and luck. If you are a skilled welder and your company lands a major underwater welding job you will undoubtedly be asked to go on the job. If you perform well, your time as an apprentice may be dramatically shortened.

Luck is also a factor in commercial diving, although we subscribe to the definition that luck occurs "when preparation meets opportunity." The better prepared you are to succeed, the better you'll be able to take advantage of good opportunities as they come along.

As a tender you will be asked to perform many tasks in support of diving operations. Generally speaking, when a diving company gets a job, the tenders are often required to help load the job out. On a big job, it may take days to pack all the equipment that's required. By doing a conscientious job of helping set things up you can put yourself in a very good position with the diving supervisor.

During the mobilization phase of a diving job you may be asked to drive a forklift, operate a crane, or use other heavy machinery. Detailed checklists of the job inventory are usually prepared to ensure that everything that needs to go offshore has been packed. On smaller jobs, you may actually end up driving the truck with all the equipment to the dock where the crew will depart for offshore. Almost every job will be different.

In the early days of commercial diving, tenders were usually assigned to work with one particular diver. The tender was expected to know what bar the diver was likely to be found in, to polish the diver's cowboy boots, and to pack and clean the diver's personal gear. Fortunately, those days are long gone...

Once you get offshore, both tenders and divers are supposed to set up the equipment for the job. However, usually the tenders end up doing the more obnoxious jobs and spend more hours working than the divers. If you want to succeed as a tender, and be quickly promoted to diver, the best thing you can do is to seek out the most obnoxious tasks on each job and do them well without complaint. Both the divers and supervisors will take notice of this and you will find yourself promoted ahead of other less ambitious tenders in short order.

Fig. 8.6 – Your early dives as a tender will usually be made in shallow water. (Photo by Steve Barsky. © Diving Systems Intnl. All rights reserved.)

While you are a tender you will get the opportunity to dive occasionally, depending upon the type of jobs you get to work on and other factors. You should take every opportunity you get to dive and strive to do your best on each of these dives. This is your chance to show what you can do underwater. Don't worry if your first one or two dives aren't outstanding; everybody makes mistakes on these initial dives.

When you dive, you will usually get some extra compensation.

With most companies you will earn depth pay for all dives deeper than 50 feet. For shallower dives you may not get paid anything.

Be cautious during your dives as a tender to make sure that you aren't making dives that nobody else wants to make. There is tremendous pressure when you are a tender to perform well, but it's foolish to put yourself in situations that are dangerous. If everyone else has said that they will not make a particular dive because they feel it's too dangerous, don't volunteer to make the dive. Learn to develop good judgment and know when to turn a dive down. Ultimately, your supervisors will respect you for this.

After you have served as a tender for some time, the next rung on the ladder towards diver is the "*diver-tender.*" This position is a "no man's land." You aren't really a tender, but you still aren't a diver. Some companies will allow diver-tenders to go out on shallow air diving jobs as divers or even air diving supervisors. This is an excellent opportunity to learn and make more money at the same time. Diver-tenders usually make a bit more money than tenders, but certainly not as much as divers. Some companies will pay a diver-tender at diver's rates on days that they dive.

Working as a Diver

Breaking out as a diver is a big day in your career. It is a time when you should take pride in your achievement. Not everybody can do this job.

If you are a good diver you will eventually be promoted to "*lead diver.*" A lead diver is considered a superior diver and is usually called upon to perform the more difficult dives. In addition, lead divers frequently get to pick which jobs they want to work on, and the dives they want to make. Of course, lead divers make more money than a beginning diver.

For people who like responsibility, diving companies are always looking for divers who have the capability to act as supervisors. Diving supervisors make a higher daily rate than divers. However, since they don't get to dive as much as divers, they usually make less money on an annual basis.

The ultimate supervisory position offshore is the title of diving superintendent. Superintendents may actually oversee several jobs in the same region at the same time. On very large or important diving jobs, where the work goes on round-the-clock, a superintendent may have two shift supervisors who report to him.

Although inshore diving can pay good money, the glamour boys of the commercial diving industry are the offshore divers. There are more opportunities to make big money offshore because there is more deep water. Since most commercial diving pay is based upon hazards, and depth is equated with hazard, it's only natural that you can usually make more money offshore. Other hazards that face the offshore diver include hostile marine life and more dangerous weather and sea conditions.

Diving work in the offshore oil fields of the world takes many forms. Although much of the work that was formerly done by divers is now performed by *ROV's (Remotely Operated Vehicles)*, there still remains a significant amount of work for divers. In fact, the robotic ROV's are often teamed with divers in an effort to get the work done as efficiently as possible.

During exploratory drill rig operations, when oil companies are searching for oil, divers are used to maintain and service the blow-out preventer (BOP) stack that is used to control the oil well. In these operations, divers work from floating drill rigs, or "jack-ups" that sit on the bottom but can be towed to new positions as needed. Divers may be required to open or close valves, attach guide wires, recover lost tools, and perform other services. In the early days of commercial diving this work was performed exclusively by divers, but today, much of this type of work is performed by ROV's.

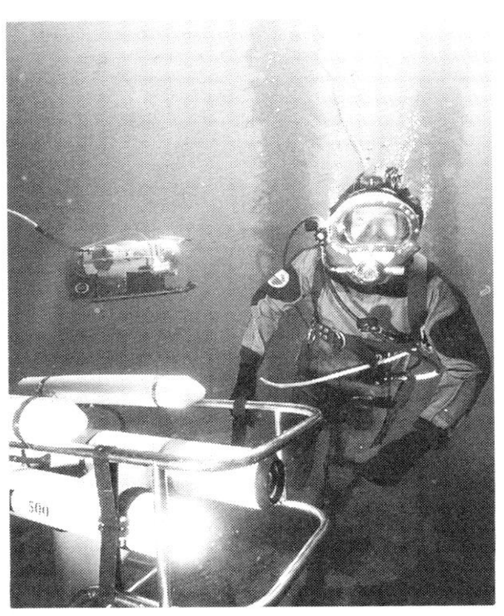

Fig. 8.7 – Much of the work formerly done by divers is now performed by ROV's (Remotely Operated Vehicles).

Once an oilfield has been located and goes into the production phase, divers are used to help complete the construction of the platforms and pipelines. The platforms are used as permanent drilling structures for the steady production of oil or natural gas. Platform installation is considered heavy construction and requires intense labor to be installed properly on the sea floor. Pilings are driven into the sea bed around each of the major legs of a platform to anchor it to the ocean floor. Divers participate in the installation phase by guiding platforms onto location, rigging pilings underwater, and cutting away fittings that were required during installation but may interfere with normal production. Divers may be called upon to connect pipelines to the platforms, inspect pipelines as they are laid, and dig trenches for pipelines to bury them below the sea floor where they are less vulnerable to damage.

After a platform has been installed and is on line there are numerous jobs for divers associated with the inspection, maintenance, and repair of the structure. During the past 15 years this has been one of the largest growth areas in diving, since many platforms are now much more than 20 years old.

At the start of a big inspection job, the first step usually involves cleaning the marine growth from a platform so the divers can closely observe the condition of the steel structure. This cleaning is accomplished with special high-speed water blasters that quickly strip away the marine growth.

Inspection diving involves additional specialized skills including underwater photography and "*non-destructive testing*" or "*NDT.*" Non-destructive testing uses a variety of sophisticated techniques to carefully evaluate the structural integrity of steel oil platforms. There are various forms of non-destructive testing, but two of the most important are the use of x-rays and "magnetic particle inspection."

The most important structural features on most offshore platforms are the "*welds*" that hold the platform together. The welds are the "glue" that connects the joints that make up the platform. In some situations the naked eye is not good enough to detect hairline cracks that may cause a platform to fail. Under these circumstances both x-rays and magnetic particles may be used.

In magnetic particle inspection a large electromagnet is attached to the portion of the platform that is in question. When the magnet is turned on, the diver applies a special fluorescent ink, containing magnetic particles, to the joint. If there are any cracks in the weld, the particles will align themselves in the joint, making them highly visible, even to the naked eye. These "indications" of structural problems are routinely photographed at this time.

In the case of extensive platform damage divers are usually called in to make repairs. In some cases, entire structural members may be removed and replaced.

To prevent deterioration of steel platforms, numerous zinc anodes are fastened to the platforms at strategic locations. These "*sacrificial*" anodes are similar to those used to protect the metal portions of power and sailboats in salt water. As these anodes are consumed they must be replaced. This is another job that is sometimes assigned to divers.

When an offshore platform reaches the end of its useful life, or if it is destroyed through hurricane or accident, it must ultimately be removed. The removal process may involve the use of explosives, underwater cutting torches, or both.

Commercial divers must be capable of using a wide variety of diving equipment. This means you must be able to take any new piece of equipment, quickly figure it out, and dive with it. You must have a very high level of comfort in the water.

Scuba gear is rarely used in serious commercial diving operations since almost all commercial dives require communications. The most common piece of equipment used to provide communications is the full face mask. As its name implies, this piece of equipment covers your entire face. By providing an air space, it gives you the ability to speak.

Commercial divers wear a variety of diving suits including wetsuits, dry suits, and "*hot water suits.*" While wetsuits and dry suits are familiar to most sport divers, hot water suits represent an entirely different type of diving. Hot water suits are baggy, loose fitting wetsuits. A manifold at the diver's waist connects to a hot water hose from the surface. Tubes inside the suit carry the hot water down each arm and leg, as well as down the diver's chest and back. Without the hot water suit, most of the deeper commercial diving done today would not be possible.

In most commercial diving operations you will be diving with "*surface supplied*" equipment, where your air and communications are controlled from topside by your support crew. For air diving, the diving system will consist of a topside compressor, an air control manifold, a communications box, a diving hose or "*umbilical,*" and the diver's mask or helmet. In the Gulf of Mexico, air diving is commonly conducted down to depths of 200 feet.

Beyond 200 feet, most diving is done with "*mixed gas,*" with the most common mixture being helium and oxygen. The helium is used to replace the nitrogen in normal breathing air to eliminate the effects of nitrogen narcosis. Surface supplied mixed gas diving is usually not conducted much beyond 350 feet. At that depth, most diving operations switch over to bell diving.

Fig. 8.8 – A diving bell is lowered from a barge with two divers inside.

Fig. 8.9 – Inside the dry environment of the diving bell, one diver tends the hose for his partner who works outside in the water.

Diving bells are typically made from steel and are used to transport divers to and from depths in a dry environment. Most diving bells have two bottom hatches. One hatch seals from the outside with external pressure, and one hatch seals from the inside with internal pressure.

Inside the bell there are lights, a heater, and communications speakers for the divers to talk with topside. The bell is supplied with its electrical power, hot water for diver heating, and communications via a large umbilical from the surface. This umbilical connects to the bell through special plumbing that connects to two short umbilicals, one for each of the divers, inside the bell.

On the outside of the bell there are external lights and large cylinders of emergency breathing gas. In the event the topside umbilical is severed, there is usually enough emergency gas for the divers to survive for at least 24 hours.

Bell diving may be done in several different ways, either "*bounce*" diving or saturation diving. In bell bounce diving, the bell is lowered from the surface with the divers inside at surface pressure and the bottom hatch closed. When the divers are at the appropriate work depth, they "*blow down*" or pressurize the bell very quickly. At this point, one of the divers puts on his mask or helmet and slips out of the bell to work. The remaining diver sits inside the bell, dry, and tends the hose for the diver outside. He also acts as a "*stand-by*" diver for the diver outside in the event he needs help or must be rescued. If the diver outside is unable to complete the work in 4-5 hours, he will return to the bell and the second diver will "*lock-out*" to do the work.

Fig. 8.10 – A diver "locks out" of a diving bell. (Photo by Steve Barsky. © Diving Systems Intnl. All rights reserved.)

At the completion of the dive, the divers close both hatches and the bell is brought back to the surface. Inside the bell, the divers are still under pressure, but have started their decompression. Once the bell is on deck, it can then be mated to a large decompression chamber where the divers can complete their decompression in comfort and greater safety. On a deep bell bounce dive, it may take more than a day to decompress the divers safely back to surface pressure.

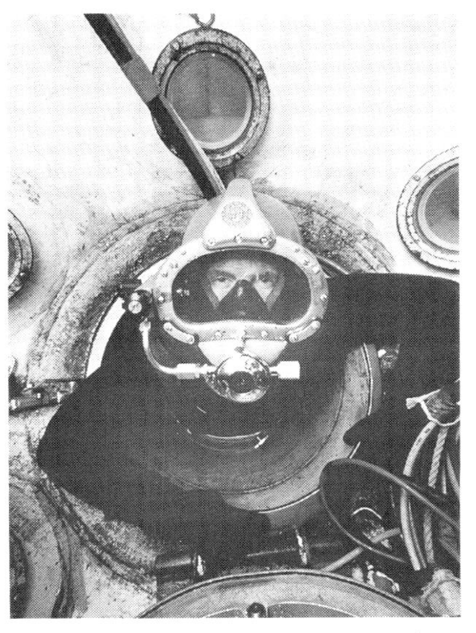

Fig. 8.11 – A diver returns to the diving bell and enters through the bottom hatch.

Saturation diving is the second diving mode that makes use of a diving bell. In saturation diving, the divers live in a large decompression chamber topside and make daily excursions via the diving bell to depth. The concept behind saturation diving is that after 24 hours at any given depth your body will be completely saturated with inert gas at that depth. This means that no matter how long you continue to stay at depth, your decompression obligation will be the same whether you stay under pressure for three days or 30 days. You only need to decompress once, at the very end of the job.

The topside decompression chamber that you live in while saturation diving is usually equipped with a special hatch or "lock" for sending food in and "locking out" trash and other materials. Most saturation systems are equipped with a special chamber that includes a toilet and shower. Some of the systems are large and reasonably comfortable, while other are so small there is not enough room to stand up!

Saturation diving is one of the highest paid forms of commercial diving. Working saturation dives have been conducted in the open ocean to depths in excess of 1600 feet. Some of the top paid divers in the industry have spent over 100 days a year in saturation on an annual basis.

Fig. 8.12 – A complete saturation diving complex on the deck of a drill rig in the North Sea.

Inland divers use most of the same equipment and techniques as commercial divers, but their work is usually quite different. Most of the work is either in harbors, or involves fresh water locks, bridges, and dams. Inland work at union rates can pay quite well.

Working conditions for commercial divers range from miserable to excellent. The accommodations on some offshore barges and rigs are excellent and the food can be delicious. In other circumstances, you may find yourself in a situation where you are ordered to sleep on deck, or even share a "*hot bunk.*" In a hot bunk situation there are not enough bunks for everyone on board. When one shift gets up and goes to work, the next shift takes their place and sleeps in the same bunks. There is no privacy offshore.

Where you work will largely determine what type of work schedule you will follow. On drill rigs the typical work schedule is usually two weeks offshore followed by two weeks of leave. During the two weeks offshore you will be expected to work 12 hours a day, seven days a week. Conversely, on a big construction job, the schedule may be 30 days offshore followed by ten days off. Again, during your 30 days at work you will be expected to work a minimum 12 hour day, seven days a week. There is no such thing as a "holiday" offshore. If you are unfortunate enough to be offshore for Christmas or New Year's, it's still a work day.

Diving conditions for commercial diving also vary from beautiful to disgusting. Diving on platforms far out in the Gulf of Mexico is like diving on a tropical reef, with spiny oysters, barracuda, triggerfish, and sharks. However, for every dive you make in clear, blue waters, you may also be asked to dive in water that is dark, dirty, or polluted. You must also be prepared to dive at night, and in rough sea conditions that most sport divers would never consider entering. You always have the option not to dive, but if you look over your shoulder, you'll find a line of apprentices waiting for their opportunity to get into the water. Survival offshore is knowing when to say "No!"

Perhaps the toughest part of commercial diving is the lifestyle. Most divers carry an electronic pager so that they can be notified of jobs as they happen. When the pager beeps, it's time to go to work. This makes living and planning a normal life almost impossible, since you never know how long any given job will last. Almost every successful diver has stories of jobs that were supposed to last for a few days that went on for months. It is difficult to sustain a normal marriage or relationship as a commercial diver.

Very few commercial divers stay in the industry for more than ten years as active divers. By that time, the majority of divers have either left the industry or gone on to management positions in the commercial diving field.

Fig. 8.13 – Jerry Clouser started his career as a Navy diver. (Photo courtesy of Jerry Clouser.)

Experiences of Working Divers

JERRY CLOUSER

Jerry Clouser is one of the exceptions in commercial diving. An instructor at Santa Barbara City College's commercial diving program, Clouser still works each summer in the industry as a diver or supervisor. He started his career as a Navy diver and moved to the commercial industry when he left the Navy. He was an early saturation diver and has thousands of hours in the water.

In 1971 Clouser went on one of the first, long duration, saturation diving jobs to salvage a platform that had been toppled during a hurricane. Clouser spent 34 days in "sat" on this first platform salvage job, working at a depth of over 300 feet. The divers used explosives and cutting torches to cut the platform into pieces small enough to lift. While the divers left the water before the explosives were detonated, they had to get back in immediately afterward due to the pressures of the job.

"It was a dangerous job," admits Clouser, "and half the divers quit because of the sharks. Each time they set off an explosive charge the sharks came in to feed on all the fish that were killed. I once got bumped in the chest by a ten foot long hammerhead."

On one of the dives, at night, Jerry's bell mate dropped down into the "stage" that hangs underneath the bell, but refused to leave the bell to work. Through the ports inside the bell, Jerry could see the sharks swirling around outside. Because of the way most diving bells are wired for communications, it's possible for the diver inside the bell to communicate with the topside crew without the diver in the water hearing his comments. When Clouser realized what was happening he told "*topside*" to turn off the outside bell lights so the diver wouldn't see the sharks. They did and the diver finally left the bell and went to work.

Like most commercial divers, Jerry has been bent several times. His most serious "*hit*" followed a 500 foot deep dive off the drill ship the *Glomar Grand Banks.* He shrugs his shoulders casually when asked about it.

"Anybody who dives commercially has to expect to get bent," says Clouser. "It's an occupational hazard. I'll admit though, that the hit I got on the *Grand Banks* was a serious one. It was a central nervous system hit and I had a mental problem for a year after the incident. When I first got hit I had such a serious pain at waist level that I couldn't stand up. It took me almost a year to fully recover."

Fig. 8.14 – "Anybody who dives commercially has to expect to get bent," says commercial diver Jerry Clouser.

ALLEN SEABREX

Allen Seabrex, 47, the owner of a commercial diving firm in the Midwest, also got his initial diving experience in the Navy. Starting as a para-rescue diver aboard aircraft carriers such as the *Enterprise* and the *Coral Sea,* Seabrex completed his tour of duty and worked as a carpenter before entering the commercial diving field. He quickly became a supervisor with Canonie Construction, a large firm in the Midwest.

Much of Seabrex's work has involved what commercial divers refer to as "*penetration,*" entering submerged pipelines or tunnels. Like wreck diving or cave diving, where it is impossible to make a direct ascent to the surface, these dives are especially dangerous. Divers usually get paid a penetration "premium" of up to several dollars a foot, similar to the depth pay provided on most offshore jobs. In one instance, Allen was working for Detroit Edison, 360 feet back inside a pipe, when a piece of metal he was cutting fell on his hose and cut it in half. Miraculously, he was able to grab the two ends of the hose, and jam them together to flow just enough air to get him back out of the pipe alive.

Yet, Seabrex continues to do penetration work and his company continues to set records for unbelievable dives. While the longest penetration dive they have completed was 5300 feet, they have also gone back 3000 feet inside a pipe in 180 feet of water. They have also done extensive nuclear reactor diving, and were the first company to dive in the suppression pool of a reactor while the plant was 100% on line.

For Seabrex, diving is a 24 hour a day business, and he is always busy. He literally lives at this business and has jobs loading out all the time. With 37 divers in his company, he has multiple jobs underway, sometimes in several states.

JON SEARS

Jon Sears attended the commercial diving program at Santa Barbara City College from 1974 to 1976. After graduation, Jon went to Scotland to work in the North Sea during the height of the North Sea oil boom. From 1976 to 1986 Jon worked for SubSea International, one of the largest commercial diving firms in the world. As a diver and supervisor for SubSea, Jon did extensive heavy construction diving. He has also been involved in salvage and inspection diving.

Fig. 8.15 – Jon Sears started his commercial diving career as a tender in the North Sea. This photo of Jon was taken in 1977 when Jon and author Steve Barsky worked on the same commercial diving job.

After leaving SubSea in 1986, Jon worked for Oceaneering International, another major diving firm. Jon's travels as a diver have taken him to Brunei, the Gulf of Mexico, and the east coast of the U.S. He has had many close calls as a diver, particularly on jobs that have involved underwater cutting.

Although Jon enjoys working in the oil "patch," today he only spends 20% of his year diving for the oil industry, and the rest of his year diving for sea urchins. With a wife and four daughters, Jon finds the time he must spend away from home to work in oilfield diving less and less acceptable.

For More Information on Commercial Diving:

For more information on commercial diving, contact the following commercial diving schools.

College of Oceaneering
272 S. Fries Ave.
Wilmington, CA 90744
Tel. (800) 432-3483

Divers Academy
2500 S. Broadway
Camden, New Jersey 08104
Tel. (800) 238-3483

Divers Institute of Technology
P.O. Box 70667
Seattle, WA
Tel. (800) 634-8377

Marine Diving Technology
Santa Barbara City College
721 Cliff Dr.
Santa Barbara, CA 93109
Tel. (805) 966-0581

The Ocean Corporation
10840 Rockley Rd.
Houston, TX 77099
Tel. (800) 321-0298

Suggested Reading:

Sisman, D., Editor. *The Professional Diver's Handbook*. Submex Ltd., U.K.

Zinkowski, N. *Commercial Oilfield Diving*, Cornell Maritime Press, Centreville, MD. 21617.

Best Publishing Co., *Commercial Diver Training Manual*, P.O. Box 301000, Flagstaff, AZ, 86003.

Chapter Nine

DIVING JOURNALISTS

Writing is something that most people hate to do. It takes a tremendous amount of concentration and effort to sit down and commit words to paper. Yet most people love to watch movies or television, and many people read books, magazines, and newspapers. Without people who like to write, these diversions and information sources would not exist.

In the diving field, there are opportunities for writers that were not available five years ago. There are more diving magazines today than at any time in the past, and the number of diving books has increased each year. This surge in diving publications is directly related to the personal computer and the phenomenon of desktop publishing, which have made it simpler to publish everything from magazines to books.

The diving industry depends on writers, for the textbooks used to train new divers, the catalogs that sell the equipment we use to dive, and the manuals that explain how to use that equipment. Diving journalists create the diving magazines that entertain and inform us, and diving script writers create the stories that underwater cinematographers capture on film.

To be successful as a diving journalist you must write about things that other writers can't or haven't covered. Or, you must find a way to cover familiar topics with a fresh slant.

Who Buys Underwater Journalism?

Just as an underwater photographer must sell photos outside the diving market to make a living, underwater journalists must do the same thing. You must find general, mass market publications that pay significantly more than the diving magazines to keep your writing profitable. Magazines that are good potential markets include regional magazines like *Sunset,* airline travel magazines, and wildlife magazines. If you have access to a truly unusual story, such as a successful treasure hunting expedition, the possibilities are enormous, provided that you are a competent writer.

Given the number of "*niche*" or specialty magazines today, the possibilities are limitless for you to create special interest stories. For example, there are numerous women's magazines that will buy stories that have a woman's slant to them. These can take the form of a feature on successful women in the diving field, or articles that explore learning to dive from a woman's perspective.

Many businesses in the diving field need people who can write for them. Manufacturers need copy written for their catalogs and equipment manuals. Training agencies need textbooks, instructional courses, and marketing materials. Resorts need brochures, informational pamphlets, and newsletters.

Fig. 9.1 – As owner of Watersport Publishing, Ken Loyst buys articles for his magazine, "Discover Diving," and manuscripts for his book division, Watersport Books.

The more different styles of writing that you can do, the more work you will get. Writing a technical service and repair manual for a regulator is very different from writing a brochure about a tropical diving resort. Not everybody can alter their style to meet these different demands. It takes practice and skill.

Training to be a Diving Journalist

There are no special qualifications or training required to be a successful writer, other than the ability to write well. What is important is that you ensure that your grammar is correct, your spelling is excellent, and your facts are accurate. Above all, you must have the ability to get the reader involved with your story. If you can't write copy that is interesting to read, if you can't make the reader anxious to read the conclusion to your story, you can't expect to make a living by writing.

Probably the most important thing that you can do to improve your writing is to read as much of other people's work as possible. Look for successful writers who write about diving topics and compare their writing to yours. Analyze other writer's work to figure out what makes their stories interesting and why they are successful.

As a writer, you must learn how to describe things simply so that anyone can understand what you have to say. You must be able to take the most complex subjects and make them understandable. Your writing should be directed at people who read at the fifth or sixth grade level, since this is where the bulk of the population's reading ability lies. Even people who are well educated prefer to read at a simpler level, rather than struggling with complex images and concepts.

Certainly, college level training in English is an asset to any writer, but there have been numerous successful writers with no training in writing beyond high school. Like any artist, most good writers have an innate skill and drive to write. It is something they have inside them. You can improve those skills through school or writing programs. If you are a nonwriter, you can learn to write clearly, but talent is something you are either born with or without.

One of the tools that can help you with your writing is a personal computer. In fact, most magazines today prefer that you submit both a "*hard copy*" (printed on paper) and a computer file on

Fig. 9.2 – The personal computer is one of a writer's most essential tools. Steve Barsky submits most of his work "on disk" to the various magazines and publishers for whom he writes. (Photo by Kristine C. Barsky)

diskette of anything you write for them. The same thing is true of book publishers. This reduces their publishing costs since you have already entered the information for them, and all they need to do is format it for their publication.

The computer can help you in several ways. First, it makes it easier to edit and revise your copy. Changes are much faster and easier. Second, the computer can check your spelling, and while it won't find contextual errors (such as the difference between *four* and *for*), it will help. Finally, there are computer software programs that can check your grammar. Keep in mind however, that most grammar checkers are not perfect. They are helpful, but they do make mistakes.

One of the most important elements to improve your writing is to find someone who is a good editor. This can be a friend, a fellow writer, or a spouse, but their most important qualifications are that they must be capable of objectivity in regards to your writing, and they must be knowledgeable about writing. Your mother is probably not a good candidate to edit your writing. Most mothers think that anything their children write is wonderful!

A good editor is invaluable as a sounding board for your writing, since they can review your work before you submit it for publication. They can read what you have written and tell you if it makes sense, if it is clear, and whether it is interesting. Good editors also help you to find embarrassing grammatical mistakes before you submit your work for consideration for publication.

If you can't find someone qualified to be an editor for your work on your own, you may want to consider joining a writing group. Most cities of any reasonable size have writer's groups or clubs where aspiring authors get together to discuss the business of writing and review each other's work. These groups are a good place to learn about the business of being a writer.

Another way to learn about writing is to attend writer's workshops or conferences. There are several of these that are held across the country on an annual basis. These programs are an excellent place to meet other writers and to share experiences.

Information and ideas on writing can also be gained from a variety of books and magazines. There have been numerous books written about writing, and there are several magazines that also explore the subject. Strunk and White's *The Elements of Style* is an excellent reference book that can help you to be a better writer. *Writer's Market* is

Fig. 9.3 – "Writer's Market" can help you to identify new markets for your writing.

an annual publication on where to sell your work, with hints on writing and interviews with writers and editors.

Although photography is not part of writing, you will be more successful in selling your work if you can take pictures to accompany your stories. Typically, editors are looking for complete packages of words and images to feature in their magazine. Given the "friendly" nature of today's automatic cameras, almost anyone can take simple photos that are adequate to illustrate an article. Learn to take attractive photos and you will sell more articles.

Conversely, certain larger magazines may want to assign a photographer to illustrate your story. If that's what the editor wants, don't argue. You must learn to work with photographers so that their images and your story compliment each other.

How to Create Copy that Sells

Whether you are writing for a magazine, an equipment manufacturer, or a training agency, you must know your topic inside and out. For example, if you are writing a catalog and must explain a new piece of equipment you haven't used, you must take the time to learn everything you can about that item. At a minimum, you'll want to see the gear and operate it on dry land, but it's always preferable to dive with it if possible.

If you are diving with a new piece of equipment it's a good idea to take a slate along with you so that you can write down your impressions as you use the gear. It is far easier to remember your thoughts by writing down a word or two during the course of your

Fig. 9.4 – If you are going to write about some aspect of diving you need to get out and dive. "Skin Diver" editor Bonnie Cardone explores a tropical reef. (Photo © Jim Church. Courtesy of "Skin Diver" Magazine, Petersen Publishing)

diving day than it is to try and remember things after you get home or on the following day.

When you start your writing career, probably the easiest place to begin is to create magazine articles. Articles take less time and energy to write than books or manuals. It's also "easier" to get an article published than a book or a manual.

When you write an article it should be with a specific magazine in mind. Most magazines have a particular style and editorial "flavor." If your writing does not match the magazine's style it will be difficult to get published there. Articles directed to the personal "you" generally have more interest for the reader and tend to get readers involved. Yet, some magazines will not accept pieces that are written this way or articles that are written in the first person.

You will do better if you start out your writing career by getting published in smaller magazines than in large ones. It is far easier to get published the first time in a regional diving magazine than it is in a publication like *National Geographic*. There are several reasons why this is true. First, the competition to get published in a periodical like *National Geographic* is intense. Unless you have exclusive coverage of a story that is exceptionally unique, the likelihood of getting something accepted at *National Geographic* as an unknown writer is slim. It's not impossible; but your chances are not good. Second, smaller regional or specialty publications are more likely to be looking for fresh talent that can bring a new perspective to their magazine.

Once you have begun to accumulate a string of credits as a writer, it becomes easier to get published in other magazines. However, you must first establish these credentials to gain some credibility with editors and publishers. As you publish more, you will eventually have editors calling you to write on assignment. This is the most desirable situation for a writer, since you are virtually guaranteed what you write will be published.

No matter what you write, it's always important to start out your story with a "*hook,*" something that will draw the reader into the story and make them want to read the whole thing. This is essential. Your hook must make an editor want to read what you have to say, as well as the reader who picks up the final printed copy. If your story is not dramatic, if it does not have something that compels the reader to read it in its entirety, than you have not done a good job as a writer.

As a diving journalist, one of your goals should be to become recognized as an "expert" in as many subject areas as possible. If you are successful in doing this, you will be the person whom editors think of first when they want to assign a story in your area of expertise.

When you write for general magazines it's important not to let your knowledge and interest in diving get in the way of your story. It's far too easy to slip into diving "jargon" that may be unfamiliar to the nondiving reader. Be careful, because this is an easy trap to fall into. If you must use diving terms, be sure to define them so that the nondiver understands what you are writing about.

When you have demonstrated your ability as a writer, you can begin to solicit work from training agencies and manufacturers for catalogs and manuals. Writing advertising copy for catalogs and technical copy for manuals is very different from writing magazine pieces.

Catalogs are created to sell products, and your copy must somehow convince the reader to do just that. Your success will be measured in terms of a customer's reaction to what you have written. If sales increase because customers have a positive reaction and buy the product because of what you have written, then you have been successful. Of course, it is possible to do a great job as a writer, but have your words become ineffective because the rest of the catalog is less than convincing.

When you write advertising copy it is essential to understand the tone and message that your client wants you to convey. This is rarely easy. Many times the client doesn't know what they want to say.

Quite often they depend upon your creativity to give them ideas. It is also not uncommon for a client to be unable to tell you what they want, only to criticize your work when you present it. They are unable to tell you what they want to say, but seem to be able to identify what they don't want to say!

Manuals are among the most difficult projects that you can be assigned to write. The best manuals are a marriage of words, photographs, and drawings. Good photographs and illustrations are essential to make your written instructions clear. Carefully written captions should accompany each photo or illustration to explain to the reader what they are supposed to do.

Whenever you write a manual it is very important to take the time to "*validate*" the manual and ensure that what you have written is understandable to a novice user. Instructions that may be clear to you, or someone who knows the product, may be unclear to a diver who has never worked with the product before.

The best way to validate your instructions is to go through the manual with someone who has never used the equipment and see if they can follow your directions. If something you have written is unclear to them, chances are it will be unclear to someone else. Find out what they don't understand, and why they don't understand it, and correct it. Have them try the new instructions and see if you have fixed the problem area. Writing text that is both clear and concise is a real art.

Manuals should always include an index, as well as a table of contents, to make it easy for the reader to locate the information they need. With the desktop publishing software available today it has become relatively easy to create an index. Ideally, you should have sufficient knowledge of desktop publishing software such as Aldus *PageMaker* or *QuarkXPress,* to assist whoever is publishing the manual in putting the index together. As the writer, you know better than anyone else what topics should be indexed. Your ability and willingness to create the index will make your work more salable.

Most of the books that are published on diving topics today are either manuals, or true adventure stories on specialty topics in diving, such as wreck diving or cave exploration. With the exception of Peter Benchley, there have not been any successful novelists who have specialized in diving or underwater topics alone.

Book publishing is generally considered to be the ultimate achievement for any writer. While there are several publishers who specialize in diving subjects today, it is still not easy for a first time author to get published. You need a unique, marketable topic that the publisher believes will sell books.

Creating a book of any length involves an enormous amount of work, as any writer can tell you. To begin, you should create a complete outline of the book, so that you understand where the work is supposed to go. This may change as the work progresses, but you must at least have an initial plan for the work to avoid going off on a tangent and wasting time.

Books are long term projects that may take months or years to create. Some writers who are excellent at putting together articles find that they do not have the stamina to sit down day after day to work on a book. Writing a book may sound "romantic," but the actual work of doing it can be drudgery if you do not have the creative drive needed to complete the project.

Fig. 9.5 – Writing a book usually entails quite a bit of library research, even if you know your topic well. (Photo by Kristine Barsky)

Even if you are extremely knowledgeable about the subject matter of your book, almost all books require the writer to do some research. If you are writing a technical book you will undoubtedly have to do a great deal of research. Your research will normally take the form of library research, correspondence with manufacturers, and personal interviews.

Library research is much easier to do today now that most larger libraries are computerized. Card catalogs can now be searched electronically, making it infinitely faster to find the information that you need. Still, it pays to make friends with your librarian, particularly the reference librarians. These people can frequently tell you where to look for materials that you never knew existed. Libraries maintained by colleges and universities are usually open to the public. They will

Fig. 9.6 – Most libraries have computerized catalogs to help you locate information quickly. (Photo by Kristine Barsky)

normally have more technical references and a wider range of journals and magazines, essential to the diving journalist.

Manufacturers are also a good source of information regarding products and how they are used. Most diving equipment manufacturers are anxious to promote their products and will help you if they can, provided you don't make unreasonable demands. You can make yourself very unpopular if you ask for, or demand, materials with an unreasonable deadline for delivery.

If you need information from a diving equipment manufacturer, you'll usually end up speaking with either their marketing or sales department. Be sure to explain what your project is about, who is going to publish it, and what specific information or materials you need from them. Find out when you can expect to receive the information and make a note to yourself in your daily planner to follow up if you do not receive the materials within a week after the promised delivery date.

When you do receive the materials from the manufacturer, be sure to follow up with a personal "thank you" note to the person who assisted you, especially if you expect to receive any assistance in the future. If you were loaned any materials, such as equipment for photos, be sure to return them promptly in good condition, or offer to pay for any damages.

Personal interviews can be the most time consuming and expensive research for any project, but they usually provide the most information. The research for this book included trips to San Diego, Monterey, San Francisco, Seattle, Los Angeles, the Channel Islands, and Orlando. If someone grants you the time for a personal interview, you should take the time to write a note thanking them for their assistance.

Probably the most difficult part of any book is maintaining a consistent style and story line throughout a long project. This is essential. Most writers find they need to reread the entire project from start to finish after the writing has been completed to put things in perspective. Again, this is where a good editor can be invaluable.

Unless your work is a novel, photographs are usually an essential part of any diving book. Even the best writers know that the first thing that most people look at when they pick up a book are the photographs. If you are not a photographer you should find a good one who will work with you to create the images necessary to illustrate your work.

Submitting Your Work for Publication

If you are a new writer, one of your first steps in getting published is to find out what magazine editors want and how to submit your materials. For this you will need a copy of *Writer's Market*. *Writer's Market* will tell you exactly how most magazines and publishers want you to submit materials.

Most magazines will want you to submit a "*query letter*" prior to receiving any work from you. In the query letter, you write to the editor of the magazine and suggest a particular story. Your letter should explain why the story will be of interest to the magazine's readers, give a sample of your writing style, and list any special support material you have to accompany the piece.

Some magazines and editors will allow you to call them to query about a particular story, but this is the exception rather than the rule. In addition, not all magazines are listed in *Writer's Market*. For those that aren't listed, it's recommended that you write to the publication with your query and request a copy of their "*writer's guidelines*" at the same time.

The writer's guidelines that are published by most magazines will usually give you specific directions regarding the magazine's audience, the type of stories the magazine accepts, and anything that they specifically do not want to receive. You will stand a greater chance of getting your writing accepted if you read and follow the guidelines they provide.

Once you begin to get published and have established a relationship with a particular magazine it may be okay to call an editor to inquire about a specific story idea. This is considered more acceptable after you have worked with an editor for awhile and they have called you to assign stories.

Some editors and publishers will allow you to submit your work without a query, or "*over the transom*" as it's known in the trade. Don't do this unless you know for sure that this is acceptable. In some cases your material may be returned unopened, while in other situations it may be thrown away!

Another unpardonable sin is to submit the same material to more than one publication without making this known to both of them. Most publications will specifically tell you that this is not acceptable. If you do this without admitting it, and manage to get the same work published in two publications, you will probably find that neither one will use your work again in the future.

If the response to your query is positive, all this usually means is that the editor is willing to examine your work. This is not a guarantee that your article will be published.

When you submit materials to a publisher there are several items that should be part of your package. First, your submission should contain a cover letter outlining what items you have included in your package. The hard copy of your manuscript should be clean and without handwritten notes on it. The manuscript should be printed on 25% cotton rag bond paper. It should not be stapled or bound. If you submit a copy on disk there should be a label on the disk identifying the contents. Each file on the disk should be appropriately titled.

Your work should be packaged in either a clean envelope with heavy, corrugated cardboard or in a sturdy manuscript box. It should be neatly packaged so it is easy for the editor to sort out your materials. How you present your work is almost as important as what you have to say. If your material is packaged sloppily, people will assume that your work is sloppy, too. The package should be marked with a large stamp, "Photos - Do Not Bend."

Your submission should be mailed via certified first class mail with a return receipt at a minimum. If you are including photographs, or if this is a particularly important submission, you should use either Federal Express, UPS, or some other private carrier who provides a return receipt. Ordinary postal service tracking and delivery are not reliable enough for tight deadlines and important parcels. You should also enclose a self addressed, stamped envelope for the return of your work.

Once you have submitted materials to an editor or publisher the best thing you can do is to forget about them for the immediate future and start working on other projects. Quite often it will be several months before you hear anything back from an editor. This is a time to be patient. Allow the editor time to examine your materials without pressure from you. Most writer's guidelines will tell you how long you can expect to wait before receiving a response to your work.

Wait the maximum time for review of your materials as listed in the writer's guidelines, then wait another two weeks before contacting the editor to check on the status of your work. At this point you may politely call or write to inquire whether they intend to use your materials. You will usually get some sort of indication at this time whether they want to use your work, or they may request additional time for review. Never be rude to an editor, or exert undue pressure to make a decision, or you may get your materials back without review.

Magazines normally purchase what is known as "*First Serial Rights*" for your articles. This means that they are buying the rights to publish that work for the first time. If your work has been previously published then the magazine will be purchasing "*Second Serial Rights.*" If you sell your work to European magazines as well as those in the U.S. you may sell "*First North American Rights*" or "*First European Rights.*"

Book Publishing

If you are trying to publish a book, most publishers will want to see a book proposal and an outline rather than an entire manuscript. Some publishers will also request to see a few sample chapters. Always follow their requests rather than creating an entire manuscript. The only exception to this would be in creating a novel, since most publishers will not commit to publishing a novel by an "unknown" author. If you want to be published as a novelist you will need to take the chance and write your entire book in a gamble to get in print. Getting published as a new novelist is very difficult.

Different book publishers specialize in different topics. Don't waste your time submitting the wrong book idea to a book publisher. For example, Sea Challengers, a book publisher in Monterey, only publishes titles dealing with marine biology. Watersport Publishing in San Diego publishes primarily titles dealing with sport diving topics. Gulf Publishing in Houston specializes in books related to dive travel locations. Best Publishing, the publisher of this book, tends to deal in the more technical topics in diving, particularly subjects that pertain to people who are professionally employed in diving.

Unlike magazines, books are normally published under very specific contracts. When you submit an article to a magazine, you will usually have little to say about how the editor changes your work and how your story appears in the magazine. This can be very surprising, especially for new writers. Conversely, when you publish a book, you will generally be far more involved in the format and final appearance of the book.

Before you deliver a book for publication you should have a firm contract in hand. The contract should explain in clear language what your responsibilities are as a writer and what the publisher's responsibilities are in his role. It should also explain how much you will be paid for each copy of the book sold and how often the royalties for the book will be paid.

Your book contract will spell out the terms and conditions set down by the publisher. Examine the contract carefully and think about what each point in the contract means to you. If there is something you don't understand, call the publisher and ask them to explain it to you. If there is something in the contract that you don't like, politely ask if it can be changed or negotiated. Above all, you should not sign a book contract without having it examined by your lawyer first. Contracts are legally binding instruments and you could find yourself in an unacceptable position if you don't have proper legal advice.

Most publishers will want to hold the copyright to the text of your book. This means that they hold all the rights to the material in the text. Your contract will generally specify that you cannot produce a competing work on the same topic for another publisher.

If you are a photographer you will undoubtedly want to retain copyright to any photos published in the book and the right to publish those photos in other places. Any reasonable publisher should not have a problem with this.

One of the things that should be clearly specified in your contract is any conditions that relate to the editing of your book. Specifically, you should know what rights the publisher expects to have in regards to changes in the manuscript and how much say you have in regards to these changes. This is especially important if you are writing on a technical topic where changes by an unwitting editor can thoroughly distort or change the meaning of what you have written.

When you deliver the manuscript for your book you will be delivering a hard copy on paper, a diskette copy, and all the photographs for the book. Each photograph should be numbered to correspond with its caption in the text. If you have multiple chapters, the photographs should be packaged in envelopes according to the chapter number. The entire package will probably need to go in a box.

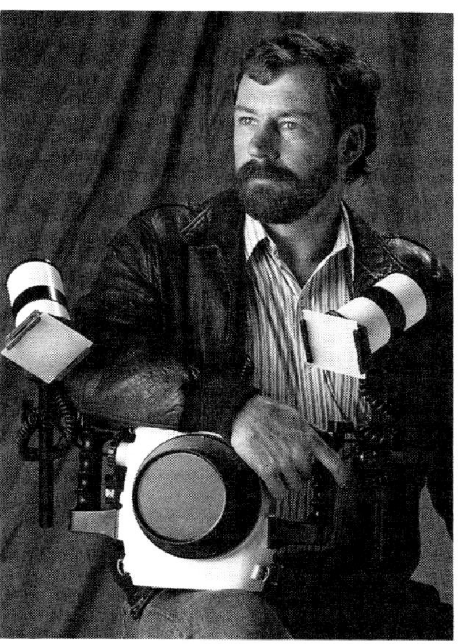

Fig. 9.7 – Ken Loyst is both a writer and a photographer, as are most diving journalists. (© Lee Peterson)

As the writer of a book, you should inspect the "*galleys*" of the book before the work goes to press. The galleys are the final layout of the book that show what the book will actually look like when it is published. In the galleys, each page is laid out to the actual size and all the photos and captions should be in their proper place.

As the writer, it is your job to carefully check the galleys to make sure that it matches your manuscript. You want to be sure that nothing was accidentally omitted, that the editors have not made any significant changes, and that the photos are cropped, sized, printed, and captioned correctly. It is not uncommon for photos to be printed backwards, or for the wrong photo to be matched with the wrong caption. The galleys are your last chance to make any corrections before your book goes to press.

Can You Get Rich as a Writer?

If all you ever publish are diving texts it's unlikely that you can get rich as a writer. However, if you can make the leap to writing novels you can make a substantial amount of money.

If you write only for magazines, you will find it very difficult to make a living as a writer unless you can get your work published in nondiving publications. Pay rates vary and the terms of payment vary from publication to publication.

Some magazines pay by the word, others pay by the page, and yet others pay by the column inch. Diving magazines may pay as little as a $60.00 a page or less, while general interest magazines can pay thousands of dollars a page, plus all expenses while you are on assignment.

Most diving book publishers will not pay a writer any sort of advance against the anticipated sales of a book. This means that you must have some means of supporting yourself while you are writing. However, if you have an unusual or unique topic that is of special interest you may be able to negotiate some type of advance to help you survive while you write.

The normal royalty rate for a book ranges anywhere from 10% to 15% of each sale. Typically, royalties are either paid quarterly or twice a year.

Diving and Traveling as a Journalist

With today's lightweight and compact electronics, it's easier than ever for a journalist to travel and work anywhere. At a minimum, all you need is a laptop computer with a fax/modem and a compact 35MM camera. Of course, if you are a serious photographer you will probably need more items than this, but the point is, that as a writer, you can work anywhere.

Fig. 9.8 – As a diving journalist you can work anywhere. (Photo by Kristine Barsky)

Eric Hanauer has written several dive travel books while on the road, traveling throughout the Indo-Pacific region. Eric travels with his dive gear, his topside photo equipment, his underwater photo gear, and his laptop computer. The final text is edited when he returns to his home in Costa Mesa, California. (For more on Eric see chapter 2 on diving instruction.)

If you are on assignment for a magazine you can send your files directly to the publisher either via your modem or as a hard copy fax. This makes you extremely versatile. With a hand held scanner or an electronic camera you could even send photographs from on location via your modem.

Experiences of Diving Journalists

BONNIE CARDONE

While most diving journalists work on a "*freelance*" basis, some writers work full time for the diving media as writers and/or editors. These positions are extremely demanding since you are constantly working under the pressure of deadlines. As a staff writer, you don't have the same freedom as a freelancer. Not everyone is capable of handling this level of responsibility.

Bonnie Cardone has one of the top positions in the world as a diving journalist. As the executive editor of *Skin Diver* magazine, she is responsible for the editorial content of more than 190 pages each month of the year.

Bonnie started diving in Los Angeles in 1973 and has been diving all over the world. Her travels have taken her to the Philippines, the Cayman Islands, Indonesia, Bonaire, the Sea of Cortez, and the Virgin Islands. She joined the *Skin Diver* staff in 1976 and has authored more than 300 articles for the magazine, most of which have been illustrated by her photography.

Bonnie's background prior to working for *Skin Diver* includes a Bachelor's degree in Communication Arts from Michigan State Uni-

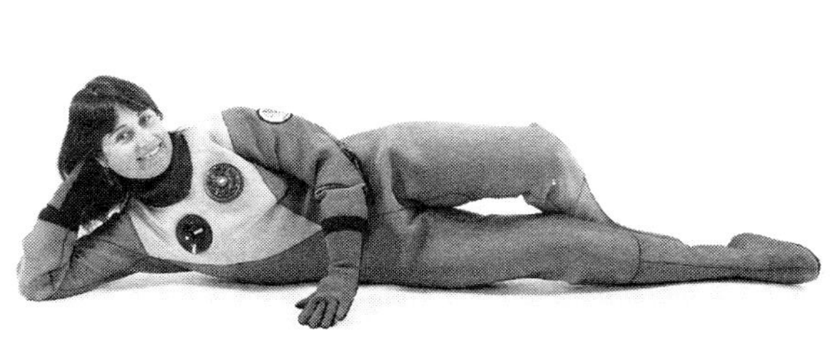

Fig. 9.9 – No, she's not lying down on the job. Bonnie Cardone models a dry suit as part of her job as editor at "Skin Diver." (Photo © Petersen Publications Staff. Courtesy of "Skin Diver" Magazine)

versity and editorial work for publisher McGraw-Hill. She has also attended numerous extension courses at UCLA including programs in TV writing and fiction.

At *Skin Diver,* Bonnie is one of two editors and shares in the proofreading and caption writing for the magazine. Her other duties include assigning articles to freelance writers, evaluating manuscripts and photographs, supervising the typesetting, and keeping track of the diving equipment reviewed by the magazine. On the average, she writes and photographs three articles a month in addition to the rest of her duties. Her articles have covered almost every topic in the magazine, including wreck diving, travel, game hunting, equipment, and celebrity interviews.

STEVE BARSKY

Unlike Cardone, Steve Barsky works as a freelance writer, but also writes and does photography for a variety of manufacturers through his business, Marine Marketing and Consulting. His writing and photos have appeared in most major diving magazines including *Skin Diver, Underwater USA, Discover Diving, Scuba Times, Ocean Realm,* and nondiving publications such as *Emergency, Rescue, Ebony, Santa Barbara,* and numerous others. Barsky has also published several books, written manuals, catalogs, advertisements, and film scripts. His clients have included U.S. Divers, Henderson, Wenoka, Zeagle Systems, DAN, Diving Unlimited International, NAUI, Scuba Schools International, and Diving Systems International.

Steve started college as an English major, but finished with a Master's degree in Applied Physiology and Applied Psychology. He completed a scuba instructor certification course in San Diego in 1970. He also graduated from the commercial diving program at Santa Barbara City College. After graduation he worked in the North Sea and the Gulf of Mexico. He returned to California in 1983 to work for Diving Systems International (DSI).

At DSI, Steve learned a great deal about producing manuals and catalogs from Bev Morgan. Bev was one of the founders of the Los Angeles County Scuba instructor's program and is an outstanding underwater photographer and writer who has written numerous manuals and articles. Bev was also editor of *Surfer* magazine for several years.

In 1987 Steve went to work for Viking America and took over the marketing for Viking dry suits. When Viking let him go in 1989, it forced him to go out and start his own company.

Steve's company, Marine Marketing and Consulting, provides a variety of marketing and consulting services to the diving industry. Most of the jobs that the company does are based upon Steve's ability to write. Although he is a good photographer, it is the combination of writing and photography that brings in the bulk of the work. His technical background from the commercial diving field allows him to write on a wide variety of topics with authority.

KEN LOYST

Although Ken Loyst makes his living as a writer, editor, and publisher of diving books and magazines, he considers himself first and foremost to be an underwater educator. He has devoted over 20 years to diving instruction, instructor training, and the development of books and other support materials for scuba diving.

Ken learned to dive in 1968 and became a diving instructor in 1972. He worked for a chain of retail dive stores from 1973 to 1977, and was the manager of the chain from 1974 through 1977. In 1979 Ken went to work for the NAUI College in Southern California and ran instructor courses all over the world. To date, Ken has directed over 75 instructor courses.

In 1980, Ken started Watersport Publishing. Initially, he published dive site and marine life identification guides, but then launched *Discover Diving,* a newspaper for divers in Southern California. Today, *Discover Diving* is a national magazine printed on glossy paper, with a circulation of over 90,000. Ken writes and photographs many of the articles in the magazine.

In 1988 Ken started an educational book division for divers, called Watersport Books. He has personally authored three titles, *Diving with Dive Computers* (with Karl Huggins), *Dive Computers* (an expanded version of the previous title), and *Night Diving* (with Marty Snyderman and Robert von Maier).

DALE SHECKLER

Dale Sheckler is the publisher of *California Diving News,* the only monthly publication devoted exclusively to California diving. Dale started diving in 1971 in Redondo Beach, California, where he grew up.

At the age of 16, Dale decided he wanted to be a commercial diver and planned his life around that goal. After high school, he earned an A.S. degree in Welding and Metallurgy and attended the Commercial Diving Center, CDC, (now known as the College of Oceaneering) in

Fig. 9.10 – Dale Sheckler is a former commercial diver who now publishes "California Diving News." (Photo courtesy of Dale Sheckler.)

Wilmington, California. He worked as a commercial diver for a company called Solus Ocean Systems, from 1978 until 1984, in places such as the Gulf of Mexico and the Persian Gulf. When Solus Ocean Systems was purchased by Oceaneering International, Dale decided to leave the company and quit commercial diving.

While he attended CDC, Dale started dating Kim, who became his wife, and eventually his partner, in *California Diving News*. They were married in 1982 when Dale was working in Houston, and lived there until returning to California.

When Dale and Kim returned to California in March of 1984, he went sport diving every day and developed the vision that led him to publishing *California Diving News*. They started the magazine in July of that same year.

Today, Dale and Kim publish *California Diving News* and run one of the most successful consumer shows for divers in the country, known as the *Scuba* show. Much of the photography and writing in the magazine is Dale's.

Dale takes a great deal of pleasure in running his own business and enjoys testing new pieces of dive gear for review in the magazine. As an "insider" in the industry, he is among the first to hear industry news and "gossip." He dives frequently and is a skilled underwater photographer.

With the demands that come with publishing a magazine and organizing a trade show for over 10,000 attendees, Dale finds that frequently he doesn't get to dive as much as he would prefer. In addition, when the economy is poor and money is "tight," advertisers frequently cut back on their budgets. This directly affects the magazine.

Dale's advice for those divers who want to enter the field of diving journalism is to find out specifically what type of material the editor desires. If you can develop your skills as a photographer, it will be much easier to sell your written pieces.

"In our publication, we're always looking for people who have a diving background and write well, but we'll take the time to edit work from a less experienced writer who has something interesting to say," says Dale.

Suggested Reading:

Kissling, M., Ed. *Writer's Market.* Writer's Digest Books, Cincinnati, OH. (Published annually)

Chapter Ten

UNDERWATER PHOTOGRAPHY & CINEMATOGRAPHY

The world's first underwater photographer was a Frenchman by the name of Louis Boutan, who began taking pictures underwater in the late 1800's. While Boutan certainly did not make a living this way, he opened the door to a field that is one of the most desired careers in diving.

Today there are more opportunities for underwater photographers than ever before, and the field keeps growing. There are numerous magazines today looking for outstanding underwater photographs, and creating opportunities for underwater photographers. There is also more television programming on network and cable channels, with a steady demand for new and exciting documentaries and stories. Unique underwater video and film footage have created career breaks for numerous divers.

Training as an Underwater Photographer

To be a good underwater photographer, it's recommended that you start out by gaining photographic experience on land before you transfer your skills underwater. Admittedly, this is not essential. There are successful underwater photographers who started out with little topside photographic experience. However, your skills will probably develop faster if you have mastered the fundamentals of topside photography before you try to shoot underwater.

Fig. 10.1 – You can get started in underwater photography with a Nikonos camera and a single flash. (Photo by Kristine C. Barsky)

There are many professional photographers who have attended photography schools, such as Brooks Institute. There are probably an equal number of photographers who have little or no formal photographic training! Whether you need to attend a school or not is a personal question based upon your individual aptitude, talent, and drive.

You can learn photography on your own, however, it may end up being more expensive than going to school. Without instruction, you'll probably end up making many mistakes during the learning process. Mistakes in photography equate to more film, photographic paper, and developing chemistry, as well as time. All of these cost money. Whether you spend your money on photo school, or the mistakes you make yourself, is a personal decision. As the old saying goes, "If you think education is expensive, try ignorance!"

If you are unsure whether or not to attend a professional photography school, take some inexpensive photo courses at a local community college. These courses are usually worthwhile and will provide you with the fundamentals of photography. They are also a reasonable way to determine whether you really have sufficient interest and ability to make it worth your time to enroll in a more expensive and comprehensive school.

Another alternative is to attend a series of short, one or two day workshops offered through any of the private professional photography schools. By attending these workshops you can get a better feel for how your skills and talent stack up against successful photographers. You can enroll in short courses in almost any subject in photography, including underwater photography. Most of today's working professional underwater photographers regularly offer week long programs at some of the top underwater resorts. These courses typically include on-site processing so you can critique your work on a daily basis.

Yet another possibility is to get a job as an apprentice with a professional photographer. There is no substitute for what you can learn from a working "pro," particularly if you are lucky enough to hook up with a real artist. Keep in mind, though, that in photography, as in most fields, there are specialists. The chances of apprenticing with an underwater photographer are pretty slim.

You can learn valuable secrets from any working pro, so don't rule out working with a successful topside photographer. A photographer who specializes in food can teach you many things about lighting and setting up a shot. Also, realize that most photographers look for apprentices who understand photography, equipment, and lighting. It may be difficult to hire on with a working pro if you don't know much about photography.

Fig. 10.2 – To be a successful underwater photographer you must be at home in the water, so you can handle large, heavy cameras and other equipment. Photographer Lance Milbrand prepares to dive with his underwater movie camera.

Apprentices are expected to do any work that must be done to keep the business rolling. This may include such activities as building sets or props, cleaning the set, loading cameras, setting up lighting, shipping product samples back to the customer, processing film, and hundreds of other chores.

As a photographer you need to have an excellent understanding of light and an eye for the way it illuminates a scene. You must have, or acquire a feel for, composition and what makes a photograph different or unusual. You must understand different films and know which film to select for a particular job.

To be a successful underwater photographer, as in any underwater career, you must be completely at home in the water. This means that your diving and buoyancy skills must be excellent. It is unrealistic to expect to produce consistent underwater photos unless you can totally concentrate on your photography without worrying about the fact that you are underwater. You must be as relaxed underwater as you are sitting at your kitchen table. This doesn't mean that you are unconcerned about your safety, but that your primary attention is devoted to producing great pictures.

Most of the world's successful underwater film makers started out as still photographers. There's a good reason for this; it's a lot less expensive to learn the basics of lighting and composition through still photography than through motion pictures. In addition, the equipment for professional still photography is also less expensive than setting up a system for professional quality video or motion pictures.

As in still photography, there are three ways that you can learn to be an underwater film maker. You can attend a film making school, you can apprentice with a successful film maker, or you can buy all the equipment and learn on your own. Of course, it is less expensive if you work in video, although a professional video camera suitable for producing broadcast quality tapes may cost over $30,000.00 when new. Add an underwater housing and you're easily looking at another $5,000.00 to $10,000.00.

Fig. 10.3 – While you can start out making videos with an inexpensive camera and housing like the one shown here, professional work demands much more sophisticated equipment.

While you can work in a less expensive format, such as hi-band 8, very few customers will accept this level of quality for reproduction purposes. Hi-band 8 is a less expensive way to get started and learn video, but in the end you will spend more money if you must replace your camera and editing equipment with professional equipment later on.

Breaking in as a Professional Underwater Photographer

If you want to be a professional underwater still photographer, keep in mind that it is very difficult to sell a sufficient number of photos to truly make a living. You can do it, but your subject matter must be exceptional. Most still photographers must also be able to write, since magazines are generally looking for complete stories that include both words and pictures. If you are not a writer, then you need to team up with someone who can write, at least initially, (see chapter 8 on underwater journalism for more information on writing and writers).

Magazines are generally looking for photographs to illustrate stories. If you work with a writer, you must understand what pictures are needed to explain the main points of the story. If you do your own writing, you should already have a good idea of what images you will need.

One of the keys to being a successful underwater photographer is to develop your own distinctive style and specialties. That doesn't mean that all your pictures should look alike, but they should have a distinct "feel" to them that sets them apart and makes them unmistakably yours. Your "signature" will generally be the lighting and composition that becomes characteristic of your photos.

Just as there are specialists in topside photography, there are also specialists in underwater photography. For example, photographers like Howard Hall, Marty Snyderman and Bob Cranston, are known for their work with large marine animals. Bob Evans, a photographer and diving inventor, is known for his distinctive lighting, and wide variety of marine life images. Dee Scarr is known for her use of marine life photos to educate divers so they won't harm the environment. Steve Barsky specializes in divers, diver training, and unusual underwater equipment. Magazine editors frequently will contact specific underwater photographers because they know they will probably have the image they need.

Fig. 10.4 – Photographer Bob Evans is known for his distinctive lighting and timeless marine life photographs.

At the same time that you are working on your style, you must also be open to experimentation.

This is where you can make creative "leaps" that lead to new and exciting images. Magazine editors are always looking for something that is new and different. To be a successful photographer you must be ready to show them things they have either never seen before, or present traditional subjects in an unusual way.

The top underwater photographers know that to make a good living you must market yourself outside the diving magazines. Diving magazines just don't pay enough money to support a working photographer. There is much better money to be made selling your photographs to general interest magazines, to advertisers outside of diving, and to book publishers who produce marine related books.

Most of the more successful still photographers eventually end up doing film work because there is more money to be made doing films than in still photography. There are also fewer people that are capable of doing film, although the video field is becoming more crowded all the time. Film projects usually last longer and are much more complex than still photographic assignments.

The most essential element to success in underwater photography, be it motion pictures or stills, is to create images that tell stories. These projects will always sell.

Setting Up Your Files

As a photographer, your photos (or stock footage if you are a film maker) become your inventory. As time goes by, you will accumulate an ever growing number of images. This is called "*shooting for stock.*" As a professional photographer, you should be continuously shooting to build your base of stock photos. Most magazines, unless you're shooting for something like *National Geographic,* would rather buy an image out of your stock files than send you "*on assignment*" to shoot for them.

When a client calls and requests a specific image it is essential to your profitability to be able to lay your hands on the exact image they need very quickly. This is where an organized photo file and database become a necessity.

There are several "canned" database programs designed specifically for professional photographers, for Macintosh, DOS, and Windows based computers. Although these programs are easy to use, they tend to lock you into a given way of entering and retrieving your data that may not best suit your needs. Most of these programs work quite well but may be expensive. If you are computer literate it is more economical to set up your own database. This will also let you organize the information in a way that makes the most sense to you.

Different photographers organize their images in different ways. For example, a marine life photographer may organize their photos according to where they were taken, and then break down the categories further by the phylum, class, and species of each subject. Conversely, a photographer who specializes in diving equipment, may need to sort images by the brand of equipment the model wears in each photo. There are no set rules for organizing your photos, except that you should use the method that allows you to retrieve your photos in the fastest way possible.

Fig. 10.5 – It is essential to edit and file your images so you can quickly retrieve them. Here, Steve Barsky reviews photos from a recent dive trip. (Photo by Kristine C. Barsky)

Generally speaking, each image in your database is assigned a number. As you get your film back from the lab, each image is marked with an individual number and goes into some type of file. Slides can be numbered directly on the side of the slide mount, while prints may be numbered on proof sheets and on individual prints. Of course, your images should always be stored in a cool dry place.

Slides are best stored in slide pages or sheets that are "*archival*," i.e., that are made from a polyethylene plastic that will not destroy the slide. Slide sheets made from PVC, poly vinyl chloride, are not archival and will harm your slides. The sheets should then be stored in one of the plastic binders that are built into a box that seals on all sides. This helps to protect your slides and keep them clean. It also allows for faster retrieval.

For print reproduction, such as magazines, catalogs, and books, color slides are the preferred media that publishers desire. Color prints can be used, but they don't reproduce as well as color slides.

For black and white reproduction, the minimum size preferred by magazines is a 5 X 7 inch print. Prints should be glossy with borders.

Dealing with Magazines

Until you get to the point where magazines are calling you and requesting your photos, you will need to send out query letters to sell your images. At this point, we should re-emphasize that it is much easier to sell a complete package including a story and images than it is to sell photos by themselves. Unless you have photos that are extremely unusual, it is hard to sell them on their own. Try to find a writer to work with if at all possible.

The query letter from a photographer to an editor is nearly identical to the query letter that is sent by a writer to an editor (see chapter 9 for more on query letters). It should be short and to the point. If you don't know the editor, it should tell him who you are, what your photos are about, and why they are significant. Many magazines will not accept your work without having received a query letter first and responding with a request for your material. Images that are sent without a "request" are called "*unsolicited images.*"

Some magazines, are very strict about unsolicited material and will return your package unopened, or worse, will not review or even return your work. To find out how to approach a particular magazine or publisher be sure to pick up a copy of *Photographer's Market,* published annually and available in most bookstores. This is an invaluable resource and provides information on many potential customers you may not know about.

If you receive a positive response to your query, then it is time to prepare your materials for shipment. Each photo that you send should be listed on a sheet of paper with its number and a caption. The caption should describe what is happening in the photograph and where it was taken. If there are people who can be identified in the photograph most magazines will want a signed "*model release*" from the person in the photo signifying that it is acceptable to them for their image to be published.

If you are sending slides, never send your originals! Always send high quality duplicate slides (dupes), unless the publication insists that you send the originals. Some magazines and other publications are careless about how they handle slides. If you send your originals you run the risk that they may be damaged or lost. There have also been cases where photographers have lost slides because the publication went out of business.

If you must send the originals, they should be sent with a "*delivery memo,*" that lists the number of the slide, a brief description of the image, and the replacement value of the image. The delivery memo should also state the date by which you expect the photos to be returned. Typically, you should allow a magazine to hold your work for a minimum of 30 days. If they need more time they will ask for it. You should include two copies of the delivery memo; one for the client to keep and another with a self-addressed envelope for them to mail back to you. The delivery memo is designed to let both parties know that the client received the work that you have said that you sent them. If they don't send the delivery memo back to you, the client's inaction is considered an acknowledgment of their receipt of your materials.

The replacement value is your cost to go back and shoot the image again. Generally speaking, most photographers will value their replacement images at $500.00 or more. However, if you have that once in a lifetime shot of two white sharks mating and the magazine insists on the original, the replacement value should be set much higher.

Never send original slides by U.S. mail, even if your client wants overnight delivery. Although their charge is less expensive than private carriers, such as Federal Express or Airborne, their delivery and tracking procedures are less than adequate. Don't risk your original slides with the postal service. In addition, the use of a private service such as Federal Express commands more attention with most clients, and conveys an unspoken message of professionalism and seriousness. Even a small business can establish an account with Federal Express, Air-

Fig. 10.6 – Never send your images by ordinary mail. Always use a private carrier, such as Federal Express, UPS, or Airborne. (Photo by Kristine C. Barsky)

borne, or U.P.S. With Federal Express and Airborne, every receipt you get identifies who signed for the package and when it was received.

Use registered mail with a return receipt only when sending dupes. Keep in mind, though, that postal carriers will not always get the return receipt post card signed, and then you will have no proof that your package was actually received.

Sometimes, if you have extremely unusual slides, such as a pair of mating white sharks, it pays to just go ahead and send your "dupes" with your query. This is definitely a case where a "picture is worth a thousand words."

Whether you are sending slides or black and white prints, always package your photos between two sheets of heavy corrugated cardboard. Don't use shirt cardboard; it's just not strong enough! You can buy 8–1/2 by 11 inch sheets of cardboard specifically for mailing photos from your local paper supply house. Your package should be neatly put together to convey that you are a professional, not an amateur.

One of the most important rules in dealing with magazines is to always ensure your material gets there on time. This can be very difficult because editors frequently will call with last minute "panic" requests and expect you to deliver the images they need overnight. Your guiding principle should be to never promise something that you cannot deliver. If you say that you will provide a photo on a specific date, be sure to do it or you may never get another request from that publication.

How Do Copyrights Apply to Photographs?

As a photographer, every time you create a new image, that image belongs to you, whether you formally copyright it or not. Copyright is a form of legal protection that, in its highest form, is achieved by registering a copy of that image with the copyright office in Washington, D.C. This takes time and costs money. Practically speaking, registering photographs is something that most photographers don't do.

To protect your work from misuse, the simplest form of copyright is to stamp your work with a copyright sign. The correct form is as shown here:

© 1992 Joe Photodiver or Copyright 1992 Joe Photodiver

The letter "C" in the circle is the universal copyright symbol and identifies that you own the rights to that image. The copyright symbo is then followed by the year the image was created and your name. Alternatively, you can use the word "Copyright" rather than the "C" in the circle. Either method signifies the same thing. Any image you send out for consideration for publication should be marked with your copyright, as well as your telephone number and address.

Before you ever release images to a publisher, be sure you understand what the terms of use are for that particular publication. There are all sorts of "rights" that publications buy, and you should have a clear understanding of what the client expects. Generally speaking, most magazines in the U.S. are willing to settle for "*First Serial Rights.*" This means that they are to be the first publication to publish a particular image. If you previously sold the work in Europe, you may end up selling a U.S. magazine what's known as "*First North American Rights.*"

At all costs, you want to avoid selling a magazine "All Rights." When you sell *All Rights* you lose control of your image and the publisher can use the photo in any way they please, over and over, only paying for the first time they are used. Since the real money in photography is to be made from selling an image repeatedly you want to avoid selling All Rights. The only time you should be willing to sell all rights is when the photo has no other value.

You must take care when you shoot photos for a catalog. The client may consider this a "*work for hire*" arrangement, where they own all the images you produce for them. If you do this type of work, you must have a good understanding with the client about what images they get to keep and which ones are yours.

Your copyright on an image is only as valuable as the amount of time, energy, and money you are willing to invest if someone uses your images without your permission. The rights of photographers to their work is quite broad today and the law generally affords good protection for you.

For more information on copyright law see *Photographer's Market* as well as some of the other publications listed at the end of this chapter.

Should You Have an Agent?

Even if you are successful selling your images on your own, you may want to consider hiring an agent. This is especially true if you start to become very successful and need to spend most of your time shooting photos. The job of an agent is to market and sell your work. For their efforts, agents take a cut of your sales in the form of a commission.

Agents, and agencies, can be both good and bad. Just as you can lose photos through carelessness on the part of a publisher, the same thing can happen with agents. On the other hand, a good agent can get you published in markets you never knew existed, and can help you further your career.

Determining What the Client Wants

If you are asked to shoot an assignment for a magazine, you need to find out exactly what the editor wants. What "slant" or perspective does the editor expect? If possible, ask for examples of other work that pleased him or her.

If you are shooting marine life you must know whether the editor also wants a diver in the photo, or whether he wants the animal by itself. What types of behaviors does the editor want to see captured on film?

Shooting products for catalogs can be one of the more difficult types of photography, especially if you must shoot the product in use underwater. It is not uncommon for a client to be unable to explain what they want in a photo, or how they want it to look. It is also not uncommon for a client who does not understand underwater photography to ask for a shot that is difficult or impossible to produce.

Fig. 10.7 – Steve Barsky pauses to direct models Gwen Murrieta and Ehsida Bissett during a shoot for U.S. Divers Co. (Photo by Kristine C. Barsky)

Some manufacturers are very particular about how a diver should appear in a photo and will want every piece of safety equipment that is normally worn underwater. Other manufacturers may want "*cheesecake,*" looking to show a diving mask on a buxom model in the tropics, clad only in a bikini. You should know what the client wants before you start to shoot.

If you are shooting for a full line manufacturer it is generally easier than if you are shooting for a specialty manufacturer that only makes a few products. The full line manufacturer will normally provide you with everything they want the model to wear, from head to toe. One of the dangers in this type of situation can be the temptation on the part of the advertising people to load the model up with so much equipment it makes them look awkward or uncomfortable.

When you work for a specialty manufacturer your job is more difficult because you must select equipment that complements their products in terms of color and application. Colors should highlight the equipment that you are trying to show. Equipment from other manufacturers should be designed for similar applications so that your photographs are technically correct. For example, you wouldn't want to photograph a minimal volume, warm water buoyancy compensator with a wetsuit that was designed for cold water diving.

Politics are another consideration when you are photographing for a specialty manufacturer. Some manufacturers have alliances with other manufacturers whose gear complements theirs and want their gear photographed together. At the same time, a specialty manufacturer of buoyancy compensators may not want their gear photographed along with a regulator from a full line manufacturer who makes competing B.C.'s. If you do this type of work it's essential to know the politics of the industry.

If you are shooting for a book that will include the work of other photographers it is essential to understand the look the editor wants to achieve. In a book, most editors want some consistency to the images. In particular, an editor may request a particular film to be used to ensure that any color work can be reproduced easily.

Film or video work is always a team effort that may involve a handful, or hundreds of people. There will usually be a producer, a director, a script writer, a camera man, lighting and prop assistants, and actors. Shooting a film or a video is extremely expensive and you must understand precisely what the client wants before you go into production. Ideally, you should have a signed contract spelling out the terms and conditions of the job.

Working with Models Underwater

If you plan to photograph diving equipment underwater you need good looking models who are excellent divers. Unfortunately, most

Fig. 10.8 – Shooting a film is a team effort. This shot was taken during the filming of the video, "Be a Responsible Diver." Left to right are director and cameraman Lance Milbrand, writer and producer Steve Barsky, actress and writer Diane Beery, and actor Richard Morton. The photo was shot by Kristine Barsky, who was also part of the crew.

modeling agencies do not have professional underwater models "on call" and available for hire.

If your photos are going to involve people underwater you will probably want to develop a working relationship with a select group of divers who can model underwater. Many of the professional underwater photographers have models who they work with regularly. The models know what the photographer expects and the photographer knows what the models can do. Even if you are the best underwater photographer in the world, a poor model can ruin your photos.

Underwater models generally need not be as attractive as topside models, because diving gear hides most imperfections in a person's figure. However, if you are shooting glamour shots of women or men, where you are advertising products such as bathing suits or dive "skins," your models should be trim and well built.

Above all, your models must be competent divers, capable of taking a new piece of gear, sorting it out, and making it work for them underwater in a few minutes. As a photographer, you cannot afford to work with a model who is not a competent diver.

Income Potential for Underwater Photographers

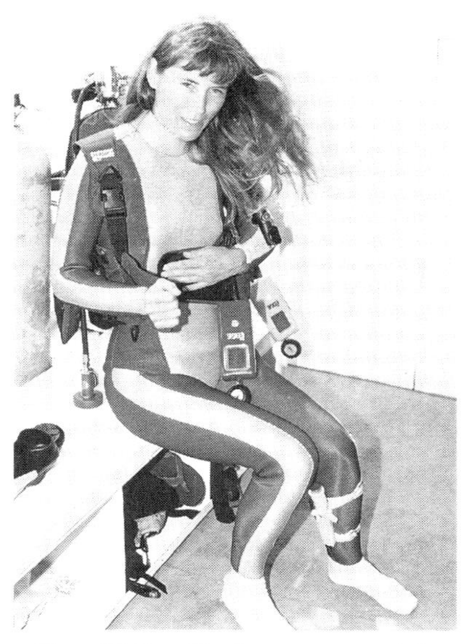

Fig. 10.9 – Underwater models must be competent divers.

Very few underwater photographers have become rich. It is difficult to make a living shooting nothing but underwater subjects, but it can be done. Most photographers must also spend a certain amount of time shooting topside subjects to supplement their underwater work. A top underwater still photographer will probably never make as much money as a top fashion photographer or celebrity photographer.

As mentioned previously, diving magazines do not pay well and the best money to be made is in selling your work outside of the diving field. Underwater film makers can supplement their work with Hollywood film projects that are quite lucrative.

The top goal for an underwater film maker is to land a contract for a special or series with a producer who makes nature films for National Geographic or PBS. These projects pay well and can make your career blossom if you handle them properly.

As an underwater photographer you can make a good living, but it is unlikely you will make as much money as a successful commercial diver. Also, you should keep in mind that as an independent photographer you must secure your own health insurance and make provisions for your retirement. While group health insurance is available through organizations like the Professional Photographers of America (PPA), your retirement income will be based upon the money you can put away while you are working. You can also buy camera insurance through PPA.

Perhaps the most negative side (no pun intended) of being an underwater photographer is the uncertainty of self-employment. As a professional photographer, unless you are under a long term contract with an organization like National Geographic, you never know where or when your next job will turn up. This type of uncertainty is not for everyone. It can be very nerve-wracking, especially if it has been some time since your last assignment. This uncertainty also means that you must be a good money manager, so you will have cash reserves available when times are lean.

Experiences of Professional Underwater Photographers

BOB EVANS

Most of the professional underwater photographers you will meet are consumed by a passion for both diving and photography. They are motivated people, self-starters with an irrepressible drive to be successful.

Bob Evans is both a successful underwater photographer and a diving inventor. Evans operates his own underwater photographic business, La Mer Bleu Productions, and is the designer and manufacturer of the Force Fin®.

Bob started his underwater photography career when he was a teenager, buying his first Nikonos camera with the proceeds from a house painting job. He took a community college course in photography and molded the course to his interests in underwater photography. Eventually, he transferred to Brooks Institute in Santa Barbara where he majored in film production and specialized in underwater photography.

When he moved to Santa Barbara, Bob found part-time work aboard the dive boat *Emerald*. This gave Bob the chance to shoot underwater on a weekly basis, helping to rapidly develop his skills.

Bob's photos have appeared in such magazines as *National Geographic, International Wildlife, National Wildlife, and Skin Diver.* He has over 300 magazine articles to his credit. He has also been published in many books including those published by the Cousteau Society and Time-Life.

Evans has a unique style that would best be described as "painterly," where most of his photos look more like paintings than they do like photographs. His approach to using light is unique. He has spent hours underwater waiting for the light to be right to create one image.

LANCE MILBRAND

A new film maker, whose career is just starting out, is Lance Milbrand. Unlike most film makers, Lance bypassed still photography and moved directly into motion picture photography.

Born in Florida, Milbrand started diving when he was 13 years old with his father. When he was 16 he moved to California and lived in a house across the street from the beach in La Jolla.

His first job in the diving business was with Diving Unlimited International (DUI) in San Diego. At DUI, Lance met Bob Cranston, another successful underwater photographer, and worked with Cranston making a video for DUI. Although Lance served as one of the actors in this video, he became more interested in working behind the camera than in front of it.

The photographers for the DUI video were Chuck Nicklin and Ozzie Wissell. Milbrand became friendly with both of them and they introduced him to video production. Nicklin in particular took an interest in Lance and taught him a great deal. Nicklin also introduced Lance to Joe Thompson, a veteran Cousteau camera man who taught Lance about film production.

Lance made his first film about diving in the waters of the Cocos Islands off Central America's coast of Costa Rica. He shot the film during a trip with Nicklin, and did all the editing, titling, and sound by himself. It was an 11 minute film entitled "*The Magic Waters of Cocos Island*" and showed at the San Diego underwater film festival.

Fig. 10.10 – Lance Milbrand edits a film at AME studios in Hollywood.

The project taught Lance that there is a tremendous difference between doing film and video. Film is much less forgiving and far more expensive than video. He learned that when you make a film, you "roll the dice" far more frequently. Lance also learned that without a big name it was difficult to get his film shown at other underwater film festivals.

Milbrand's next big project was a film called "*Quintana Roo,*" about diving in the waters of Cancun and Cozumel, Mexico. This film was 26 minutes long. To make the film, Lance got ten of his friends to request free sample film stock from a manufacturer who was giving away promotional sample cans of film. Each can held 400 feet of film and Lance needed 4000 feet to make his film. With the film in hand, Lance traveled to Mexico and made the movie. It won a golden eagle trophy from CINE, the Council on International Nontheatrical Events, a prestigious film society.

More recently, Lance has shot for NAUI and for the Scuba Diving Resource Group (SDRG), a non-profit safety oriented organization in diving. He has the drive and determination needed to be a successful film maker.

Lance is in transition in his career as a film maker. Like many people who work in diving, Lance must constantly "hustle" to find the next film project. Meanwhile, to support his film making career, Lance cleans boat bottoms when he is not working on films.

Fig. 10.11 – Bob Cranston has shot some incredible shark footage for television. (Photo courtesy Bob Cranston)

BOB CRANSTON

Bob Cranston began working in the diving business when he was in his teens, working for Diving Unlimited International when the company owned a dive store in San Diego. He gained further experience when DUI began manufacturing hot water suits for commercial diving. Because of this work, Bob had the opportunity to gain valuable commercial diving experience with mixed gas and deep diving systems.

Through DUI, Bob became friendly with underwater photographers in the San Diego area, most notably Howard Hall and Marty Snyderman. They encouraged Bob to work on his underwater photography.

On the side, Bob began running shark diving trips, using a stainless steel Neptunic shark suit and steel cage. This gave him the opportunity to work with, and photograph, many large sharks. It was a unique opportunity for him to photograph a subject that commands attention.

Bob also learned to use closed circuit scuba rebreathers that produce no bubbles, and allow him to get close to animals that might otherwise be frightened by a diver's regulator exhaust. The use of this equipment has allowed Bob and Howard Hall to photograph schooling hammerhead sharks in Mexico.

Bob also started working part time with Howard Hall on Mutual of Omaha's *Wild Kingdom TV* series. Together, they did ten shows before they lost the contract. As Bob puts it, "It was a blessing in disguise, because it forced us to go out on our own to solicit work."

Working with Howard Hall, Bob has participated as a camera man, stunt diver, and safety diver on numerous projects. Some of his credits include *Dolphins, Whales, and Us, Seasons of the Sea, and Sharks - Fact and Fantasy.* He has worked for Audubon, National Geographic, CBS, and Nature.

HOWARD HALL

Howard Hall was originally educated as a marine biologist at San Diego State University. This training gives Howard a competitive edge in his underwater film making, because he knows where to look for those unique shots of exotic marine creatures.

Fig. 10.12 – Howard Hall is one of the top underwater film makers in the world today. (Photo courtesy Howard Hall)

Howard is both an extremely successful photographer and a writer. While he started out shooting stills and writing articles, Howard quickly made the leap to film. However, he still writes regularly and is a contributing editor and photographer for *Ocean Realm* and *International Wildlife.* He has written numerous articles on underwater photography as well as a book on the subject. Hall's film credits include work for PBS Nova, ABC American Sportsman, National Geographic, Nature, and Audubon.

DEE SCARR

As mentioned previously, Dee Scarr considers photography to be another tool that she uses to educate divers about the delicate nature of marine life. Through her *Touch the Sea* program, she has educated thousands of divers about the underwater world.

Fig. 10.13 – Dee Scarr uses photography as an educational tool. (Photo © Michael Weinberg)

Dee received both her bachelor's and master's degrees from the University of Florida. She taught high school for six years, and it was during this period that she became a diver and scuba instructor. In 1978 she took a position as a dive guide on the island of San Salvador in the Caribbean. She started doing underwater photography and went to Bonaire to work as an underwater photo professional in 1980.

Dee's articles and photographs have been published in *Skin Diver, Underwater USA,* and *Sea Frontiers*. Her first book, *Touch the Sea,* was published in 1984. She has also published *Coral's Reef,* a children's book, and *The Gentle Sea,* which was published by PADI in 1990.

BILL MACDONALD

Bill Macdonald is another professional underwater film maker and producer with numerous productions to his credit. Bill started diving when he was 12, and has been filming underwater scenes since 1960. He became a diving instructor in 1967, and directed one of the first advanced diver programs in the country. He also worked full time for U.S. Divers Co., and for the Cousteau Society during the late 70's. Currently Bill is the Director of Production for Bill Burrud Productions, as well as an underwater cameraman. In addition, Bill worked with the late Jack McKenney.

Bill has filmed a variety of different underwater subjects for different clients. In 1992 he was completing a shark documentary for the Discovery Channel, on cable television. He has also filmed other specials on seals, whales, and dolphins.

Bill finds many things to enjoy about his work. When he worked with the Cousteau's he would routinely lecture to groups as large as 1,500 people. Now, he reaches audiences as large as 5,000,000 people through television, which he finds very exciting. Every show he works on is different and the variety is stimulating. Bill particularly likes the talented people he gets to meet through his work.

Fig. 10.14 – Bill Macdonald has been filming underwater for over 30 years.

Perhaps the only downside to working as a documentary film maker is the monetary sacrifice one must make to do this job. Your income is generally not comparable to the levels made by people who make films for theatrical purposes. Yet Bill concedes that he is enriched by his experiences working in "educational" television.

Macdonald's advice to anyone considering a career in film making is to keep in mind that no one person can tell the whole story of the oceans; there are lots of opportunities. "The ocean is full of stories," says Bill.

"Given the excellent video systems available at the consumer level, it's possible for an amateur to get started through local cable access. There are people at the local stations who will teach you how to edit and put together a program for very little cost," notes Bill. "The most important thing is to have something to say." By availing yourself of the public access programming in your area, you can keep your current job while learning how to put together a professional presentation.

LYNN FUNKHOUSER

Lynn Funkhouser started diving in 1967. She earned her B.S. degree from Bowling Green University in 1964. She is an extremely accomplished underwater photographer and writer. Her photos have

Fig. 10.15 – Lynn Funkhouser runs her underwater photography business out of Chicago. (Photo courtesy of Lynn Funkhouser.)

been published in *Audubon, Ocean Realm, International Wildlife, Sierra, Skin Diver, and Outside Magazine.* Currently she is working on two books entitled *The Secrets to Successful Underwater Modeling and Reflections in a Mermaid's Eye.*

In addition to doing underwater photography, Lynn also does nature and architectural photography. She frequently leads dive tours to the Philippines.

Training in Underwater Photography:

Brooks Institute of Photography, 801 Alston Rd., Montecito, CA 93108. Tel. (805) 966-3888

Suggested Reading:

Hall, Howard. *Howard Hall's Guide to Successful Underwater Photography,* Marcor Publishing, Pt. Hueneme, CA. 1982.

Kopelman, A. and Crawford, T. *Selling Your Photography.* St. Martin's Press, New York, NY. 1980.

Roessler, C. *Mastering Underwater Photography.* William Morrow & Co., New York, NY. 1984.

Sharbura, R. *Shooting Your Way to $-Million.* Chatsworth Studios, Ontario, Canada. 1981.

Willins, M. (Editor). *Photographer's Market.* Writer's Digest Books, Cincinnati, OH. (Published annually)

Chapter Eleven

SEARCH & RESCUE DIVING

Search and rescue diving is probably the most psychologically demanding diving career that a person can pursue. Most search and rescue diving takes place in low or zero visibility conditions, and frequently involves the recovery of dead bodies. This is very stressful for most divers who do this type of work.

Search and rescue divers are what is known as "*public safety divers.*" They are usually employed by either law enforcement agencies or fire departments. Law enforcement divers may be called upon to do rescues, body recovery, and evidence recovery. Those who work for fire departments may also do rescue and body recovery, as well as waterfront and under pier fire fighting. They may also be involved with the containment and cleanup of toxic spills.

Most public safety diving takes place where underwater conditions are very poor. It is not uncommon for these divers to work in harbors, drainage canals, and rivers that are highly polluted. They must wear special diving equipment, such as dry suits and helmets, to protect themselves from the hazards in these waters.

The typical public safety diver dives in addition to the rest of his duties. If he is a policeman, he will ordinarily have patrol duties in addition to his diving duties. Certain teams dive more than others, usually because of their proximity to water. For example, the New York City Police Department has a dive team that is dedicated 100% of the time to diving and waterfront patrol.

Fig. 11. 1 – Most search and rescue diving takes place in conditions that are not pleasant. Divers with the Rochester Police Dept. regularly conduct searches below the ice in upstate New York. Lt. Scott Hill directed this particular operation. (Photo © Dennis R. Floss)

The Los Angeles County Sheriff's Department has a dive team that is devoted to search and rescue. The L.A. Sheriff's search and rescue team does all the rescue work for the county, as well as handling the SWAT (Special Weapons and Tactical) responsibilities. Given the county's miles of ocean shoreline and numerous lakes this is not surprising. One day they may be recovering a body from a mountain lake, the next day they may be at the scene of an aircraft disaster off the coast, and the following day be called to dive at Catalina Island to recover a murder weapon in deep water.

Other law enforcement agencies also use divers, including such organizations as the Federal Bureau of Investigation (FBI), the Secret Service, and the U.S. Border Patrol. These divers are usually engaged in evidence recovery. It would be rare for them to be involved with rescue work.

Fire department divers usually handle fire fighting duties in addition to their diving. Like their law enforcement counterparts, some fire fighting teams dive more than others. For example, cities with major waterfront areas like New York, San Francisco, Miami, and Los Angeles, usually have hundreds of wooden docks and pilings. Fighting fires under these structures may only be possible with divers in the water. This is especially hazardous work.

Training to be a Public Safety Diver

Training to be a public safety diver usually takes place after you have joined a public service agency. To dive for a police or fire department you must normally already be part of the department, and then volunteer and be selected for diver training. Even if you are already a certified diver, you will usually be required to complete the department's training to ensure that everyone on the dive team is trained to the same standard and follows the same procedures.

Your initial training in law enforcement or fire fighting will usually take place at some type of formal academy. Different departments have different programs, but the typical program will usually last several months. Of course, there is continuous training while you are on the job, and most departments require people to requalify for certain skills on an annual or semiannual basis.

As a public safety diver you will be asked to dive under a wide variety of conditions and with many different types of equipment. You must be competent with all your gear and completely relaxed in the water.

Aside from their basic diving skills, probably the most common requirement for all public safety divers is the ability to execute a variety of underwater search patterns. There are many different types of search patterns, and public safety divers must be proficient in a wide

Fig. 11.2 – Members of the San Diego County Sheriff's Department dive team prepare to conduct a training dive off the coast of California. They use a customized dive van as their base of operations.

variety, since varying situations call for specific search patterns. Running an effective search pattern in zero visibility conditions is much more difficult than running a pattern in clear water.

Many public safety divers must dive either under the ice during winter months, or in exceptionally cold water. Ice diving adds additional danger to search and rescue diving. Winter diving operations are much more demanding.

Law enforcement divers must be trained in the special techniques of underwater crime scene investigation. While many elements of crime scene investigation are applicable to underwater situations, there are special considerations when dealing with underwater evidence. For example, while murder weapons are normally tagged and bagged topside, a gun recovered from an underwater crime scene should be kept in water for transportation to the crime lab to prevent corrosion that would destroy the evidence. This is especially important for any items that have been submerged in salt water.

Underwater photography is an important skill for public safety divers, but particularly for those involved in law enforcement. Underwater photographs can be essential as evidence in a criminal investigation. Both still and video photography are used, and law enforcement divers should be competent in both. The ability to take photos or video under low visibility conditions is especially important.

Since many of the dives that are performed by public safety divers are conducted in polluted water, many dive teams now use specialized equipment for diving under these more hazardous conditions. Divers must commonly contend with water that is biologically and/or chemically polluted. There may even be rare circumstances where there is radioactive pollution.

Fig. 11.3 – Weapons must be recovered in special canisters to prevent rust by exposing them to air. (Photo by Steve Barsky. © Diving Systems Intnl. All rights reserved.)

Diving in polluted water requires highly specialized equipment to prevent contaminants from contacting the diver's skin or being accidentally inhaled or swallowed. To prevent this from happening divers wear vulcanized rubber dry suits and either full face masks or diving helmets. This type of equipment is becoming more common as divers recognize the dangers of exposure to different contaminants. Fire fighters who work under piers and docks are vulnerable to exposure to creosote, a toxic chemical used to protect wood from marine life and the effects of salt water. Smoke from creosote is a serious health hazard.

Divers who regularly work in polluted water must be knowledgeable in hazardous materials or "*haz-mat*" operations. They need to have an excellent understanding of the variety of hazards they may encounter, and the effect of those hazards on their equipment and the human body. Polluted water diving operations are conducted according to a very strictly defined protocol that spells out detailed procedures for every step of the dive.

One firm that specializes in training public safety divers is Dive Rescue International, out of Ft. Collins, Colorado. Dive Rescue trains divers in many different specialty areas of public safety diving including underwater crime scene investigation, polluted water diving, ice diving, and swift water rescue. In addition, they have assisted numerous dive teams in their formation and basic training, and provided information on obtaining funding and team organization. They have trained many dive teams across the country as well as internationally, including divers from the FBI, the U.S. Coast Guard, the Secret Service, and the New York City Police Department. They are the most respected group in law enforcement search and rescue training in the United States.

Fig. 11.4 – Diving in polluted water requires specialized equipment like this vulcanized rubber dry suit and full face mask.

Most public safety agencies use a combination of in-house training and outside experts to train their dive teams. It is not uncommon for dive teams to send team members for certification as diving instructors. As an example, the Los Angeles County Sheriff's dive team sends many of their team members though the Los Angeles County Underwater Instructors Certification course.

When search and rescue divers aren't on an assignment, they are constantly training to maintain and upgrade their skills. Even with a busy team, there can be weeks or even months where there are no emergency rescues to perform. To maintain proficiency, especially in more complex skills, regular training is essential.

Working as a Public Safety Diver

Public safety divers must have exceptional diving skills to cope with the demands placed on them by their work. Many public safety divers have died in the course of their jobs.

Like military divers, public safety divers are usually volunteers. Generally speaking, nobody forces them to join a dive team, and they are free to leave the team at any time. Most departments recognize that you cannot force someone to be a diver. They either want to do it or they don't.

Every public safety dive is always evaluated in terms of a risk/benefit equation. Specifically, what are the risks involved in making a certain dive and what are the benefits to be gained? While there may be enormous pressure to recover the body of a child who has drowned, no body recovery is worth the life of a living person. Many dives are just too hazardous to make.

Fig. 11.5 – Many search and rescue dive teams have inflatable boats as part of their equipment. (Photo © Lt. Scott Hill)

Employment as a public safety diver can be tremendously rewarding and satisfying. There is the satisfaction that comes from doing a job that few other people can do, or are willing to do. There are also tremendous psychological rewards when you can save the life of a person trapped in a vehicle underwater, or some other similar situation.

Most public safety occupations have demanding hours and frequent changes in schedule. It is common for public safety personnel to work nights, weekends, and holidays. In addition, public safety divers are usually "*on-call*" and may be expected to come to work in an emergency situation when they would otherwise be on leave.

Law enforcement and fire agencies usually have a paramilitary organizational structure. Most public service agencies have a strict chain-of-command that must be observed at all times. If you have a difficult time dealing with this type of organization, employment in the public sector is probably not for you.

Employment in the public sector usually carries good benefits and is reasonably secure. Most departments have excellent health and retirement benefits. The pay scale for law enforcement and fire fighting personnel is usually good. Public safety divers frequently receive an additional bonus to their pay for "*hazardous duty.*" The majority of public safety positions provide for early retirement at age 55 or younger with a full pension.

Above all, search and rescue divers must be able to function as part of a team. They must be able to get along with fellow team members, and follow the direction of the team leader. There is no place for heroics or grandstanding on a search and rescue team. Your fellow team members must be able to trust you, and you must be able to trust them. In the L.A. County Sheriff's Department dive team, no one is invited to join the team unless all the members vote them in.

Stresses of Public Safety Diving

Working as a public safety diver is a highly stressful experience, and is not something that everyone can handle. There are many stresses to this type of work, both on and off the job.

Probably the greatest stress of search and rescue diving is the tragedy of recovering a person who has died in the water, particularly if that person is a child. Locating a body by feel in zero visibility water is not a particularly pleasant task. There have been many divers who were eager to participate on a diving team that have found that they could not handle this particular experience.

If the job of recovering a body isn't bad enough, probably the next most difficult part of the job is notifying the next of kin when a person has died in a water related accident. The trauma of dealing with a grieving family is not something that anyone is eager to do.

During the course of a search operation there will frequently be curiosity seekers present who want to watch the divers in action. In addition, the press will usually show up, particularly in the case of a rescue or body recovery. Dealing with the public and the press can both be difficult, especially during a dangerous or emotion filled incident.

The responsibility for dealing with the press and the public usually falls to the dive team leader. The team leader or other spokesperson must be sensitive to the family of missing victims, and be mindful of the image of the dive team and their department any time they deal with the press or the public. Handling these types of situations requires excellent public relations skills.

The risks involved in public safety diving include all the normal risks in diving, as well as those caused by the more demanding environments where search and rescue dives normally take place. Because many search and rescue dives take place in harbors or other busy waterways, entanglement is a constant threat for these divers. There is also a very high risk of injury when diving on airplanes or other vehicles that have accidentally entered the water. Torn and twisted metal can be unusually sharp and extremely hazardous.

Exposure to contaminated water is a threat during many public safety diving operations. Some divers find they cannot handle the psychological stress of wearing the special equipment required for conta-

Fig. 11.6 – Many aspects of public safety diving are dangerous. Helicopter operations require special training and precautions. (Photo © Steve Linton, IADRS.)

minated water diving. In addition, during warm weather, contaminated water diving equipment places a high thermal stress on the divers who use this specialized gear.

Public safety divers can be subjected to a great deal of psychological tension to complete an operation, especially when there is a crisis or when the media is present to observe operations. There can be high pressure to "get the job done" and to "make the department look good." Each diver must remember that he always has the right not to dive, especially if he does not feel well or is uncomfortable about a dive for any reason. No one should ever be forced to make a dive when they don't feel right about it.

"*Survivor guilt*" can be crippling to the dive team who has lost a team member during the course of an operation. Survivor guilt is a feeling of responsibility for the person who died, especially if the diver's buddy blames themselves and feels there is more they could have done to save their partner. Good divers have been known to act irrationally as a direct result of this condition. Survivor guilt is often characterized by unnecessary risk taking; but may also take the form of a sudden dependence on drugs or alcohol, or inappropriate emotional behavior. Dive team supervisors must keep a vigilant watch for survivor guilt any time a team loses a member through the course of an operation.

Experiences of Public Safety Divers

SGT. TOM BENNETT

Tom Bennett is a sergeant with the San Diego County Sheriff's Department, based out of the city of San Diego. A 15 year veteran with the department, Tom is one of two sergeants with the Special Enforcement Detail or "SED." In San Diego, the SED's primary responsibility is the Special Weapons and Tactical (SWAT) team, and diving is just another special skill that is part of their job.

As a member of the SED, Bennett's duties include high risk arrests, swift water rescue, dignitary protection, supervising diving operations, and teaching at the San Diego SWAT academy. The dive team has a core of six Department divers, supplemented by reserve officers who are volunteer divers from the public. Tom notes that the Department is heavily dependent on the volunteers to supplement their team. In fact, the diving instructor for the Department is Mike Downs, a Ph.D. in anthropology, who volunteers his time to assist the Department with their diving operations.

San Diego's dive team normally makes two training dives a month, often in conjunction with other agencies. For example, they frequently dive with the California State Lifeguards, since some of the beaches in the county are state operated beaches. Cooperation with other agencies is especially important on large or hazardous operations.

Fig. 11.7 – Sgt. Tom Bennett supervises a dive for the San Diego County Sheriff's Department.

The diving equipment used by the San Diego team includes both scuba and surface supplied gear. They use both wetsuits and dry suits.

Ironically, San Diego's Sheriff's Department divers receive hazardous duty pay for diving operations, but no extra compensation for SWAT operations. In San Diego, officers can take full retirement as early as age 50. There is no mandatory retirement age.

Bennett sees many positive aspects to his job. Perhaps one of the best things is that everyone he works with is highly motivated to do well. There is an intense team spirit, coupled with respect for the individual. Tom especially likes the diversity of their assignments, and the opportunity to help other people.

On the negative side, the deputies of the Special Enforcement Division are on call 24 hours a day, seven days a week. They carry a pager with them everywhere they go. When there is an emergency they must respond. This means that every time a team member goes out to dinner with his family, they must always have a backup plan in the event they must leave them. During holidays, only a few team members may be on vacation outside the county at any one time. They must always be able to provide a full team when needed.

STEVE LINTON

Steve Linton is the former president and founder of Dive Rescue International and is the executive director of the International Association of Dive Rescue Specialists. In 1972 when Steve formed the Larimer County Dive Team in Ft. Collins, Colorado, he had no idea that his involvement would lead to the formation of the largest underwater search and rescue organization in the world.

Steve's background in law enforcement started in 1974 when he became a sheriff's deputy for Larimer County, Colorado. He worked full time in law enforcement until 1977.

From 1977-1979 Steve was the National Director of Education for Scuba Schools International (SSI). By that time, the need for an organization dedicated to dive rescue specialists became apparent to Linton. In 1979 he formed Dive Rescue International.

Fig. 11.8 – Steve Linton is the executive director of the International Association of Dive Rescue Specialists and former president of Dive Rescue. (Photo courtesy of Steve Linton, IADRS.)

While president of Dive Rescue, Steve annually trained over 4,000 divers in sophisticated water rescue and investigative techniques. He is also the author of the *Dive Rescue Specialist Training Manual* and the *Ice Rescue Text.*

When Steve started Dive Rescue there was no national certifying organization for public safety divers. Everything they did was new; there were no "old ways" of doing things. The techniques Steve developed for training public safety divers were based upon methods that worked in the "real world." Dive Rescue has trained divers from the FBI, the NASA Space Program rescue teams, and the Royal Canadian Mounted Police. They train approximately 10,000 divers each year.

SCOTT ROMMÉ

Scott Rommé is the new President of Dive Rescue International and has been with this organization since 1989. At Dive Rescue, Scott is responsible for developing training programs, marketing, and conducting training courses both nationally and internationally.

Scott first started diving in 1976. He became involved in public safety diving while employed as a fire fighter in Cincinnati, Ohio in 1984. He worked for the city from 1984 through 1989, and instructed the dive rescue team in river rescue, ice rescue, and open water rescue. During that time he received several awards, including the Cincinnati Firefighter of the Year and the Mayor's Award for Heroism. Scott has also trained in the control and containment of hazardous materials.

Fig. 11.9 – Scott Rommé instructs dive teams in river rescue, ice rescue, open water rescue, and other specialty areas. (Photo © Steve Linton, IADRS.)

For Scott there has been tremendous satisfaction in working on the Larimer County Dive Team with true rescue and response capability. He has the opportunity to save lives and not just recover bodies. He dives regularly as a member of the Larimer County Dive Team in Colorado.

At Dive Rescue, Scott enjoys working with the paramilitary structure of those dive teams with high levels of organization. His experience has led him to believe that this paramilitary structure results in a high level of professionalism.

Rommé believes that with the trend towards public safety organizations that are more civil service oriented, many police and fire departments have lost their "edge." This has directly affected the capabilities of some dive rescue teams. He has also observed that with the budget restrictions that most departments face today, many organizations expect too much from their members. There is real apprehension on the part of some dive teams that they will be asked to do something that is beyond their capabilities. These situations can potentially result in accidents or even fatalities on the dive team.

At Dive Rescue, Rommé has the opportunity to see the challenges that all dive teams face. As a consultant to dive rescue teams across the country, Rommé is witness to the highs and lows of search and rescue diving. He hears from the public safety divers whenever they have a failure or a success.

Fig. 11.10 – Lt. Scott Hill is in charge of the dive team for the Rochester Police Department in New York state. (Photo © Dennis R. Floss)

LT. SCOTT HILL

Scott Hill is a lieutenant with the Rochester Police Department in Rochester, New York. Scott has been in law enforcement since he graduated from Northeastern University with a Bachelor's degree in Criminal Justice. Prior to joining the Rochester Police Department, he worked for the Monroe County Sheriff's Department and with another police department in New York state.

Hill first learned to dive while at Northeastern University in 1971, but his enrollment in the recreational diving course there was purely a matter of luck. He needed two athletic courses to graduate from school and diving sounded interesting, so he enrolled.

Scott first coupled diving with law enforcement when he worked for the Monroe County Sheriff. He joined the dive team there as a working member, and recalls that he had much to learn about search and rescue diving. On his first working dive one of the hoses on his double hose regulator fell off the first stage.

Since that time Hill has become a recognized expert in public safety diving. However, he has not gotten there without experiencing some of the heartache of search and rescue. In 1984 Hill was involved in a mutual aid operation, involving several dive teams, in the recovery of a body from a double drowning. The scene was a boating accident where two vessels had collided at night. One victim was found floating on the surface, while a second sank to the bottom of the lake. The call for the dive team came at 11:00 P.M. on a Saturday night. "We were ill prepared for what we had to do," recalls Scott.

The dive plan called for teams of two divers to be towed by separate underwater sleds to search for the body at a depth of 70 feet. The water temperature was a chilling 39 degrees. Scott and his partner made the first dive, which almost ended in an accident. They were diving with "J" valve tanks, and neither Scott nor his partner knew that Scott's partner's "J" valve had been installed backwards. When Scott pulled the lever down on his partner's "J" valve it shut off his air! Neither Scott nor his partner were equipped with octopus rigs or other alternate air sources, and after an aborted buddy breathing attempt, Scott's buddy made an emergency swimming ascent.

Although Scott's dive buddy survived the incident with no ill effects, the next team's dive ended in tragedy. As the next two divers rode their sleds across the bottom, their tow lines became tangled. The divers signaled topside to discontinue the tow and dropped to the bottom to try and untangle the sleds. As they worked to disengage the lines, they stirred up the mud on the bottom of the lake until the visibility dropped to zero. With the stress of the dive, the low visibility, and the cold water, one of the divers ran out of air very quickly.

The dive team tried to buddy breathe and ascend together, but since neither diver was wearing a buoyancy compensator they were not rising in the water. Sadly, they did not realize that they were only a few feet off the bottom, kicking hard, but going nowhere. When they were both out of air, one of the divers dropped his weight belt and made it to the surface, but the other panicked and drowned. To this day Scott says that every time he drives by the lake he feels a sense of profound loss for the diver who died.

In 1985, Hill became the dive team leader for the city of Rochester, New York. He has worked on numerous underwater operations, from the recovery of evidence to bodies. Scott has also worked on innovative techniques to produce underwater crime scene photographs.

In 1988 Scott's team participated in the recovery of a three year old child that had fallen through the ice on a frozen river. Six different dive teams participated in the operation that went on for several days. This time his team had all the right equipment; dry suits, stabilizing jacket style B.C.'s, and electronic underwater communications.

The local fire department had cut holes in the ice, with each hole 200 feet from the last one. Each dive team was assigned a hole to search. Scott and his teammates were a mile down the river when one of the divers signaled that he had located the child. When the diver surfaced with the child and removed his mask he had tears in his eyes. For him, and for all the members on the team who had children, it was as though that child was their own.

Hill notes that his team has worked hard to develop a rapid response capability in the hopes that they will be able to save lives rather than just recover bodies. With the current medical knowledge and techniques on cold water drowning, it is recognized that if you recover someone in under an hour, you stand a good chance of successfully resuscitating them to their full capabilities. Although the Rochester team has had several recoveries that have been well under an hour, they have yet to experience that type of success.

For Scott Hill the positive aspects of public safety diving are that the work is always interesting, never boring. He enjoys the managerial aspects of organizing the team and coming up with new dive techniques.

Scott concedes that when there are no rescues to be made it can be very difficult to keep the dive team members motivated. His Department only allows the team one training day a month. Although the team members strive for excellence, it can be difficult to juggle the demands on their time with the finances of the Department. While the city supports them well and gives them time to train, during that one day each month they must also take care of gear maintenance and other team duties. Because of these demands Scott must rely on those motivated team members who will do something extra, above and beyond their responsibilities.

Almost all the diving done by the Rochester Police dive team is done in black water. While most people would not find this pleasant, Scott still loves the diving. He is more distressed by the violence that law enforcement must contend with today, than diving in cold or dirty water. The only other negative aspect Scott finds in his work are the irregular hours and the time he must spend away from his family.

Training Programs:

Dive Rescue International, Inc. 201 N. Link Lane, Ft. Collins, CO 80524
Tel. (303) 482-0887

Suggested Reading:

Barsky, S. *Diving in High Risk Environments.* Dive Rescue International, Ft. Collins, CO. 1993

Linton, S. Rust, D., and Rooney, L. *The Dive Rescue Specialist Manual.* Dive Rescue International, Ft. Collins, CO. 1986

Chapter Twelve

MILITARY DIVING

Like commercial divers and public safety divers, military divers must dive under some of the most demanding and dangerous conditions imaginable. Of all the divers covered in this book, military divers usually have the least choice about when and where they must dive.

While most people immediately think of the Navy when they think of military diving, the reality is that there are also divers in the Army and the Marines.

Military diving also presents one of the greatest varieties in types of diving operations and divers. Military divers include construction divers, such as the Navy's Construction Battalion, known as "Seabees" for short, and combat divers, such as those in the Marine's Recon groups, the Navy SEALs (Sea, Air, Land), and the Army's Rangers. There are also salvage and ship repair divers, and another whole group that specializes in nothing but Explosive Ordnance Disposal (EOD).

Military divers use a wide range of diving equipment, from open circuit scuba to saturation diving techniques. The military also probably makes greater use of closed circuit diving apparatus or "*rebreathers*" than any other diving group.

Most military divers have other primary assignments and diving is a secondary part of their job. A ship's repair diver might be a gunner's mate, a pipe fitter, or be responsible for other duties when not diving.

In this chapter we will not cover every military diving specialty in every branch of the armed services, but we will explore at least one of each major classification in military diving.

Fig. 12.1 – Army Special Forces divers exit the water during a training exercise. The equipment they use is very similar to that used by Navy SEALs and Marine Force Recon.

Training to be a Military Diver

Training to be a military diver is highly specific to the type of diving that you do. In addition, unlike most other diving careers, military divers probably do more continuous training than other divers. Military divers must regularly requalify in every area of their diving expertise.

The Marine Force Reconnaissance Company is an elite unit that performs many of the same missions and duties as the U.S. Navy's SEAL teams and the Army's Rangers. Force Recon has specifically been tasked with "deep reconnaissance" forward of the battlefield, behind enemy lines.

Recon personnel are trained as paratroopers (parachute qualified) and as divers. They are considered elite units and all three units, SEALS, Recon, and Rangers, attend many of the same specialized schools. These units all fall under the title of "*Special Warfare,*" or "*SPECWAR.*" The men in these units are all volunteers.

To qualify for Recon training you must take a strenuous physical test that includes swimming, an 11 mile run, push-ups, and other exercises. Your vision must be at least 20/70, correctable to 20/20. The final hurdle is a personal interview, where you must demonstrate that you are a highly motivated individual.

Like the SEALs and Rangers, Recon training is designed to prepare you to operate behind enemy lines. Recon training may include inflatable boat operations, basic explosives, rappelling, radio operation, helicopter deployment, and hydrographic surveys. Individuals may be specially trained in areas such as photography or other skills.

SEAL Team training is divided into three phases, and each phase lasts for two months. This training takes place at the Naval Special Warfare Center at Coronado Island in San Diego, California. It's also known as "SEAL Boot Camp."

Phase One is strictly conditioning and includes the infamous "Hell Week," where recruits are kept awake for a week straight and run through constant physical testing. There is continuous harassment from the staff during Hell Week and usually not more than half of those who start are still left at the end of the week. You can quit any time during the week by ringing a large bronze bell located near the bunk house. During Hell Week the average recruit burns between 6,000 and 8,000 calories a day.

Fig. 12.2 – Close-up view of Special Forces diver during training exercise. Note the closed circuit rebreather, automatic rifle, and waterproof bag for carrying radios and other equipment.

Phase Two for the SEAL trainees is diving with open circuit scuba and with the Draeger closed circuit breathing apparatus. They learn how to use the Draeger rig in tactical situations.

Phase Three of SEAL training covers land warfare. This portion of the training includes land warfare, small arms, land navigation, demolition and explosives. Once the trainees complete this program they are posted to their respective teams, either on the east or west coast of the U.S.

Another elite group that is picked from within the SEAL team graduates are the divers who join the SDV teams. "SDV" stands for SEAL Delivery Vehicle. An SDV is a large, open "wet" submarine that carries divers wearing closed circuit rebreathers to conduct special missions against enemy targets. The subs are used in situations where it is too far for a diver to swim to his objective. Once the sub reaches its target, the divers leave their seats and swim a short distance to perform their oper-

Fig. 12.3 – Special Forces divers using a radio on dry land during a training exercise.

ation, then return to the sub and pilot it back to their mother ship or base of operations.

SDV Team training includes instruction in piloting and operating the wet subs and extensive courses in navigation. The basic training for SDV operations lasts for 12 weeks, but there is normally another year of practice before divers participate in a real operation. The SDV extends the work that a SEAL team can perform. It allows the divers to carry far more equipment than could be managed by a free swimming diver.

The Navy operates several schools to train divers for salvage and ship repairs. The ability to clear a harbor of a damaged ship or to recover classified information from a plane or ship that is underwater is extremely important to the military.

Second Class Diver School is a 13 week school that trains divers for air diving operations. This is the first school that all Navy divers attend. Divers at Second Class School are trained in the use of scuba and surface supplied air. The divers learn to use several different full face masks, including the AGA, the Jack Browne, and the MK I. They also learn to use the MK 12 helmet. Second Class divers are qualified to dive to 190 feet on air.

Navy scuba divers are not Second Class divers, but are an entirely separate classification. All Navy submarines have at least two scuba divers on board.

The next training course for Navy divers is the First Class Diving School. To attend this school you must have served a minimum of one year as a Second Class diver and have an "E4" classification. An E4 is the equivalent of a Third Class Petty Officer. At First Class School the training includes mixed gas diving (helium and oxygen), diving supervision, and sophisticated ship repair techniques. First Class diver candidates practice air diving to 285 feet and mixed gas diving to 300 feet.

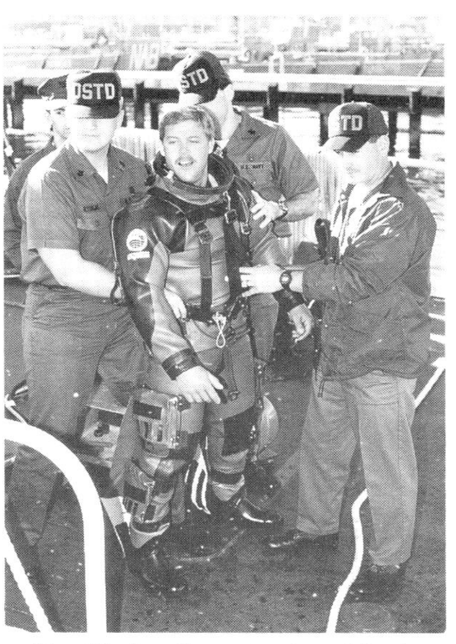

Fig. 12.4 – Dressing in with the Navy MK 12 helmet.

To attend a Navy Master Diver's course, you must have at least two years of experience as a First Class diver and be an "E7" or above. An E7 classification is equal to a Chief Petty Officer. In addition to these other qualifications, you must have previously qualified as a diving supervisor and served in a mixed gas command. You must also pass a written exam on diving to qualify for the school.

Each Master Diver course is limited to four students and there are only five classes offered each year. In a typical year, only a small number of candidates satisfactorily complete the course. There are never enough Master divers to fill the Navy's demands for them.

The evaluation and training of Navy Master diver candidates takes six weeks. The last three weeks of the course are spent at sea, where each candidate acts as a diving officer and learns to handle simulated diving emergencies from a supervisory standpoint. Each day the candidates supervise a diving operation with a different type of gear. You are evaluated on how you handle problems and are observed by as many as nine evaluators at one time. Each day is critiqued. Some people have gone through the Master Diver's School as many as four times before graduating successfully.

Fig. 12.5 – The Navy MK 12 diving helmet is used for surface supplied diving.

To attend saturation diving school, where diver's live in a pressurized habitat and work out of a diving bell, you must have a minimum of one year of experience as a First Class diver. Saturation diving school lasts for approximately six weeks.

Explosive Ordnance Disposal (EOD) is another Navy specialty classification. EOD divers receive the same training as the divers who perform ship's husbandry. They then receive more specialized training in mixed gas diving from small boats and in the techniques for disarming chemical, biological, nuclear, and conventional explosives.

Working as a Military Diver

Of all the military diving duties, divers who are engaged in Special Warfare probably face the highest risks, since they are regularly involved in combat situations. In addition, today's SEAL teams are now involved in antiterrorist operations, another especially hazardous duty.

The typical SEAL team member is either a young man straight out of boot camp or a seaman who has been in the fleet for several years and is bored with ordinary shipboard duty. However, the majority of recruits enter the teams when they are young, and most of them stay in for their entire career. On the whole they are an arrogant group, and probably need to be to survive in their type of warfare.

There are no women in the SEAL teams, and it seems unlikely there will be any in the near future. Their operational requirements frequently demand that the men be naked and closely huddled together for extended periods of time. It's doubtful that the military will be willing to place men and women together in this type of combat situation, even if other restrictions on women in combat are lifted.

Like most diving jobs there are periods where SEAL team divers are in the water daily, and other times when they do no diving at all.

During their period of enlistment they are shifted back-and-forth between shore duty and sea duty. Shore duty tours last from 3 – 4 years and are Monday through Friday jobs. Sea duty tours involve periods at sea of continuous work, seven days a week; and last an average of five years.

SEAL team dives are usually heavily dependent upon the diver's ability to navigate underwater. This is essential, especially when a mission may call for a dive team to penetrate to the very back corner of a complex harbor. Many of these dives are at night. It is not uncommon for practice compass courses to include up to 37 different turns. Some of these dives may last for up to three hours, with the divers using closed circuit scuba apparatus. For specific missions they train with other specialized equipment, such as dry suits.

There are risks to each type of SEAL team duty, whether it is diving in a harbor or parachuting. As most team members will tell you, they have been on operations that have made Hell Week look easy. They train in the jungle, the Arctic, and the desert.

SDV operations include the use of a wide range of equipment. On a single sub mission the divers may use open circuit scuba, the MK 15 rebreather, and the Draeger Lar V all on the same dive. The divers wear dry suits since their dives usually last for many hours. Most of the work done by the SDV divers is intelligence gathering.

The SDV wet sub is approximately 20 feet long and equipped with obstacle avoidance sonar and a Doppler navigation system. The sonar can be used to detect mines, as it was during the operation in Desert Storm off the coast of Iraq. The SDV's can be transported to the scene of operations on the rear deck of a nuclear sub.

Fig. 12.6 – A Navy EOD diver checks over a scuba compressor after an operation.

The stated mission of the U.S. Navy EOD is to "*eliminate hazards from ordnance which jeopardize operations conducted in support of the national military strategy.*" In actual practice, this might include disposing of old munitions from World War II, finding and destroying underwater mines that block harbors, and support of the U.S. Secret Service in protecting dignitaries aboard ships. Anything that potentially involves explosives below the waterline is the responsibility of EOD, as well as certain specified above water operations.

EOD is one of the groups within the Navy that uses marine mammals, such as dolphins and sea lions to do their job. Dolphins are used in the detection of enemy swimmers or divers, while sea lions are used in the recovery of weapons from the bottom. According to the Navy, marine mammals are not used in combat roles.

The typical EOD dive team consists of four or five divers operating out of an inflatable boat. All the diving equipment they use is "*non-magnetic,*" which means that it will not trigger the magnetic switches used in mines or other ordnance that respond to the presence of steel, as is found in the hull of a ship, to set off the explosive. Almost all the diving they do is with self-contained equipment, either ordinary compressed air scuba or the closed circuit MK 16 rig. The Navy's philosophy is that in the event an EOD diver makes a mistake and triggers an accidental explosion, they will not risk the lives of hundreds of other men aboard a surface support vessel. This is the reason for the small teams in an inflatable boat. Like the SEAL team divers, EOD members are volunteers.

There are several different types of EOD teams where a diver can be posted. Some teams are posted aboard ships, while others work with the marine mammals. There are teams that specialize in mine countermeasures, while others are considered "mobile detachments," ready to travel on short notice. The creed common to all EOD divers is, "You call, we come." In a catastrophe, an EOD team may spend weeks or even months away from their normal base working on a particular operation.

While in the past EOD teams might have gone in and blown up a potentially explosive weapon where it lay, those days are gone. Today they concentrate on doing their job without creating an environmental hazard or killing wildlife. Due to the complex nature of modern weapons an EOD team may spend weeks planning an operation.

To be a good EOD diver you must have an inquiring mind and be long on ingenuity. You must want to understand why and how things

Fig. 12.7 Navy Master diver Jeff Royse checks out a diving umbilical for surface supplied diving.

work, and what makes things "tick," in the most literal sense. There are some women in the EOD teams.

The typical EOD detachment is comprised of ten members. Each group has a lieutenant, a warrant officer, and eight enlisted sailors.

Most Navy fleet divers have some other primary classification apart from their rating as a diver. They may be a welder, a machinist's mate, an engineer, a mechanic, or a rigger ("Bosun's mate"). As of 1992 there were approximately 25 women divers and one female Master diver in the fleet.

Fleet divers do just about anything that has to do with maintenance and repair of naval vessels. They may replace propellers, salvage equipment or ships, clean seawater intakes on ships, service buoys, or other tasks. They dive as needed under conditions that are rarely pleasant.

Experiences of Military Divers

Due to the sensitive nature of certain military operations, some of the divers we interviewed for this book asked not to be photographed or identified by their full name. We have honored their requests and hope the reader will understand why.

NAVY CHIEF "DUANNE"

Duanne is a Navy Chief on a SEAL team and a career Navy man. He notes that as a SEAL, he is "paid to work out." The divers in the teams consider themselves to be "warrior athletes."

SEAL team members are tested annually for their physical fitness, notes Duanne. He enjoys the team camaraderie and the goal oriented nature of the men. There is extensive travel in the job, and the pay is good.

On the negative side, the extensive travel required of SEAL team members can get old. During Duanne's first three years of enlistment he traveled for 18 months. This is one of the reasons why there are few married team members.

Although the risks the SEAL teams take are part of the excitement of the job, they are also indicative of the injuries and physical pain the men must endure. In addition, the aches and pains that annoy an older team member are more easily ignored by the younger men in the outfit.

The employment benefits enjoyed by the SEALs are the same as those of other branches of the military. After 20 years military personnel can retire with half their base pay. While in the service they receive 30 days of paid vacation each year. Their health and dental benefits are excellent, even after they have retired. With the GI bill, the government will match your education expenses, dollar-for-dollar, after your retire.

SDV TEAM MEMBER "SCOTT"

Scott is a graduate of SEAL team training who volunteered to join the SDV teams. He entered the Navy at 19 when he was living on the east coast. He joined the SEAL's after basic training when he became "fed up with boot camp." He has been in the military for 19 years. During the course of his enlistment he has traveled to South America, Northern Europe, and the Mediterranean.

Scott finds that the positive aspects of his involvement with the SDV teams include the variety of the work, the camaraderie of his team mates, and the travel. SDV team members also make more money that regular SEAL team members.

On the negative side Scott admits that the military way of life is difficult. The demands of the military make it impossible to live a normal life. Risks are a way of life for the SDV teams.

For a person considering joining the SDV teams, Scott notes that despite the hardships of the job, being a member of the SDV teams is a worthwhile experience. Most of the people who become an SDV team member stay in for a full career.

EOD TEAM "LARRY"

Larry is a Warrant Officer in the Navy EOD. When he originally enlisted in the Navy, in 1977, his intentions were to get in, learn a trade, and get out. His initial training was as a pipe fitter for the

Navy's Construction Battalion Team, better known as the "Seabees." Several events, including his marriage and an attractive offer for posting to Bermuda, conspired to change that, and he has been in the military ever since.

When Larry went to Bermuda he became interested in diving, although he had no prior diving experience. Since the only divers posted to Bermuda were EOD divers, he talked with them about diving. He admits that prior to meeting the EOD divers he didn't realize there were so many different possibilities surrounding diving in the Navy. He decided that EOD offered him the most potential and left Bermuda early for EOD training.

Larry attended diving school in Panama City, Florida, and took his first EOD course at Redstone Arsenal in Alabama. His first EOD assignment was in Hawaii. Since that time he has attended advanced EOD courses in explosives, terrorism, and other topics. For him, working in EOD is like a big chess game. "People build stuff (explosives), and you have to figure out how to take it apart," explains Larry.

As an EOD diver, Larry averages approximately 100 dives a year. He observes that in EOD, "there is a bona fide opportunity to get hurt or killed."

"There are many good things about serving in EOD," says Larry. "All the people who are here are in it because they want to be here. The caliber of diver we have in EOD is second to none. This is a small, tightly knit community. If I need help, I can pick up the phone and call people all over the world who are happy to share their information with me. We have no discipline problems because everyone who is in EOD wants to excel."

EOD is demanding work, and like most military jobs, it calls for regular periods of separation from one's family. The job also requires lots of paperwork. The hours are long, with the typical day running anywhere from a regular eight hours to as many as 10 – 11, even when the teams are posted on shore. During diving operations or when a crisis occurs the days may run 15 or 16 hours, seven days a week.

Larry's advice to someone who is considering enlisting in EOD is to get as much education as you can. Be honest with yourself about what you want to do. As he puts it, "Don't join EOD for the monetary gain or the promotional opportunities. Do it because this is what you want to do, because you want to be a part of the team." EOD is very demanding, both physically and mentally, for long periods of time.

Fig. 12.8 – Master diver Jeff Royse inspects a trailer of helium breathing gas.

MASTER DIVER JEFF ROYSE

Jeff Royse is a Navy Master diver with over ten years experience in the service. He had been in the Navy for five years as a welder and ship's hull technician prior to enrolling in dive school. In 1991 he logged over 300 hours of bottom time.

As a Master diver Jeff supervises a team of men who are constantly engaged in maintenance and training whenever they are not working on an actual operation. He particularly enjoys the people associated with Navy diving, and finds them a cut above the average enlisted person. He also enjoys the variety of the work and the equipment he uses.

The only negative factor Jeff finds in his work is the uncertainty of never knowing when your career as a diver might end, due to the Navy's stringent medical and physical requirements. There is always the potential to get hurt while diving, and the possibility that an injury may preclude you from diving in the future.

Suggested Reading:

Supervisor of Diving. *U.S. Navy Diving Manual.* Best Publishing, Flagstaff, AZ.

Chapter Thirteen

SEAFOOD DIVERS

In ancient times man gathered shellfish for food at low tides and by breathhold diving. Abalone shells have been found with Indian remains from coastal tribes that date back 7,000 years. Mussels, clams, oysters, and other shellfish have also been utilized through the centuries by people on the coasts of the U.S. Although local populations of shellfish were affected by this gathering, the elimination of a species was not a threat.

Today, with the modern technology available to the commercial seafood diver, it is easy to over harvest a population of shellfish. Other factors also affect marine life populations, such as pollution, elimination of habitat, disease, predators, introduced species, and even water temperature and storms. The eastern or American oyster, *Crassostrea virginica,* was decimated by a combination of the factors listed above. The fishermen and divers on the east coast who harvested this species lost their livelihood. The message is this: as a seafood diver you must have a concern for the species, and be ready to get politically involved to change the human factors that negatively impact your fishery. It is possible to achieve a continued annual harvest, or what fisheries scientists refer to as a "*sustainable yield.*"

Equipment and techniques vary between individual divers and fisheries. However, the basic equipment required for dive fisheries is minimal compared to other fisheries, so the monetary investment is low. Divers require a wetsuit at a minimum, although some divers use dry suits. Working on the bottom really tears the suits up quickly.

Seafood diving is primarily a male occupation. It takes a great deal of physical strength and stamina to haul your equipment and the animals you harvest around. Certainly you have to have good judgment and skill. Weather and sea conditions limit the number of days it is physically possible to dive.

As a seafood diver you are your own boss, so you have to be a self-starter. You also have to manage your income well since it doesn't come in on a regular basis. "*Ex-vessel price,*" the price the diver actually gets paid for his catch, varies with the fishery, but is usually market driven. Since abalone, sea urchins and sea cucumbers are principally exported, the price fluctuations are frequent and varying.

Metal and salt water are not a happy combination, so dive boats require constant maintenance, as does your diving equipment. Fuel cost is another major expense.

You have to be very knowledgeable of the species you are seeking, or be a quick learner. You can't afford to spend hours diving in the wrong area for the species you're seeking.

There are lots of regulations in almost every state governing the species that will be discussed in this chapter. Enforcement of these regulations is frequently not good, since most states have limited finances and manpower. The temptation to break the rules is strong. Many of the divers have formed associations to tax themselves for research, enhancement, and enforcement relating to the species for which they dive. They're also making efforts to self-police themselves since they realize their livelihood depends on a healthy resource.

Abalone Fishery

Abalone along the Pacific coast were utilized by the Indians before the arrival of white men. This single shelled mollusk has a large foot that can be "steaked" into a delicious meat. In the mid-nineteenth century Chinese immigrants started harvesting abalone along the California coast with long, hooked poles. They were replaced by Japanese "barrel divers," so called because they were free divers and rested on a barrel in between dives. Local ordinances excluding the take of abalone in shallow water eliminated the Chinese and pushed the Japanese into hard hat diving in deeper water. The Japanese dominated the fishery until World War II interrupted their activities. After the war, "*hookah*" equipment replaced the hard hats and that is the industry standard now.

Fig. 13.1 – Abalone diver Mary Stein checks out her catch of red abalone off the California coast. Mary is one of the few women abalone divers. (© D.B. Pleschner)

Fig. 13.2 – Diver Jon Sears fills the gas tank of his hookah compressor, common to both abalone and urchin divers.

Hookah equipment is the efficient and mandated method of commercially diving for abalone in California. The diver uses a first stage regulator that is attached to a hose. The hose length varies from several 100 feet to over 1000 feet. The hose is attached directly to an air compressor, or a "surge tank," that serves as a small "reserve" air supply. The size of the compressor and the volume of air it pumps determines how many divers it will support, and how deep they can dive. Some divers also use scuba gear to scout new areas to see if they will be productive.

Abalone fishermen carry a specific tool to harvest that species. An "*abalone iron*" in California must be less than 36 inches long and 3/4 inches wide, with all edges rounded. The iron may be straight or with a curve, having a radius of not less than 18 inches, nor less than 1/16 inch thick. Ab divers also carry a fixed gauge or "*mike*" to measure the greatest diameter or length of the abalone shell. The four species that comprise the commercial fishery in California are the red *(Haliotis rufescens)*, black *(H. cracherodii)*, pink *(H. corrugata)*, and green

(H. fulgens) abalone. Different size limits apply to each species, which are found in different depth ranges. There are also restrictions on the number of abalone that can be harvested per day. The fishery is completely closed three months of the year.

California has close to 120 licensed commercial abalone divers or "permittees." This fishery became limited entry due to dwindling stocks of abalone. A minimum landing requirement of 1200 lbs. or 320 abalone is needed to renew the permit annually. In 1991 a regulation was passed allowing a fisherman without a license to purchase two abalone permits from other divers, and trade them in to the state for one abalone permit. A further requirement of this ruling is prior experience as an abalone diver's tender.

Abalone are also harvested on the Baja California peninsula of Mexico. There is a small fishery for the pinto abalone, *Haliotis kamtschatkana*, in British Columbia.

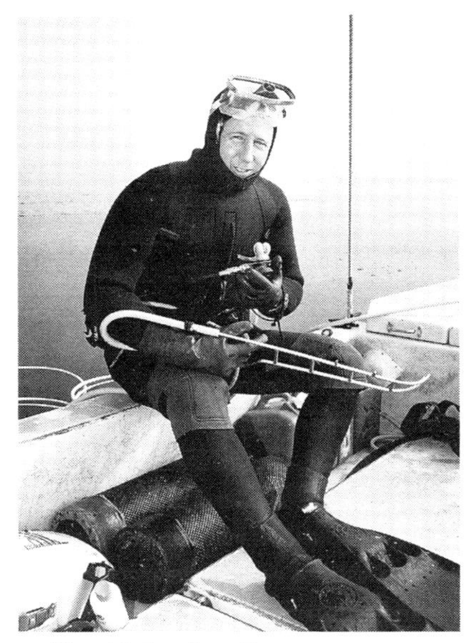

Fig. 13.3 – Jon Sears prepares to dive for urchins at Santa Rosa Island. Note his special collecting rake and hookah hose in the water behind him. Jon is wearing a thick, 3/8" wetsuit.

Sea Urchin Fishery

Sea urchins belong to a group of invertebrates known as "*echinoderms.*" Sea urchins can best be described as balls of spines. They are harvested for their five, orange slice shaped sex glands, known as "*gonads,*" that are considered a delicacy by many people particularly in the Orient.

In the early 1970's a fishery for the red sea urchin, *Strongylocentrotus franciscanus,* developed on the west coast. Commercial divers collect this species in British Columbia, Alaska, Washington, Oregon, and California. On the east coast the green sea urchin is harvested commercially in Maine. Sea urchin gonads are referred to as "*uni*" in sushi bars.

The purple sea urchin, *S. purpuratus,* another smaller

species found right alongside the reds on the west coast, is beginning to be harvested now. Their small size makes them very labor intensive to process. Presently they are being exported whole to the Orient.

Fig. 13.4 – A collecting bag full of sea urchins is unloaded into the hold of his boat by Jon Sears.

Every sea urchin fisherman has a tool called a "*rake*" they use to gather and bag the urchins. These rakes are usually personally designed by each individual diver. The diver's arm and hand are used to manipulate this tool that's normally equipped with a rounded, hooked end. The fishermen also carry a fixed gauge, or "*mike*" to measure the size of the animal. The diameter of the shell, also known as the "*test,*" is measured, not the test and the additional length of the spines. In some states there's not only a minimum size limit, but a maximum one, too.

Divers use collecting bags and baskets to carry the urchins to the surface. A collecting bag is usually a ring of heavy conduit with a mesh bag attached. A medium bag will hold 250 pounds of urchins. Some divers use a bag and a basket, others will use one or the other, exclusively.

Boats suitable for harvesting urchins sell for $20,000-25,000, at the low end. Mid-range boats are $35,000-60,000; and high end boats can go for $150,00-250,000. Used boats are cheaper, but it's tough to find a bargain. The boats are usually worked hard.

Close to 550 urchin diving permits are held in the state of California. Additionally there are roughly 75 apprentice urchin diving permits. Apprentices enjoy all the privileges of an urchin diver, except they must be in the company of an urchin permittee when they dive. The lottery for urchin apprentice permits was initiated in 1989 after the fishery went limited entry in 1987. Twenty landings a year, of at least 300 pounds of urchins, is required to maintain both these permits. The goal of the limited entry system in California is to reduce

Fig. 13.5 – Boats suitable for harvesting urchins are expensive.

the number of urchin diving permits to 400. Size restrictions and a reduced number of harvest days are now in place.

Oregon's red sea urchin fishery got started in 1986. A limited entry permit system was initiated in 1988, with 92 permits as the maximum to be issued. The maximum number of permits to be issued has been reduced to 46, but the number of permits still active is close to 60. A size limit and minimum harvest depth are in effect. A 20,000 pound landing requirement every two years to renew the permit was changed to an annual requirement. Harvesting occurs in the summer, when gonad quality and price are low, because of harvesting closures in other states.

Landings of red sea urchins began in Washington in 1971, the same time landings began in Southern California. In 1976 upper and lower size limits, seasons, and rotating fishing districts were established. The divers formed an association and together with the Washington Department of Fisheries produced a limited entry system that went into effect in 1989. Further modifications and restrictions went into effect in 1990, limiting the days that can be fished and the number of divers that can work off a boat at the same time. Currently, there are just under 80 vessels in the fleet. Washington's permit system issues licenses to vessels, not divers. The goal is to reduce the fleet to 45 vessels.

Alaska's red sea urchin is largely unexploited, but the Alaska Department of Fish and Game has taken a conservative management approach. Annual assessments of the abundance of urchin stocks are made by the Department and only a 3% rate of harvest is allowed.

Fig. 13.6 – Urchin diving is hard work.

With the exception of Alaska, the urchin stocks on the West coast of the United States have all been heavily harvested. Limited entry restrictions in all the states make entry into urchin diving a challenge.

The green sea urchin, *Strongylocentrotus droebachiensis,* has been harvested from the Gulf of Maine for the past 15 years. There is an eight month winter harvest season. Supply shortages have occurred in the past couple of years. In the absence of any licensing or other regulations the future of this fishery appears bleak.

Sea Cucumber Fishery

Like the sea urchin, the giant or red sea cucumber, *Parastichopus californicus,* is another member of the echinoderm family that lives on the bottom of the ocean. Sea cucumbers are roughly the same size as the salad vegetable from which they get their name, only they're a pale orange color, soft and flexible. They feed on dead matter on the bottom in a manner similar to the earthworm.

Sea cucumbers have five sets of longitudinal muscles that are considered a delicacy. Additionally after the animal is gutted the whole body is boiled and then dried. This product, known as "*trepang*" or "*beche-de-mer*" is highly prized by the Chinese. Salted intestines are also used in Japan, and the product is referred to as "*konowata.*" In Japan the dried

Fig. 13.7 – Sea cucumbers are considered a delicacy in the Orient. (Photo by Kristine C. Barsky)

sea cucumbers are known as "*namako.*" British Columbia, Alaska, Washington, and California have dive fisheries for *Parastichopus sp.*

Cucumbers are picked by hand and put in collecting bags by divers. Divers started harvesting sea cucumbers in the state of Washington in 1971 without restriction. In 1987 the state was divided into four harvest districts by the Washington Department of Fisheries and a five month season was initiated. The harvest areas are rotated annually. At the end of 1989 the fishery went limited entry. To maintain the permit, 30 landings of a minimum of 10,000 pounds must be made each year.

The sea cucumber fishery in Alaska began in 1987. It was restricted in 1990 because the number of divers and harvest grew so quickly. A rotational management system was implemented. Logbooks were also mandated.

California's sea cucumber fishery went limited entry in 1992. One of the permit requirements was filling out a logbook. In California, the majority of sea cucumbers are harvested with a bottom trawl net towed behind a commercial fishing vessel.

Scuba and hookah divers have collected *Parastichopus parvimensis,* the warty sea cucumber, that is more common inshore on the California coast. *P. parvimensis* yields a better product so the divers get a higher price.

Geoduck Clam Fishery

Geoduck clams (pronounced "gooey duck") are large, meaty clams that are harvested recreationally along the west coast. In Washington there is a commercial fishery for geoduck clams, *Panope generosa.* Alaska and British Columbia also have fisheries.

Commercial divers in Washington use a high pressure stream of water from hand-held fire hoses to free geoduck clams from the bottom. The nozzle size on the hoses used is restricted. The clams burrow from 1-1/2 to 4 feet deep, and are carried to the surface in baskets once they are retrieved.

The number of boats in the Washington geoduck fishery fluctuates from 8 to 26, and is highly regulated. Only two hookah divers per boat are allowed. Harvest hours are 9 A.M. to 4 P.M., Monday through Friday, and a compliance boat from the Washington Department of Fisheries is on site while you work. Divers have to work in specific areas, and only in depths of 18 to 70 feet.

A public auction is held annually where bidding for the "*right to harvest*" takes place. The bid price is what the diver pays over and above the price paid to the state for every pound of clam harvested.

Alaska's commercial fishery for geoducks is small. British Columbia has a large fishery that has had quality problems, which impacts market acceptance of the product.

Scallop Fishery

The deep-sea scallop, *Placopecten magellanicus,* is found from Labrador to Cape Cod in depths up to 600 feet. Off the coast of Maine it's found in shallow water, and there is a sizable fishery for this large scallop. Several hundred licensed commercial divers use their hands to gather scallops. The season is open in the winter for 5-1/2 months, but this is subject to change. The only other regulation is that the scallops have to be shucked upon delivery. Many of the scallop divers are also urchin divers. The scallop stocks are declining rapidly, and the future of this fishery is bleak.

Diving on the east coast is heavily regulated in many of the states. Fishermen involved in long established dredging fisheries see "divers" as another threat to their already declining fisheries. For example, there is a deep water diving fishery for *Placopecten* in Massachusetts. However, it's very restricted and involves less than a dozen divers. It came into existence because dredges couldn't be used in the areas that are fished.

Fig. 13.8 – Jon Sears sorts out his hookah hose after a dive. Note the scooter that Jon uses to check out new dive areas.

Experiences of Seafood Divers

JON SEARS

Jon Sears dives for sea urchins off his own 26 foot vessel in California. He started diving in junior high in 1969. After graduation from high school he traveled to Europe and Jamaica. For a time he cleaned boat bottoms for a living. Then he went through the Marine Technology Program at Santa Barbara City College in Santa Barbara, and was a full-time commercial oil field diver from 1976 to 1986.

In 1987 Jon started diving sea urchins on the side. He spent more and more time harvesting urchins in the following three years. Jon finally decided he wasn't interested in working in the offshore industry to the extent he had previously, and bought himself a boat to dive for urchins.

Jon averages 10-11 dive days a month, although some months it's 14-15 days, and in the winter months it can be only four. On an average day he'll spend 3 - 5 hours in the water. He spends lots of time in the 20 to 40 foot depth range, but goes as deep as 110 feet. He needs to harvest 600 pounds of urchins to meet expenses, while a good day would be 1200 pounds sold for $1000.00 or more.

Jon likes being his own boss, and having the freedom to put his own schedule together. He loves being at sea, and the lifestyle is wonderful for him. He feels that if he works hard he reaps the benefits. He likes being completely responsible for his own business.

Being a diver still takes Jon from his family for extended periods of time, although its much better than commercial oil field work. He usually leaves home at 4:30 a.m. and might not return for 4 – 5 days.

Jon is concerned about his general health and safety while diving. Despite the fact he's never been bent (which is unusual), the possibility is always on his mind. Urchin spines are a common injury, and if not taken care of can be a serious problem. Being at sea and doing strenuous work means you must concentrate on avoiding strains, sprains, breaks or worse.

Jon recalls a dive day at San Miguel Island when the visibility was 3 – 5 feet and he saw a torpedo ray (electric ray) early in the day. Late in the afternoon as he was surfacing he saw a bright flash. He discovered the ray was two feet from his head. Although he wasn't shocked he had to push the ray away and continue beating it off until he got on the boat.

Jon's advice to someone considering this occupation is to go out and try it. See if it's something you really like. As an urchin diver you're on a small boat in a rough ocean, and it's always damp, even in the cabin. Many people find this a miserable experience. To be successful you must also understand decompression tables and diving physiology, and have some knowledge of first aid.

Jon notes that it's easy to push yourself too hard underwater, because the more time you're underwater the more money you make. However, by being steady and following the dive tables or your computer you'll be more productive in the long run. The temptation to violate the fishing regulations is always there, especially since most states don't have adequate enforcement.

Jon notes that it's important to protect the resource. If it goes, so does your career! However, Jon does feel it's a renewable resource if treated with respect. Sea urchins are a valuable product for trade with Japan.

Jon makes use of a pick-up boat. For a cut of his ex-vessel price, an operator will pick up the urchins Jon has collected that day and deliver them to the processor. The pick-up boat might charge 5 – 6

Fig. 13.9 – A pick-up boat collects the day's catch after dark from an urchin boat at San Miguel Island, off California.

cents a pound regardless of the price the fisherman gets at the dock. Jon likes it because he can stay out for 4 – 5 days and work steadily at the Northern Channel Islands. He doesn't waste time motoring back and forth from the mainland. He also doesn't get as fatigued, so his susceptibility to the bends is decreased. Conversely, some divers feel pick-up boats put more pressure on the resource because it allows divers like Jon to extend their diving time.

MARY STEIN

Mary Stein has been an abalone diver in California since 1976. She started snorkeling as a child when she spent her summers at Catalina Island. Mariner's Scouts in high school is where she learned to sail. She continued to sail while she got her Bachelor's in Art from UCLA.

After graduation from college in 1972, Mary got her first 50 ton Captain's license. She worked sailing charters seasonally for about four years, and she did whale watching trips in Baja California. Although the work wasn't lucrative, it was fun. Mary recalls applying for a deckhand position at H & M Landing in San Diego. The gentleman in charge refused to hire a woman to be on deck even though she was the most qualified applicant for the job. Mary was offered a cook's position in the galley instead. She took it and spent her spare time in the wheel house with the Captain on her first trip. The next trip Mary was on deck.

Mary was driving the shore boat (water taxi) at Avalon (Catalina Island) in 1975 when she first met the abalone diving fleet. A trip on a pick-up boat to San Clemente Island is when she made her decision to be an abalone diver. She still remembers Seal Cove at San Clemente with all the abalone boats anchored together waiting to get supplies from the pick-up boat. It was the lifestyle that caught her.

To Mary, being outdoors and interacting with nature is to be a part of "the real world." Mary took the Fish and Game test required to become an abalone diver in California in 1976 (the test is no longer required) and passed. Although Mary was a water person, she had never done any compressed air diving. Her next hurdle was learning hookah diving.

Stein started out by tending the hose for two abalone divers. The senior diver taught her how to use hookah. Since he did decompression diving, that's what she learned and did for a couple of years. She routinely worked at depths of 150 feet harvesting white abalone, *Haliotis sorenseni,* and selling them to the restaurants on Catalina Island.

In 1979 she moved from Catalina Island to San Diego with her boyfriend. They picked urchins together for a year. She didn't like harvesting urchins and moved back to Catalina Island minus her boyfriend.

Mary then tried to find a boat to work off to dive for abalone. She had a difficult time because even her friends told her their wives and girlfriends wouldn't allow it. That year she hooked up with Randy Brannock and his dive buddy. Randy and Mary worked well together and decided to build their own vessel. The *Amais* is a 25 foot boat with their own innovations.

Randy and Mary's relationship blossomed and they're now a permanent team. Together they purchased Catalina Diver's Supply with another diver, John Mello, in 1986. They diversified because abalone stocks were dwindling and the sport diving industry was growing. They were also concerned about educating the sport diving public. In 1985 they designed and manufactured a "Conservation Abalone Iron," with an informational leaflet for sport divers.

Mary and Randy now split their time between the store and abalone diving. They usually tend for each other. In fact, if Randy hadn't been tending Mary the day she encountered a belligerent sea lion, she's sure she would have been bitten. They have always been careful to avoid sea lion rookeries. On the day of the incident, Mary was diving in 30 feet of open water in a cove at Catalina, when a bull sea lion started threatening her. It bared its teeth and bit a fish in half in front of her face! Mary surfaced and Randy started pulling her hose back to the boat. She put her floater bag between herself and the sea lion and kept waving her abalone iron in front of his snapping teeth. Everyone agrees that it was unusual behavior for a sea lion, so they dubbed the location "Mad Dog Cove."

Mary still loves the lifestyle associated with abalone diving. She recommends that you try it before you make the commitment. She emphasizes that you must understand that the income is very unreliable, making credit hard to get. The dive store has given Mary and Randy a credit standing, and the cost of boat insurance has been reduced since they're both licensed captains.

Your health is also critical to your earning power. A serious injury could reduce you to bankruptcy. Mary tries to use her brain more than her muscles, but the job is physically demanding .

Fig. 13.10 – Bruce Steele delivers a load of urchins to the dock. (© D.B. Pleschner)

BRUCE STEELE

Bruce Steele has been a sea urchin diver all his adult life. While in high school he had an opportunity to take a marine biology course sponsored by Southern California Edison at a local junior college. One of the things he was encouraged to do in association with this class was to learn how to scuba dive. He recalls two lectures by outside speakers in this course. One was given by Dr. Wheeler North, a kelp specialist. Wheeler told the students about the "terrible sea urchins" that overgraze the giant kelp off Southern California. He also mentioned that the Japanese were interested in purchasing sea urchins, and that maybe something could be worked out.

Bruce also remembers a hard hat diver coming to class and explaining how diving was a way to make a living. Bruce was 17 when he graduated from high school early and went to Oakland, California to learn to be a commercial diver at the Coastal School of Deep Sea Diving. He went back home to Oxnard, California after he completed the program and scraped enough money together to go to Louisiana in April of 1973. He got hired on as a tender with McDermott Diving and "starved for three months." He gave it up because jobs were scarce at that time and there was little hope of him breaking out into a diver position in the near future. He felt that nobody took him seriously because he was so young. The climate in Louisiana also didn't agree with him.

In 1974 Bruce got a job as a diver on an urchin boat out of Oxnard where the urchin fishery/business got started. Oxnard is only 11 nautical miles from Anacapa Island where there was an abundant source of urchins. There were probably 30-40 fishermen in the fishery initially.

Bruce recalls motoring out to Anacapa Island at 8 a.m. and collecting 2,500-3,000 pounds of urchins in a regular work day. He was working then as a "*split diver*" with another diver, taking turns diving and tending. Since Bruce didn't own a boat he'd go out on another diver's boat and give him 50% of his harvest for the service. At that time Bruce was making eight cents a pound. Today split divers usually give the boat 40%.

After close to two years Bruce moved to Santa Barbara and leased his own boat. He recalls that one of the first boats he leased at the age of 21 was on the condition that he hire the owner's son as his deckhand. When he moved to Santa Barbara he started diving the more northern Channel Islands and he utilized a pick-up boat. He'd meet the boat at Johnsons Lee, at Santa Rosa Island, and the operator would take the urchins back to Oxnard. In those days Bruce was diving in the 30-40 foot depth range. When he had collected his poundage he'd get out of the water and enjoy the environment.

When the El Niño event of 1982-83 occurred it was a tough time for the industry. The influx of warm water caused the kelp to die and all the grazers (like abalone and sea urchins) suffered. Although many of the sea urchins survived on their fat reserves their gonads were nonexistent or of unmarketable quality. Bruce says December 15, 1983 is a date he'll always remember. The water temperature dropped 10 degrees that week, and there was a tremendous burst of life on the bottom. As the urchins recovered the fishery revived.

In 1985 a few divers, Bruce included, moved to Northern California to harvest urchins. Bruce left his 26 foot vessel in the slip in Santa Barbara and worked as a split diver again. He was getting 20 cents a pound. That Christmas the price went to 50 cents a pound. He achieved his personal best that month and for three days in a row, he collected 6,000 pounds a day.

Bruce knew he was harvesting old animals, or "*virgin stock*," that had built up over time. He saw few young animals, and knew it was just a matter of time before the fishery in Northern California would start to decline. To keep making money, Bruce went to Oregon for a month or two every year. Here again he found he was harvesting big, old urchins in concentrated beds. He gave up his Oregon urchin permit in 1990.

Trailering his boat to Northern California and Oregon was what Bruce calls, "a white knuckle affair." "You put almost 7,000 pounds of boat on a trailer and hook it to a truck, and you're at the mercy of other drivers. You can't bring that kind of weight to a sudden stop if someone cuts in or slams on their brakes," says Bruce.

Bruce spends about 120 days a year in the water now. From 1985 to 1990 it was 200 days. He finds that controlling his overhead is part of the key to success. If your boat, trailer, and pick-up truck are paid for, your overhead is lower, and you can make more money in less time.

Bruce has always been a "chicken." He never pushes the tables, and he doesn't do decompression diving.

"It's hard to compete with people who are crazy. Divers in their 20's are risk takers. Alcohol and drugs probably go along with that. Most divers in their 30's or 40's change or die," observes Bruce.

Steele loves going to sea and living in a "wild environment." Underwater he becomes part of an environment that is very new for humans and feels he's a pioneer of sorts.

"Every diver wears the same gear, but they don't see the same things," says Bruce. For him, observations and familiarity with this underwater environment have nurtured an empathy for the ocean. His work allows him to live in Santa Barbara and spend the rest of his time in the mountains, another wild place.

When asked to comment on negatives of his career Bruce thought of the responsibility he has for the safety and welfare of his crew. He also believes he bears responsibility for the resource. He feels that most urchin processors aren't concerned, many environmentalists are misdirected, and the majority of fishermen are apolitical. Bruce has been on the Board of Directors of the California Urchin Diver's Association (CUDA) since it was organized during the '82-'83 El Niño. He also represents divers on the Director's Sea Urchin Advisory Committee (DSUAC), that advises the Department of Fish and Game. DSUAC was created when California's urchin fishery went limited entry.

Bruce is a dual permittee, meaning that he also has a permit to harvest abalone. He only collects 360 abalone a year to maintain his permit and keep his limited options open.

Bruce 's advice to people considering this career is "you had better love the ocean. Diving is painful." Cold is part of the pain. You have to be strong, agile, and literally have the right physiology for diving. He went on to say if you're not willing to take risks forget it. But don't take risks that jeopardize your life. Expect that it will take two to three years to get good enough to compete with other divers.

"Copy the best people as best you can. Innovate after you've figured out what you're doing. Don't innovate first or you'll die," warns

Bruce. He also cautions that, "when you're in the ocean nobody can help you, and you can't depend only on your equipment."

Bruce has had a number of close calls. His most vivid near miss took place when he was unloading urchins onto a pick-up boat while both vessels were underway. The pick-up boat had lost its neutral. The transfer of urchins went smoothly until the two boats were about to separate. Bruce was on the stern of his boat and the Captain of the other boat was on its bow when both got ready to cast off the lines. Bruce cast his line off just as the boat kicked into reverse, throwing him overboard. He'd had gymnastic training in school and managed to hold onto the boat. At that point the boat was thrown back into forward. Bruce did a "*muscle up,*" boosting himself back on the boat just before the boats crashed together. He said there was dead quiet as eight men who had almost seen him crushed between two boats regained their composure. He had escaped death by seconds.

GARY JOHNSON

Gary Johnson had been out of high school for ten years when he ran into a buddy from high school who was diving for abalone out of a 17 foot skiff just north of Santa Barbara, California. He tended for three months for his friend, and received 20% of the diver's harvest for his efforts. Although Gary was a surfer, he was afraid of everything underwater when he first tried hookah diving. His friend had taken a job elsewhere and had left Gary the skiff and dive equipment. Without formal lessons, and wearing a borrowed wetsuit, he ventured underwater by himself to collect abalone off the coast. In 1969 Gary was getting a dollar an abalone, and there was no difficulty finding them.

Fig. 13.11 – Gary Johnson performs regular maintenance on his boat, the "Hot Chocolate."

The year 1975 was a fateful one for Gary. In July, Gary was diving alone as he usually does, in 25 feet of water off the Pt. Conception light. He had his arm clear up to his shoulder under a rock ledge, and he was fighting to retrieve an abalone he hadn't completely "popped" when something hit his fins hard. When he turned around he saw a large animal doing a 180 degree turn and coming back toward him. That's when he realized that it was a 15 foot white shark.

The animal was so awesome Gary said he just couldn't think for awhile. The animal passed by him close enough for Gary to feel its pressure wave. When the animal started to come around again Gary headed for the surface. He screamed at the tender who had accompanied him that day to pull his hose in. When he got to the boat Gary was so weak he couldn't crawl back in. The tender had to drag him aboard. Although the physical damage was only a couple of slices in one fin, the mental damage was worse. Gary got back into the water the next day, but shadows and dirty water brought back vivid memories of the incident.

Late in 1975 Gary got the "bends." He had been doing decompression diving, and the "hit" was in his left eye. Not realizing that his vision problem was related to his diving, he didn't seek immediate medical treatment. By the time he was seen and treated by several ophthalmologists, he'd lost all the peripheral vision in his eye. He was also told to give up diving.

For the next five years he worked for Tidewater Marine as a deckhand on the oil crew boats. It was a job of which he was not fond. In 1980 he went back to diving. By that time the abalone fishery had gone limited entry and he couldn't get an abalone diving permit, so he started fishing for urchins out of a 20 foot skiff. However, he immediately wrote and called the California Dept. of Fish and Game to try and get his abalone permit back. He kept up constant pressure and contact with the Department and was given his abalone permit back in August of 1980.

Gary has been a dual permittee ever since. He enjoys the variety of having two fisheries to work in.

In 1985, Gary bought a 24 foot boat, the *Hot Chocolate.* He started making two or three day diving trips. Now he probably dives 100 days a year.

Gary loves his career because "he does what he wants to do." He smiles when it storms and goes down to the harbor to have breakfast with his buddies.

"It's an honest living. The harder you work the better you do," says Gary.

Gary likes the solitude when he's diving, although now he'll have five or six boats following him to "his spot." The camaraderie in the business is disappearing.

Unfortunately, Gary sees things changing as the resources get scarce. He sees no future in abalone or urchin diving. Gary's great interest is in mariculture, farming the sea. He feels that harvest of the sea should be like a well managed farm. That's the only way he believes his career will survive.

Suggested Reading:

Pacific Fishing Magazine, published by Salmon Bay Communications, 1515 N.W. 51st Street, Seattle, Washington 98107. Published monthly.

National Fisherman Magazine, published by Journal Publications, 120 Tillson Ave., Rockland, Maine 04841-0908. Published monthly.

Browning, R. *Fisheries of the North Pacific*, Alaska Northwest Publishing Co., Box 4 - EEE, Anchorage, Alaska 99509. 1980.

Fig. 14.1 – Every aquarium and marine life park depends upon specimens from the wild for their tanks. The Living Seas exhibit at Epcot Center in Orlando, Florida is no exception.

CHAPTER FOURTEEN

MARINE AQUARIST & COLLECTORS

There are several groups of people that collect invertebrates, fishes, and algae from the ocean. These people are generally known as "marine collectors." Scientific marine collectors capture specimens for educational purposes. For example, some coastal universities have a collector on staff, while others use contract personnel.

Many institutions, especially high schools and landlocked colleges, buy specimens from biological supply houses. The biological supply houses usually have a regular staff, and use contract collectors for special orders.

Every aquarium and marine life park in the United States depends on specimens from the wild for their tanks. Again these organizations usually have a combination of collectors on staff and on contract. It takes thousands of specimens to keep the Monterey Bay Aquarium looking great year-round. These attractions have become very popular with the public.

Home aquarium systems are now relatively inexpensive. Unfortunately the mortality rate of fish and other invertebrates in salt water systems is often high. Consequently there is a steady demand for aquarium specimens from existing aquarium owners, and from those new to the hobby. Naturally people are attracted to colorful specimens and creatures with status or charisma, such as small sharks. There is a whole network of small companies and collectors who fill the needs of the aquarium trade.

One of the most famous marine biological collectors was Ed Ricketts, who formed the basis for the character "Doc" in John Steinbeck's book, *Cannery Row.* Ricketts himself was one of the coauthors of the book, *Between Pacific Tides,* considered an essential book for any west coast marine biologist. To read more about the life of Ed Ricketts, be sure to read the book, *The Log from the Sea of Cortez* by Steinbeck, particularly the preface, *About Ed Ricketts.* Although Ed Ricketts wasn't a diver, his spirit is certainly characteristic of many of the divers we know.

Aquarists are the people who maintain marine aquariums for scientific or public institutions. These people specialize in knowing what it takes to keep marine creatures alive and healthy in captivity.

Fig. 14.2 – Collectors use a variety of tools to get the job done. This collector is using a "slurp" gun to collect small fish.

Scientific Collectors

Any collector on staff with a university or other scientific institution is usually required to have a bachelor's of arts or science degree (B.A. or B.S.) in the biological sciences (see chapter 5). The collecting they do is for specific courses or research projects. Generally speaking, these people are extremely knowledgeable about the behavior, habitat, and dietary needs of the creatures they collect. The collecting is done on tight schedules and sometimes very short notice.

Collectors don't always have the luxury of collecting when conditions are optimal. The local tidal cycle will frequently determine when a collecting trip must be scheduled. They collect year-round under all sorts of conditions. A collector on staff with an academic institution dives under the school's scientific diving regulations, just as the scientists do (see chapter 7). Marine collectors need to be highly experienced divers.

Scientific collectors usually have a permit to gather specimens from the fish and game agency of the state where they reside. Records of all species collected and their deposition have to be turned in to the permitting agency on a regular basis. The school will also require accurate records on the species collected, which will include dates and collection sites. In addition, OSHA (Occupational Safety and Health Administration) has paperwork dealing with the use of formaldehyde or any other preservatives or anesthetics used. There is purchasing and accounting paperwork required by the university. The records and associated databases are expected to be maintained on a computer.

In an academic institution, where animals are used for lab work, setting up the laboratories with the species that have been collected may be either the collector's responsibility or the aquarist's responsibility. Retrieving the specimens and equipment after their use is also part of the job.

The maintenance of the tanks, pumps, and all other equipment associated with collecting are also the responsibility of the collector. Many collectors use a small power boat when collecting at sea. Knowledge and skill in boat handling and maintenance is a requirement. Although the collector is expected to act independently, they're considered a representative of the institution that employs them . Therefore they must demonstrate tact and public relations ability.

Fig. 14.3 – Small boat handling is an important skill for a marine collector.

Independent collectors have to be reliable. If you promise a researcher 50 specimens by a certain date, and they don't arrive on time, that researcher will find a new supplier. The creatures delivered also have to be healthy. Fifty sick and dying animals benefits no one. When you have established a reputation for reliability, researchers and institutions are loathe to try someone new. Price is not the only motivating factor in this business.

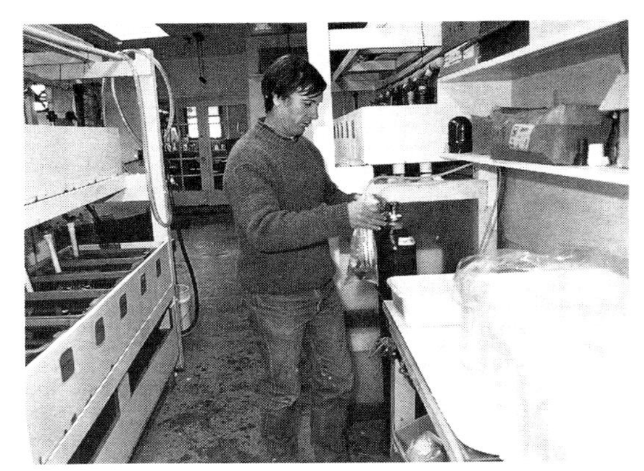

Fig. 14.4 – Aquarium trade collectors must be able to get their specimens to customers quickly. Mike Morris of Sea Life Supply prepares specimens for shipment via an overnight service. Note the oxygen cylinder for filling the bags the specimens are placed in before they go into the insulated Styrofoam container.

Aquarium Trade Collectors

These divers are very active in Florida and Hawaii despite the fact some highly restrictive legislation has been passed that directly regulates their business. California's aquarium trade has been growing; but the impact of new regulations that went into effect in January 1993 remains to be seen.

Aside from their scuba gear, collectors need hand nets and buckets. Many collectors use an anesthetic, such as quinaldine, to aid in capturing fish. Other standard equipment includes tanks with aeration to keep the specimens alive until they are shipped or delivered.

Saltwater fish tanks take up a great deal of space, and they have to be housed away from the elements to maintain such critical factors as proper temperature. Although some collectors make the salt water for their specimens with packaged ingredients, it's often necessary to treat domestic water supplies to remove chlorine and other chemicals before using it in their tanks. Shipping is generally a stressful event and many animals are lost during the transport process. The collector is only paid for the fish that arrive alive and healthy.

If you want to use the same area again and again for collecting you have to be a good manager. You can't disturb or destroy plants or animals while collecting a particular species. Biologists use the term "*ecosystem*" when referring to the interrelationships of a particular habitat. If your collecting eliminates or severely impacts selected species you will affect the whole ecosystem in that area.

Working for or with another collector is how many people get started in the business. You can learn the "tricks of the trade" and avoid costly mistakes this way.

Collectors in the U.S. have to compete with native collectors from other countries who are not regulated, or who may not be as concerned with preservation of the environment or the animals.

Fig. 14.5 – Aquarists need to have a broad background to be successful. Floyd DeWitt at the University of California, Santa Barbara (UCSB) is responsible for the salt water system on campus.

Aquarist

Aquarist is the title usually given to biologists who work for aquariums and marine life parks. They usually have a degree in the biological sciences.

Sometimes aquarists are involved in collecting animals for display. However, their primary responsibility is the care and feeding of marine life once they're resident in tanks. They must know how to keep these creatures alive and healthy, and this is a big commitment. Aquarists must tailor their work schedules to the needs of their charges. This may mean working nights and weekends.

In certain situations the aquarist may actually need to dive inside the aquarium to check on the health or behavior of certain creatures. This is particularly true when the aquarium includes large display tanks like those found at the Monterey Bay Aquarium, the Boston Aquarium, or Sea World.

As an aquarist you must possess many construction skills. You have to know how to plumb a display tank so that creatures that need wave action get it. If you can't do it yourself you have to be able to work with somebody who can get the job done. You have to become very sensitive to little details about your fish. Did the garibaldi not eat today because he's started guarding a nest, he's ill, or just because he's not hungry?

Aquarists must also be keenly aware of how different species interact. Not all creatures can live together harmoniously in the same tank.

The job market for aquarists looks promising. As of 1993, it was estimated that there were as many as 70 new public aquariums in various stages of evaluation, and more than two dozen are in advanced planning stages. Many existing aquariums, such as the Chicago Shedd Aquarium and the Monterey Bay Aquarium are in the midst of major expansions.

Fig. 14.6 – Dave Powell checks out the top of the Monterey Bay tank at the Monterey Bay Aquarium. The tank is kept dark to simulate the conditions found in the deeper depths of Monterey Bay.

Experiences of Aquarists and Collectors

DAVE POWELL

Dave Powell is the Director of Husbandry at the Monterey Bay Aquarium in California. In this capacity he is responsible for all the fish and other animals on display at the aquarium.

As a child Dave was always interested in marine life. He was born in South Africa of American parents, and moved to England with his family at the age of five. At 18 he moved to the United States and joined the military.

Dave went to UCLA after his military service and received a Master's degree in Marine Biology. In 1952 Dave started scuba diving. He shared the expense of purchasing a single scuba rig with his cousin because neither of them could afford to buy it by themselves. He read a diving manual, and went out and taught himself to dive. There were no formal instruction courses in diving at that time. Although his cousin dropped out of the sport after a year, Dave was a natural.

Dave started collecting animals for the Biology Department at UCLA while he was enrolled there. He built an 18 foot inboard boat and went to Catalina Island and started night diving. He quickly realized that the best time to collect fish was at night.

After graduation, there were few jobs available for biologists, so Dave went to work for a sewage plant. When an aquarist position came open at Marineland of the Pacific, on the Palos Verdes peninsula south of Los Angeles, he got the job. Dave collected for Marineland and also sold marine animals on the side. He worked at Marineland from 1959 to 1962. While there Dave tried to recreate what the real underwater world looked like for the public. He would bring back rocks with animals living on them to the aquariums. Marineland had a good sea water system so Dave was able to refine his techniques while working there.

Dave left Marineland to take a position with the Steinhart Aquarium in San Francisco. He got people diving at Steinhart and started meeting diving professionals like Al Giddings, the famous underwater photographer. Dave worked at Steinhart until 1965 when he was recruited by the president of Sea World to work for them.

Dave spent nine years with Sea World, collecting and designing their marine exhibits. He learned a great deal and had lots of freedom. While at Sea World he made more than ten major collecting trips to Mexican waters.

In 1974 Dave went back to work for Steinhart again. The construction of the Aquarium's "Roundabout" tank was underway. This was to be a unique circular tank with a winding ramp inside it for the visitors to view the fish. A strong current was generated inside the tank by electric motors for the fish to swim against. It was the first exhibit of its kind.

Dave went to the Comoro Islands in the Indian Ocean with Dr. John McCosker (the Director of Steinhart), Al Giddings, and Dr. Sylvia Earle in search of coelacanths. The coelacanth is a rare and unusual fish that scientists had presumed was extinct until one was caught in a fisherman's net by accident. Although Dave's expedition was not able to return with any live specimens, they brought back two dead coelacanths for further study and some of the first live flashlight fish to be displayed in a public aquarium.

In 1979 the Packard family (of Hewlett–Packard fame) invited Dave down to Monterey, California to review their plans for a new and exciting aquarium to be built along the old cannery row. Dave consulted for the Packards until the following year when they offered him a permanent job. The aquarium opened in 1984. Dave's first years were spent in exhibit design and major collecting efforts. In 1983 he hired a collector. Dave doesn't get to do as much diving now, and he has people who dive in the aquarium's tanks and do the collecting.

Powell's responsibilities include designing all living exhibits, for everything from sea otters to jellyfish. Dave determines what animals to exhibit, and supervises the support staff that feed and maintain all the aquarium's marine life. Dave also works on plans for new exhibits. The Monterey Bay Aquarium is planning an open sea, or "*pelagic,*" and deep sea exhibit. Planning involves figuring out how to collect the animals, and how to keep them alive and healthy once you have them.

Dave also responds to visitors' concerns and comments about the animals displayed at the aquarium. With 1.7 million visitors a year he receives a large quantity of correspondence. Dave answers all questions relating to live animals.

Creating exhibits that accurately depict the undersea world gives Dave great pleasure. He tries to make the habitats at the aquarium so much like their real home that the animal will live a normal life and reproduce. Dave enjoys working at the aquarium, watching and listening to visitors having a good time, and learning in the process. He enjoys working with highly motivated people and learning from those people, just as he shares his knowledge with them.

Dave's list of negatives was short. At times there are too many meetings, and he does not enjoy the frustrations of dealing with government agencies.

Dave's career advice was to forget about this career unless you really love the animals. In this line of work, your attitude truly makes a difference. You must always think of the needs of the animals for which you are responsible. You also shouldn't expect to make a lot of money.

Dave firmly believes that you should only pursue an occupation in something you enjoy. For the career of aquarist a good general background in biology, as well as basic chemistry and physics is essential. A B.A. or B.S. is required and a masters is preferable. Volunteer at a facility if you have the opportunity. Monterey Bay Aquarium has hired many people who started as volunteers.

FLOYD DEWITT

Floyd DeWitt is the aquarist at the University of California, Santa Barbara (UCSB). It's a position he's held since 1976 when it was first instituted and advertised. Floyd has always been interested in the ocean. He started snorkeling when he was eight years old. He received his B.A. in Biology from Cal Poly Pomona.

After graduation Floyd spent three years in the Navy. Following his discharge from the service he went back to his home town of Santa Barbara and got a Master's in Marine Biology at UCSB. He worked as a research specialist for the Marine Science Institute, which is affiliated with UCSB, for several years. In 1974 he received a grant from the EPA to do an oil spill literature search, and spent a year putting a current bibliography on the subject together. The following year he worked for Dr. Mike Neushul, a kelp researcher. Floyd took care of Neushul's greenhouse at UCSB where he grew algae. He also did research diving for Neushul at a site adjacent to the campus.

In 1976 UCSB put in a new salt water system. It consisted of two pipes, 12 inches in diameter, that extend 1,500 feet offshore. They're made of polyethylene, and are anchored every ten feet with concrete collars. The system delivers 500 gallons per minute of salt water. The school advertised for an aquarist to take care of this system. A Bachelor's degree in Biology was required for the job. Diving certification and small boat experience were also required. Floyd was overqualified for the position, but he got it. Certainly his long association with the school and familiarity with their previous salt water system helped.

Floyd calls himself a "saltwater plumber" - "more mechanic than scientist." He is peripherally involved in science, but he doesn't do the "hard core research." Floyd is not officially the curator of any marine creatures, but in conjunction with facilities management he oversees the sea water system, pumps, tanks, and other associated equipment. He does lots of consulting with salt water users. Floyd designs and oversees all the salt water system installations on campus which often includes plumbing in filters or rigging ultraviolet lights. Sometimes the sea water isn't even being used for animals. For example, the laser unit on campus is cooled with fresh water that is cooled by sea water from Floyd's system.

Floyd dives once a month to clean the intake structures on the saltwater intake pipes and to swim the length of the pipes to make sure there are no problems. He works an eight hour day, but has the freedom to arrange his schedule as he sees fit. He works in the bioscience shop, fabricating equipment, during slack times. Sea water systems constantly corrode, so failure is expected, it's just a matter of when they occur. The "when" is usually on weekends, and in the middle of the night, and Floyd must respond when they fail.

Floyd gave up "hard core biology" for the security of a permanent job in a place he wanted to be. He's very happy with his work, even though it wasn't the job he foresaw in college.

CONSTANCE GRAMLICH

Constance Gramlich is the scientific collector for San Diego State University (SDSU). She credits her love of the sea to her parents who took her to Laguna Beach, California from the time she was very young. She has a vivid memory of two scuba divers coming out of the ocean when she was seven and handing her a variety of snails. Right at that moment she decided that she wanted to dive and gather marine creatures, and followed up by learning how to dive in high school. In college, at UCLA, Constance had a bent toward the natural history of marine creatures, but was diverted away from diving.

Fig. 14.7 – Constance Gramlich knew she wanted to work in biology from the time she was young.

Constance earned her bachelor's degree and did additional graduate level work before leaving school. One of her first jobs was to sample fish caught by anglers on open charter boats for the California Dept. of Fish and Game. She then spent five years working for Dr. Rim Fay at Pacific Bio-Marine Laboratories, where she did scientific collecting for his firm.

For the next 2-1/2 years of her life, Constance participated in research and management at Channel Islands National Park, where she was part of their kelp forest monitoring dive team. She went to work for San Diego State University in 1990, where her collecting position is permanent and full-time.

Constance loves learning new things and having the time and the justification to study some things in depth. She has a regular opportunity to visit new diving and collecting sites. She collects on mud flats, beaches, in tide pools, off harbors and piers, and offshore in her university skiff. She enjoys having students and faculty coming to her as an information resource on marine creatures.

Like all government employees, Constance has to regularly cope with increasing budgetary constraints. The University is a bureaucracy so there are rules and paperwork that must be followed. She works long hours, under all sorts of conditions. Because the environment and teachers' needs dictate when she collects, she has to be able to juggle her schedule. Her personal life is impacted by the demands of her work.

During the summer term Constance's collecting schedule is not as intense as it is during the regular school year. Constance tries to gear up for the fall schedule during the summer. She also deals with lots of loose ends. She has to take care of things like straightening up the microscope slide collection; which includes cleaning, repairing, and replacing slides.

Constance greatly enjoys the freedom and variety associated with her position at SDSU.

SHANE ANDERSON

Shane Anderson is a collector/naturalist for the University of California, Santa Barbara (UCSB). It's a position he's held since 1974. Shane learned to dive while he was pursuing an Associate of Arts degree (A.A.) in Biology at Santa Barbara City College. He received his B.S. in Biology through Cal State Hayward in 1971, although he did most of his course work at Moss Landing Marine Lab.

During his summers and for about six months after graduation Shane worked for Bill Jorgensen at Western Marine Laboratories in Santa Barbara. From 1971-1972 he worked for Dr. Rim Fay at Pacific Bio-Marine. He returned to Western Marine Labs from 1972-1974 and did extensive underwater photography. Western Marine produced audio-visual aids for schools, primarily in the form of filmstrips. Following his work at Western Marine Labs, Shane was hired at UCSB.

Shane's job has evolved over time. He now has four boats available to him to use for collecting. His job description includes the responsibility of "launch master." This means that he schedules the use of university boats by graduate students or other researchers, and must ensure that they're checked out for safety and in boat handling techniques. He also lets the maintenance staff know when the boats need repair or attention.

Shane normally spends 2 – 3 days a week diving. He also does low tide work in waders and surfsuits on mud flats and in sloughs. He does 80% of his collecting within 11 miles of campus, so he must be a

Fig. 14.8 – Marine collectors Shane Anderson and Jim McCullagh service their underwater scooters in preparation for another collecting dive.

careful harvester. Since 90% of the work with live animals at UCSB is observational, many of the animals are returned to the ocean. He is also fortunate that UCSB has an excellent saltwater system, allowing him to collect specimens in advance of when they are needed.

Shane enjoys being in charge of his time. When he receives a written order for animals from an instructor or researcher it's up to him to fill it the way he chooses. He's free to be innovative. He frequently counsels and consults with graduate students and visiting researchers not familiar with the local animals.

As a marine collector Shane experiences and sees things most people never see. His experiences underwater and on the ocean are always new and changing. A few years ago Shane and his dive buddy were able to swim with a school of close to 50 basking sharks. They're large filter feeders about which little is known.

Shane has written an aquarium manual and contributed to a number of scientific notes. When he sees things that are unusual, he contacts the appropriate researcher to verify that information. Shane observed surface feeding by a gray whale, normally a bottom feeder. He discovered leeches on newborn angel sharks.

Shane's list of the negatives about his job was short. Working in bad weather or zero visibility underwater is not fun and can be quite uncomfortable. Although many people envy his job, they don't realize that it can be hazardous, and the hours long and unusual.

JIM MCCULLAGH

When Shane Anderson first started working at UCSB he hired students on an hourly basis to assist him with his diving. He quickly found it was not an efficient way to get the job done.

In 1983 the university funded a full time Assistant Collector/Naturalist position and Jim McCullagh got the job. Jim had been an aquatic biology major at UCSB, and while doing his undergraduate studies had volunteered to assist instructors and other researchers with their diving. During that time he met Shane and got exposed to the collector career path.

In his senior year, Jim arranged his class schedule so he could work entire days with Shane. Although skill level is important, compatibility with your assistant/dive buddy is critical since you spend so much time together. Because of his pleasant nature and "can-do" attitude Jim was a natural choice when Shane had a position to fill.

Jim was born and raised in Hawaii, and has always loved the water. He learned to snorkel at an early age. He expressed interest in scuba diving in high school, but his parents thought it was too dangerous, and were unwilling to fund lessons. Jim had to wait until he was a freshman in college before he could learn to dive. Although he'd entered college as a biology major, the diving steered him toward marine biology. Jim put in his "time" while he was in college. Volunteering was his key to success.

"If material things are your goal, this is not the profession to get into," says Jim. "Expect to spend several years getting where you want to be. Be persistent, since jobs are limited, your determination is crucial to your success."

The most attractive part of Jim's job is working outside and observing nature in general, and specific animals in an ever changing environment. Collectors are always in a position to learn and discover. Jim has had wonderful experiences with elephant seals, gray whales, sharks, and killer whales. Being in the vicinity of large animals, even if you're not actually in the water with them, is inspirational.

Jim expresses the negative aspects of his job nicely when he says, "I don't like my job everyday."

Working outside during winter storms and other weather is not pleasant. Sometimes the job is more physically demanding than mentally demanding. Everyone else thinks you have the best job in the world, as long as the sun is shining.

Jim gets recruited into other jobs that the biology department needs done to function. He runs the campus scuba tank fill station, including maintenance of the tanks and record keeping. One day he may drive a truck and pick up equipment, the next he may be moving supplies or equipment around the campus.

Fig. 14.9 – Bill and Chris Parks get ready for a dive off the Florida coast. (Photo courtesy of Bill Parks.)

BILL AND CHRIS PARKS

Bill Parks is a private marine collector in Florida where he has lived his whole life. He started snorkeling in fifth grade, and took up scuba in 1975 after high school. He has a B.S. in Ocean Engineering from Florida State. Bill started collecting the same year he learned how to scuba dive. In 1978 he went into the collecting business full time. Reef Hopper, Inc., his current business, was launched in 1983. Bill married in 1986 and his wife, Chris, is in business with him.

Together, Bill and Chris spend 7-1/2 - 9 hours a day on the water about 150 days a year. Their actual "in water" time is about 2-1/2 hours since they're regularly diving in depths of 80 – 100 feet. They use nitrox to extend their bottom times. The Parks' deliver their fish once a week to a wholesaler. Most of their fish end up in Los Angeles.

Bill loves his work. He likes the freedom and being outdoors. Even after 17 years, he still learns something new whenever he gets on a reef. He's very sensitive to the life cycles of hundreds of reef dwellers and enjoys that intimacy.

The Parks' are alarmed by the increasing population along Florida's coast, and the associated pollution. They are angry and frustrated by the destruction of the reefs and their inhabitants. This destruction has forced them into deeper water to do their collecting. Bill is trying to organize a limited entry fishery for collecting in Florida, and estimates that there are about 150 active collectors in the state.

"If you're interested in this career you have to approach it realistically," explains Bill. "You have to put the resource first, and realize that your business will impact the environment. You can't look the other way when you see people destroying the resource."

MIKE AND GAY MORRIS

Mike and Gay Morris operate Sea Life Supply in Seaside, California. They're a private company devoted to scientific collecting, and they've been in the business for 25 years. Mike received a Bachelor's degree in Biology from Cal State Hayward in 1968. He started diving in college, and when he married Gay, in 1967, she was already his dive buddy. Mike recalls that his first sale in college was a shipment of amphipods (tiny shrimp-like creatures) to one of the biggest biological supply houses in the country at that time, a company called Turtox (now out of business).

Fig. 14.10 – Getting paid is important! Gay Morris of Sea Life Supply prepares a bill as her husband Mike looks on.

Mike and Gay moved to Monterey in 1968. Mike decided he didn't like working with preserving fluids, and he wanted to concentrate on live specimens. He met Dr. Rim Fay, who has a biological supply business called Pacific Bio-Marine. Mike got Rim's catalog and then went through the Bioabstracts to find out what species scientists were working with.

The Morris' produced their own catalog and bought a mailing list of biology teachers to whom they promoted it. They sent a post card out to everyone on this list giving them the opportunity to request their catalog. Business growth was slow, and Gay worked as a medical technician initially. Although she worked part-time for Sea Life Supply throughout the years, she didn't join the business full-time until 1980.

Mike collected by himself until 1984. That year he started raising sea hares, *Aplysia sp.*, in a culture lab, and hired a number of employees to assist with the operation. The sea hare is the marine equivalent of a giant slug. He raised the sea hares for Howard Hughes Medical Institute where the animals were used for neurological research. Hughes built their own Aplysia lab in 1988 and the contract with Mike was terminated. Mike and Gay shut things down and went to Australia for two years to dive and travel about.

When they returned in June of 1990, Mike started collecting for hobbyist's tanks with two partners. They called their business "California Reef Specialists." They advertised in aquarium magazines, and published and sold books on how to keep aquariums. They also sold chillers and aquariums, and went to trade/pet shows across the country. To set up a basic cold water aquarium with a chiller runs about $2,000.00.

When the recession hit it became difficult to sell big ticket, luxury items like home aquariums. Recent legislation has also made it difficult to sell to hobbyists. Tropical tank enthusiasts are now purchasing chillers to keep the temperature of their aquariums at about 75 degrees. Corals can't tolerate the high temperatures generated in heated tanks with lights.

Mike's main customers today are universities and educational institutions. He dives 1 – 2 days a week, and has a diving buddy, but most of his diving is done alone in depths less than 70 feet. The majority of his diving is done at 40 feet. Since Mike only collects invertebrates, they're usually found in shallow water.

Mike tries to avoid decompression diving. He uses the Navy tables and doesn't use a dive computer. Despite the cold water in Monterey he wears a wetsuit.

Mike collects his invertebrates by hand and puts them in net bags for transportation. He uses a knife when removing anemones from the rocks. He has a 19 foot fiberglass skiff that he uses for diving.

Sea Life Supply occupies 2,000 sq. feet of space in Mike and Gay's home. Since he does not have a saltwater pipeline, once a week Mike takes a large trailer–mounted tank down to the harbor to fill it with fresh sea water for his animals.

Mike enjoys the fact that diving is part of his business. He likes being self employed and interacting with scientists. Financially it has been good, and you make more being in business for yourself. Mike has a good feeling about what he does. It's a public service providing resources to schools.

Despite his love for diving, even Mike doesn't like to dive when the ocean is rough and the weather nasty. However, when you have orders to fill, you can't wait for optimum conditions. Mike is not pleased with the California Dept. of Fish and Game's newly enacted regulations governing collecting for the aquarium trade. He attended meetings on his own time and expense to give input on the development of these regulations. There were many interest groups involved and it was hard to produce a document that would protect the state's resources and not put undue hardships on the aquarium trade collectors.

Mike's advice to people considering this career is that it's a difficult business. There are only a few animals that you can make a living selling. Research labs are more concerned about a reliable supply of animals then price and it's difficult to establish a business relationship with them. Schools don't have money for specimens anymore. If Mike and Gay weren't also selling equipment they'd have a difficult time staying in business. A significant part of their business is the research labs.

Suggested Reading:

Steinbeck, John. *The Log From the Sea of Cortez.* The Viking Press, New York. 1971

Ricketts, E. and Calvin, J. Revised by Hedgpeth, J. *Between Pacific Tides.* Stanford University Press, Stanford, CA. 1968.

CHAPTER FIFTEEN

DIVING EQUIPMENT MANUFACTURING: IN-HOUSE POSITIONS & SALES REPRESENTATIVES

Diving equipment manufacturers employ many divers in a wide variety of interesting and challenging positions. Manufacturers need engineers who are divers to design equipment, and salespeople who are divers to talk to customers. Successful manufacturers have discovered that even their marketing people are more productive when they have a diving background. Independent sales representatives may work for a variety of diving equipment manufacturers, receiving commissions on sales from each product line they sell.

Training Required to Work for Equipment Manufacturers

Given the wide variety of jobs involved in the equipment end of the diving industry, it's impossible to suggest a single general path to prepare yourself for a job in this field. You must decide which area you want to become involved in and prepare yourself accordingly.

Some manufacturers, like U.S. Divers Co., Inc., use in-house sales representatives to service their dealers. Their logic is that they do not want their representatives to have divided loyalties. Many smaller manufacturers cannot afford to have full time sales representatives and instead make use of independent outside sales reps. Other manufacturers, like Diving Unlimited Intnl., make use of a combination of inside sales personnel and independent outside "reps."

To be successful as a sales rep does not require any formal training, although in today's highly competitive environment it is becoming increasingly more difficult to be successful without some form of education. At a minimum, you should have some training in sales. Additionally it is helpful if you also have knowledge of marketing, advertising, and "*demographics,*" the study of consumer profiles and behavior. Although it is not essential to be proficient in these areas, the more abilities you have, the more valuable you will be to the companies who employ you.

The position of sales manager for a diving equipment manufacturer is normally a full-time, in-house position. Sales managers not only must be knowledgeable about sales, they also must understand marketing and have the people skills to manage a sales force. All the sales representatives in a company will usually report to a single sales manager.

While in the past most of the presidents and senior executives in diving equipment companies were divers who learned the business from the bottom up, today's new managers usually have solid business backgrounds. Many even have Masters' degrees in Business Administration (MBA's). The ideal background for a senior executive in the diving industry today would include extensive experience in diving, a scuba instructor's rating, practical experience working in dive stores, a Bachelor's degree in Business, and a Master's degree in Business Administration.

Fig. 15.1 – The manufacture and sale of diving equipment has become highly competitive. The climax of the annual sales efforts of most companies takes place at annual industry trade shows, such as the DEMA (Diving Equipment Manufacturer's Association) show. This is the Sherwood exhibit from a recent DEMA show.

Marketing is a separate area that is distinct from sales, although most diving equipment manufacturers are too small to have separate sales and marketing departments. The function of marketing is to educate the consumer, to make them familiar with the company's products, and to help them select products from the company when they are finally ready to buy. Conversely, the function of the sales department is to complete the sale when contact is made with the customer. While sales and marketing should complement each other, they are quite different things.

Working in marketing requires a good background in consumer psychology. You must understand why divers behave the way they do and what motivates them to buy a particular product. People who work in marketing must be effective communicators, and must have the ability to write. They should understand graphic arts and photography. Marketing people should be able to work with designers and advertising agencies in the development of advertising materials.

Fig. 15.2 – Electronics have become very important in diving. This technician is testing a dive computer at Oceanic's plant in San Leandro, California.

If you want to design diving equipment, you should be an engineer with a background in diving to understand the demands made on gear that must operate in a variety of underwater environments under harsh conditions. Much of the diving gear that we use today was designed by divers with no formal engineering background, but this is becoming increasingly rare.

The new breed of diving engineer must have both the ability to dive and the ability to utilize the most sophisticated computer assisted drafting (CAD) programs. Without a practical background in diving it is easy to design equipment that won't work in the marine environment. For example, it is possible for engineers to design equipment parts that have threads that are too fine for operation in salt water. Corrosion or salt deposits can make it impossible to remove fine threaded screws or nuts for maintenance or repair of dive gear.

One of the most important aspects in the engineering of diving equipment is human factors engineering or "*ergonomics.*" This is an interdisciplinary field that combines elements of physiology, psychology, statistics, and engineering. The human factors specialist participates in the design team to design diving equipment that is user friendly and ergonomically correct. For example, a human factors specialist would evaluate a new weight belt buckle design to ensure that the buckle is equally easy to operate in both warm water and under ice diving conditions while wearing three finger mitts.

Electronics are becoming more important in diving gear all the time, and the ability to design electronic equipment for diving is extremely valuable. It has been a short time from the introduction of the first electronic dive computer, the EDGE, back in the 80's, to the wide proliferation of dive computers available today. To successfully design and market a diving computer requires a team of people who understand diving, mathematics, diving physiology, electronics, machining, human engineering, marketing, and sales.

The Job of the Sales Representatives and Managers

Whether a sales representative works full-time for a single diving equipment manufacturer, or as an independent, their job is much the same. The best salespeople have a passion for their products and have an excellent understanding of how they are used.

Even if you are selling excellent products, it's essential as a sales representative to get out and see the dealers in your region. While sales visits are expensive, in terms of both out-of-pocket expenses and time, there really is no substitute for the personal touch of a knowledgeable sales representative.

As a sales representative you must be able to talk to dive store owners, dive store employees, and customers. The concerns of each of these groups of people can be quite different. When a new product is presented to a dive store owner, his concerns will probably include the profit margin on the product, how well the product will sell, how quickly the manufacturer can ship, what sort of credit terms are available from the manufacturer, whether the manufacturer has product liability insurance, and how well the manufacturer will stand behind its warranties. The sales representative must be ready with the answers to these questions and more.

The employees of the dive store may have a different set of concerns than the store owner in examining a new product. They are more likely to be concerned with how to sell the product and present it to the customers, how it interfaces with other equipment, and how to instruct the customers in the use of the product. In this situation, the sale representative must be prepared to train the store personnel in the right way to present the product to consumers. The rep may also be expected to have the ability to train the store personnel in minor or complete repairs.

Frequently, manufacturer's reps will be asked to make appearances or assist at special seminars or sales at a local dealer's store. In these circumstances the representative must be able to talk knowledgeably with avid divers who may be as well informed about certain diving products as the rep. In these situations, you are seen as a direct representative of the company, and the manufacturer's image is your responsibility.

If you are an independent sales rep your income will be based solely upon commissions from your sales. Most independent reps work on an 8% sales commission. It is essential to track your sales to measure your success and to ensure that you have been properly reimbursed by the companies you represent.

Probably the most difficult part of working as an independent sales rep is securing enough product lines to make a comfortable living. As an independent rep, none of your product lines can compete with each other. For example, if you represent a line of buoyancy compensators like Zeagle, you would be unable to also represent a line like Dacor, who manufactures their own buoyancy compensators. You would have to find "complimentary lines," such as a specialized wetsuit manufacturer and a specialized regulator manufacturer.

Most independent sales representatives work out of their homes, rather than maintaining a separate, off-site office. You will probably need to outfit a complete home office to work effectively. At a minimum you will probably want a separate business phone line and a fax machine. As your business grows you will probably find that you need a home computer, a printer, file cabinets, and a copy machine. If you spend a great deal of time on the road, a cellular phone is indispensable to keep in touch with your dealers and family.

As an independent sales representative all your expenses are your own. Generally speaking, none of the manufacturers will provide you with any support other than your sales commission. If you have a family to support, working as an independent rep can be difficult. As

Fig. 15.3 – Sales representative Jon Hayes checks out a new product at Oceanic USA's warehouse.

an independent you have no health benefits or retirement benefits, and must give serious thought to setting up programs to take care of these matters on your own.

Not everyone is capable of working as an independent sales representative. To work at this kind of job you must be self-motivated, since the only income you make will come from the equipment you sell. Many people cannot live with this uncertainty and the fluctuations in their income.

In-house sales representatives may work in either telemarketing, outside sales, or some combination of both. Depending on the size of the company you work for, you may work on some combination of salary plus commission, straight commission, or straight salary. However, in-house reps normally have the benefits of supplied office space and equipment, health benefits, and retirement.

Sales managers will normally have several sales representatives who report to them, and may also have a telemarketing crew as well. The sales manager must coordinate with the marketing department, and will also normally interface with engineering, accounting, production, and top management.

The sales manager will typically be responsible for developing sales forecasts, analysis, budgets, and managing the staffing of both trade and consumer shows. At the big diving trade shows, like the Diving Equipment Manufacturer's Show, or "DEMA," manufacturers meet with dealers to write orders and sign up new dealers. At consumer shows, like *Beneath the Seas* in New York or the annual *Scuba* show put on by *California Diving News,* manufacturers display their newest equipment to consumers and provide support to their dealers.

Fig. 15.4 – The marketing department makes predictions about how many products will be sold, so that manufacturing doesn't produce too many products. These buoyancy compensators are undergoing final assembly at Oceanic USA.

Marketing Diving Equipment

The marketing department of a major scuba equipment manufacturer can be a very busy place. In addition to developing advertisements, ads must be scheduled and tracked to monitor the response to them. There are also the responsibilities of producing an annual catalog, developing promotional films, working with independent photographers and film makers, producing point of purchase displays, and creating a wide variety of promotional literature and photographs.

When producing a catalog or ad, the marketing manager must ensure that all products and equipment are portrayed correctly and project the image that the company wants to show to the diving public. It's unreasonable to assume that you can hand over your products to an outside advertising agency or photographer and they will know how to show your products to best advantage. Similarly, even if your company uses outside writers to develop product literature, the marketing manager must be familiar with the products to ensure the copy is technically correct. This knowledge is best developed by diving with the equipment.

Efficient marketing managers know that they must leverage every advertising dollar to make their company successful. This means that the company should be sending out a steady stream of press releases, photographs, and promotional articles.

One of the most important responsibilities of the marketing manager is to develop an annual marketing plan. The marketing plan is a road map that outlines how the company will market their products each year.

To write an effective marketing plan, you must have an intimate knowledge of the diving business. You must understand all the factors that influence the market and be able to predict what changes will take place. For example, with the profusion of electronics in diving, it is not difficult to foresee that electronics will be integrated with regulators and buoyancy compensators. The trick will be to predict how these innovations will change the way we dive, and what influence they will have on equipment sales.

Writing a marketing plan also means that you must be able to take a wider view and look at other factors that will ultimately influence recreation and lifestyles. How will changes in the price and availability of petroleum affect the price of gasoline, diving equipment, and air travel? How will changes in the air travel industry affect dive travel? How will environmental changes affect the quality of diving in popular diving locations? The wise marketing manager takes into consideration as many factors as possible in their decision making process.

In the highly competitive scuba equipment manufacturing business, getting close to the customer is essential. A good marketing manager knows that it is essential to develop a high level of customer service. You must respond promptly to customer inquiries, so that there is little delay between the time a customer requests product literature and the time they receive it.

Marketing managers must be experienced in database management. This is essential to tracking the demographics of your customers. It is difficult to know how to conduct an advertising campaign without knowing the demographics of your customer base. By constructing a computer database, it is possible to track and analyze large amounts of information. Customer information from warranty cards and product inquiries can be fed into the database. The database can rapidly calculate such information as the average age of your customers, the percentage of males and females, and the types of diving your customers enjoy.

Designing Diving Equipment

Developing new diving equipment is one of the biggest challenges in the scuba equipment business. Most manufacturers are constantly looking for new and innovative products to maintain a competitive edge. For every new product that makes it to market, there are literally hundreds that never are manufactured.

When you work full time for a diving equipment manufacturer as a design engineer you must be a team player. Although you may have personal ideas about how a piece of equipment should be designed, you must be open and sensitive to input from the marketing and sales departments regarding customer needs and wants.

It's possible to design a great piece of diving equipment that is too expensive to manufacture, or too costly or difficult to maintain. Most of the equipment you find in the dive store today is designed in the U.S., but the tooling and parts are made overseas, usually in Taiwan. The cost to build molds and to mold the parts is much lower overseas than in the U.S.

As a diving equipment designer, you must be a very competent diver, particularly if you test dive new equipment. Even if you are a good engineer, it is always possible for a new piece of equipment to fail.

Fig. 15.5 – Skip Dunham, president of Diving Systems International, a manufacturer of commercial diving helmets, works with the company's product design engineers and test dives new products. (Photo by Steven M. Barsky, © Diving Systems International. All rights reserved.)

Generally speaking, anything you design while employed by a diving equipment company becomes the property of that company, even if you design it on your own time. This means that the manufacturer will hold the "*patent*" on the product. The patent is the manufacturer's right to produce that product, and affords them protection from other manufacturers who would try to copy it.

Working as a design engineer for a manufacturer is quite demanding. The hours are frequently long and these positions are usually salaried with no overtime compensation.

It is also possible to work as an independent equipment designer and design and test dive equipment on your own. Many diving equipment manufacturers purchase the manufacturing rights to new pieces of equipment from independent designers on a regular basis. In most cases, the designer holds the patent and the manufacturer licenses the right to produce the equipment.

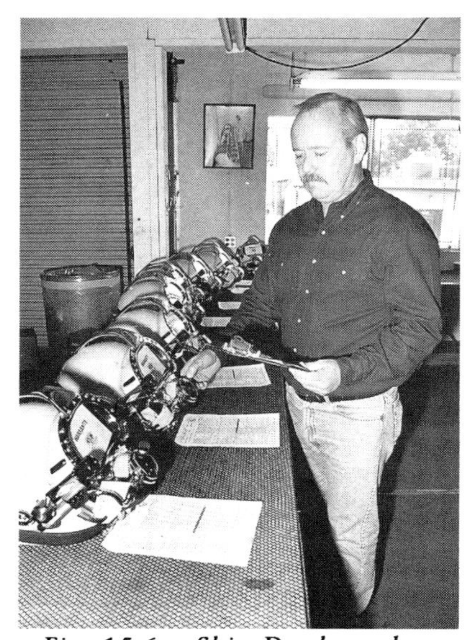

Fig. 15.6 – Skip Dunham does the final inspection on a batch of new diving helmets that are ready for shipment. Each helmet is thoroughly tested to ensure proper performance.

It can be difficult to get started as an independent designer, since most manufacturers want to see a working prototype of any piece of gear before they will commit to produce it. In addition, it is quite expensive to secure your own patents.

Another pitfall of working as an independent equipment designer is dealing with product liability. If your product proves defective in design and leads to accidents, the manufacturer may try to recover their financial damages from you. Once the product is licensed to the manufacturer, you will generally have very little to say about how the product is manufactured or marketed. If the manufacturer does a shoddy job of producing the product, your reputation as a designer may suffer along with their reputation as a company.

Experiences of Sales Reps in the Diving Industry

RON RUSSELL

One of the most successful independent sales representatives in the diving industry is Ron Russell, who represents Zeagle Systems, Body Glove®, Viking, Force Fins®, and several other lines. Ron has worked in the diving business since 1986 and is highly respected in the industry. He works out of his home in the Seattle area and covers the entire Pacific coast for most of his lines.

Ron started diving in 1970 at the University of California at Santa Cruz where he was studying biology. After graduating from school he held several different jobs including working for West Marine, a major distributor of equipment and supplies for boaters.

Ron met Jim Wittstruck, another Zeagle sales rep, through a chance encounter at a dive shop in California. Zeagle was a relatively new line in 1986, and their buoyancy compensators were quite different from most of the other models available then. Wittstruck introduced Ron to Zeagle's management, who negotiated an agreement with Ron to represent their products in the California market. Shortly after that Ron took on the Poseidon and Denizen lines.

Fig. 15.7 – Ron Russell is one of the most successful sales representatives on the west coast of the U.S.

Ron makes a real effort to help his dealers see how they can run their businesses more efficiently and more profitably . He makes an extra effort to understand the viewpoint of the dealers and help them in any way possible. "Just knowing about diving or diving equipment is not enough," observes Ron.

As an independent "rep," Ron enjoys a tremendous amount of freedom to structure his work as he sees fit. This doesn't mean that he doesn't work hard; it just means that he has some flexibility in scheduling his work. In addition to writing orders and making sales calls, Ron actually helps his manufacturers develop their marketing materials. He has participated in the production of numerous catalogs and promotional materials. There are few independent reps who put in as much effort as Ron.

One of the things that Ron enjoys most about his work are the interesting people he meets in the diving business. He also notes that most years he is able to make a better than average living through his sales as a rep.

Ron finds that one of the negative aspects of being an independent rep is the extensive amount of travel that the job requires. There is also a certain amount of insecurity in his job, since he is dependent upon the "pleasure" of the manufacturers to maintain his representation of a given line. "Even if you do an outstanding job for a manufacturer, it's still possible that you can lose an important line through politics or other unforeseeable circumstances," says Ron.

JON HAYES

Jon Hayes has been with Oceanic since 1975. Through a chance meeting with Bob Hollis, president of Oceanic, Jon landed a job with the company which has grown steadily since that time. He learned to dive as part of his job.

Hayes started out doing telephone sales for the first few years he was with Oceanic. As the company grew and orders increased, more salespeople were added. Currently Jon is responsible for sales in California, one of the largest diving markets in the U.S.

Having a good product makes Jon's work very enjoyable. He finds dealing with the people in the industry, particularly his dealers, is usually very enjoyable and interesting. Working for Oceanic is fun for Jon because the company is very innovative and always developing new ideas.

Jon finds the negative aspects of being a sales rep are dealing with credit problems and collections. As a rep, he sets his own hours and sometimes finds himself working more hours than he would like due to the demands of the job. It's also unpleasant dealing with competing manufacturers who offer deep discounts as they attempt to win business away from Oceanic.

Jon's advice to a person who wants to work for a diving equipment manufacturer is to get as much knowledge of the company's products as possible. If you have experience as a dive store employee or an instructor this is advantageous, but not essential. As in many other professions, most people can learn to dive, but not everyone can be effective as a salesperson. You must have the ability to sell, and you must enjoy it to do well in sales.

Experiences of Engineers in the Diving Industry

MARK WALSH

Mark Walsh is a product engineer with the Dacor Corporation in Illinois. He started diving in 1962 as a result of his participation in competitive swimming and after watching the program *Sea Hunt* on television. He was 14 years old when he was first certified.

Upon graduation from high school, Mark enlisted in the Navy and went through UDT/SEAL training (see chapter 12 for more information on this type of diving). He learned to use closed circuit rebreathers and attended Second Class Diver's School before he left the service. At Second Class school he trained in the use of surface supplied diving gear.

After leaving the military, he became a PADI instructor and enrolled at Northeastern Illinois University where he received his Bachelor's of science degree in Ocean Technology in 1974. While attending college, he also set up the University's recreational and scientific diving programs. His course work included a heavy emphasis on physics, earth sciences, and math. He also attended graduate school where he took some engineering courses.

When he finished college, Mark sent out 185 resumes and got two responses back; one was from the Lockheed Ocean Systems Lab and the other was from Northrop Services, Inc. At the time, both of these space oriented companies were involved in major ocean engineering projects for the military. The jobs Mark was offered were excellent. He credits his naval experience in helping him get his foot in the door.

Mark made the decision to work for Northrop and worked as a systems engineer on a design review of the Navy MK I mask (based on the Kirby-Morgan band mask). He worked on the MK 12 surface supplied helmet, and the MK 14 Push-Pull system that was designed to recover the diver's exhaust gas when breathing helium-oxygen mixtures. He also developed the maintenance, operation, and emergency procedures for the Navy's Deep Diving System.

One of the keys to Mark's success was that throughout his career Mark had the advantage of having "mentors," experienced people in the industry who took an unselfish interest in his career. He discovered that the diving industry is so small that he would eventually cross paths with the same people over and over again. He realized the importance of maintaining good relationships throughout the industry.

In 1975 Mark went to work for Ocean Systems, Inc. (OSI), an early leader in the development of deep saturation diving techniques. When he joined Ocean Systems they had deep diving systems and a handful of submersibles scattered across the world. Mark worked as the Safety and Training Coordinator, and reviewed the decompression procedures for every dive made, whether it was on air or mixed gas. While at OSI he met Dr. Chris Lambertsen, a diving physician, who became one of Mark's mentors.

Mark's next job was with Comex Marine Services, Inc., the French diving company, where he had the position of Operations Manager for North America. As he puts it, they "made him an offer he couldn't refuse." Mark negotiated with Pemex, the Mexican national oil company, and Comex got the first two contracts for the Bay of Campeche off the coast of Mexico.

Fig. 15.8 – Mark Walsh was the chief designer of the Omni Pro®, Dacor's air integrated computer.

Mark left Comex to try his hand at independent consulting, and did that successfully for two years. He consulted to several commercial diving companies, and wrote a manual for Chicago Bridge and Iron, a diving contractor in the midwest, to help them meet OSHA (Occupational Safety and Health Act) standards.

Coming full circle, back to sport diving, Mark was hired by Dacor in 1979. He had been sending them resumes since 1974. He signed on as a design engineer, and his first project was the Vista mask, which represented the first new generation of masks for Dacor. In the time he has been at Dacor he estimates that he has had some involvement with at least 65% of their product line.

Mark was very close to the late Sam Davison, a true diving pioneer and the founder of Dacor. To Mark, Davison was an advisor and friend, besides being his employer. Mark tells an interesting story to explain his relationship with Sam Davison.

"His (Davison's) expectations were high and praise did not come often. In 1984 he approached me to navigate a working cruise through the Bahamas on the DACOR DIVER (the company boat). For weeks ahead we laid out courses that would lead us from Florida to a final destination on Great Exuma. He insisted that during the trip I would act as navigator only and not touch the helm. To say that there were a few tense moments between us would be an understatement. That trip brought us closer together than one could imagine. We returned home with a mutual respect not previously known. The years passed in this spirit.

Although his health was declining, Sam chose to continue working. Just prior to his death, Sam sent his son Jeff to pre-

sent me with a prized possession. Placed into my hands was a World War II sextant that Sam wanted me to have. Silent emotions swept over me as I realized the impact of this gesture. I thanked Sam and shortly he was gone. The memory of our relationship lives forever."

For the past five years Mark's principal responsibility has been the design of Dacor's dive computers and other instrumentation. He is the chief designer of the Omni Pro®, Dacor's air integrated computer.

Designing diving equipment that makes "sense" is one of the things that Mark likes the most about working at Dacor. He enjoys testing equipment that he has developed in a wide variety of environments, especially under demanding conditions. "We test in both fresh and salt water, under the ice, and in wreck diving situations," explains Mark.

Working with dive computers gives Mark a sense of "deja vu," since many of the people who are developing the algorithms for today's computers were involved in the development of the decompression tables for commercial diving. He enjoys attending industry workshops on dive computers and meeting with many of the people who were his mentors. "The camaraderie at these events is great. With my background I'm both a participant and a contributor at these gatherings," says Mark.

As materials change, Mark finds an ever increasing challenge to develop new equipment. "A lot of the ideas that we are looking at now are really old ideas that couldn't work in the past. Now that the material has caught up, we have the chance to make many of these ideas into products. The challenge is still there," declares Mark, " and there is no way to get bored with this job."

Mark finds the frustrating part of his job is the difficulty in bringing new products to the market. He admits, "There are so many things in making a piece of equipment work properly – the environment, dealing with suppliers, and numerous other factors – that it can be very discouraging at times."

Engineering can also be tedious, especially when you consider the amount of paperwork involved. "You must work by the book and keep good records," Mark declares, "because if something occurs down the road you've got to be able to explain why. We are working with life support equipment and we have more responsibility than when you are working with non-life support gear."

To be a good diving equipment designer you've also got to be a good diver. Mark notes the importance of developing your skills at a pace where you can absorb what you've learned so that you're not just "collecting badges." On the academic side, he advises attending a college prep program that will gear you up for the sciences, including the earth sciences and environmental science.

"You need to appreciate where the gear will be used," explains Mark, "what effect the environment will have on the gear and what effect the gear will have on the environment."

Mark strongly believes in the mentor system and that you must serve your apprenticeship as you develop your career. You should learn what you can from the people who have the experience in diving. He observes, "Many of our mentors are starting to retire, and once they are gone you won't be able to access them." Some of the other people who have had a strong influence on Mark's career include Jim Stewart, former diving officer at Scripps Institution of Oceanography, and Dr. Glen Egstrom, retired diving researcher from UCLA.

BOB STINTON

Fig. 15.9 – Bob Stinton is vice president and general manager of Diving Unlimited Intnl., and is still heavily involved in the engineering end of the company.

Bob Stinton is vice president and general manager of Diving Unlimited International, Inc. (DUI), one of the world's largest manufacturers of dry suits and accessories. While Bob has many responsibilities at DUI, he has been mostly involved with engineering there. He has a degree in manufacturing engineering and holds six patents for projects he developed with Dick Long, president of the company.

Bob started snorkeling, like many divers, after watching the television program *Sea Hunt* in 1963. In 1964 when he was 14, he built a surface supplied diving "system" with his brother. The "system" consisted of a lawn edger motor, a paint spray compressor, a garden hose, and a mask with built-in snorkels. The garden hose was connected to the snorkel so the diver could breathe. Bob and his brother put the whole system on a small wooden boat built by his brother and the two of them went diving.

By coincidence, Bob took his first scuba lessons at the age of 15 from Dick Long, who became his lifelong friend, collaborator, and employer. At the time, Long owned a dive store that was called Skin Diving Unlimited. Bob started helping with classes, volunteering his time in trade for boat trips to go diving.

When Bob graduated from high school he went into the Navy as a hospital corpsman. Following his honorable discharge, he went to work full time for Dick Long. Initially he was responsible for the care and maintenance of all the dive gear in the shop's extensive rental and training inventory.

In 1973, Bob became a diving instructor and moved into government sales. Skin Diving Unlimited manufactured custom wetsuits and did extensive business with the Navy in San Diego. Eventually the name of the company was changed from Skin Diving Unlimited to Diving Unlimited International.

When Dick Long came up with the concept for the hot water suit for commercial diving, Bob became involved with the sales and training for these systems. He also participated heavily in the design and test diving of each new generation of hot water system. He went to France in 1974 to train their Navy in the use of the hot water system in preparation for their 900 foot deep dive.

Bob took over manufacturing for DUI in 1975, and in 1977 began to devote himself full-time to research and development. He spent 100% of his time on government funded research. Bob would write the research proposal, get the money, and do the project.

Some of the projects Bob has helped develop under patent at DUI include the following:

> *NRV Hot Water Suit: This is a unique hot water suit that has a special valve system. In most hot water suits, if the diver loses his hot water supply, for any reason, the hot water just flushes out of the suit and the diver gets chilled very quickly. In the NRV (Non-Return Valve) model, the suit can be sealed by the diver, using a special valve in the suit, to trap the hot water inside. This gives the diver enough time to get back to the diving bell safely.*

CF200 Material: CF200 material is a crushed neoprene material that is made under a special process that is unique to DUI. The material is used to make DUI's CF200 dry suit, waterproof bags for the military, and other products. DUI is the only company that uses this durable, yet flexible material.

Dry Suit Seams: This is a special double folded seam process that helps ensure the watertight integrity of DUI dry suits.

Self-Donning Dry Suit: Bob developed the self-donning suit originally to allow a military diver to wear a shoulder holster under a dry suit. The design permits access to the diver's weapon when they're topside and the suit is unzipped. Self-donning dry suits have become extremely popular with sport divers, because they can be put on without assistance.

Weight and Trim System: The Weight and Trim system is similar to a commercial diver's weight harness, but the similarity ends there. The system allows a diver to quickly change the amount of weight carried, and the weights can be ditched through a quick release. The diver has complete control of where the weights are positioned on his torso, allowing for perfect adjustment of trim underwater.

Low Friction Seal: This is a unique type of dry suit seal that offers watertight integrity, but makes the suit easy to don.

In 1990 Bob was promoted to general manager, and in 1991 he assumed responsibilities for sales and was promoted to vice president. Because DUI is a small company, Bob is still intensely involved with the engineering aspects of all new products.

Bob likes the people in the diving industry, and the fact that everyone in it shares a common interest. For people in diving, "*shop talk*" is also recreational talk.

"The sea is the last remaining frontier on earth, but it has all the same problems as space travel. Yet we can go to the beach, 20 minutes from home, and have a true adventure. As divers, we are pioneers," observes Bob.

Bob makes approximately 100 dives a year, although some years he has made as many as 300 dives. His lifetime total is well in excess of 5000 dives.

If you want to work in the engineering end of the diving industry, Bob warns that it can be very tough for a new person to get started. You will frequently have to start at the bottom.

"As an engineer you can make a lot more money in other places, but in diving you have the opportunity to be a pioneer," says Bob.

Experiences of Sales Executives in the Diving Industry

UTE PACKI

Ute Packi is the sales manager for JBL Enterprises, Inc., a manufacturer of spearguns, pole spears, and other diving accessories. She first came to the United States from Germany, at the age of 19, with a background in accounting and bookkeeping.

Ute's first job in the diving industry was with Healthways, an early manufacturer of sport diving equipment. She started with Healthways in 1967 as Export Manager and remained there until 1975. Healthways was an early manufacturer of single hose regulators.

Ute wasn't diving when she worked for Healthways, due to the multiple demands of her job, her marriage, and her two children. She didn't learn to dive until her daughter, who is her youngest child, was old enough to be certified. Then the whole family participated in the sport. When her daughter turned 12 and was certified in 1983, Ute also learned to dive. Today she dives regularly in the Caribbean and California.

Fig. 15.10 – Ute Packi is the sales manager for JBL Enterprises, Inc. (Photo © Joe Packi)

After leaving Healthways in 1975, Ute joined Seatec and handled both military and international sales. The people at Seatec would kid her in a good natured way. They said they could always tell when she was coming down the hall, since she was the only person who ran everywhere she went. The sound of her high heels racing through the building was distinctive.

In 1988 Ute left Seatec and started working as an independent sales representative. Initially she handled Choice Swimsuits, Sierra Scuba, JBL, and Diving Star. A year later, JBL asked her to manage their domestic sales, which was a new challenge to her. To understand their business better, she also took on the domestic territory of Oregon, Washington, and Utah. She traveled through this territory for several years before turning it over to another sales rep.

Under Ute's direction, JBL's sales have grown every year, despite the negative press spearfishing has received in recent years. She manages a sales organization for JBL that includes ten sales representatives. Her husband Joe, who retired as an engineer with the telephone company and took a second career in diving, is one of JBL's reps.

To communicate with her reps Ute sends out a sales letter at least once a month. The letter helps keep them informed of changes in the company and the market. While she runs her personal rep business out of an office in her home, she travels to the JBL office at least once a week. Today, in addition to JBL, she handles export sales for Diving Star and Zeagle buoyancy compensators, and domestic sales for Danicorp, a supplier of high pressure and low pressure hoses for diving equipment manufacturers.

Ute conducts most of her business via the phone and fax machine, although she travels extensively and has many customers visit her at her home. Her travels take her to the annual International Sporting Goods Show (ISPO) in Munich, Germany, and to the Caribbean each year. She has also been to Australia, New Zealand, Fiji, the Far East, and Puerto Rico as part of her job.

Ute credits much of her success to the personal relationships she has developed over her many years in the industry. She has been doing business with some of her customers for over 20 years and they have followed her from line to line with her career changes. They do business with her based primarily on this relationship, and because she provides a very high level of service to her clients. She makes a point of being available to them 24 hours a day and frequently takes calls for customer orders even on weekends.

As an example of her personal relationships, Ute cites a customer, Dave Evans, from Fiji, who first contacted her in 1967 when he was "just a diver" and editor of the newspaper, the *Fiji Sun.* Evans sent Ute $3.00 with an order for parts for his Healthways regulator because he didn't know what they would cost. The $3.00 didn't begin to cover the cost of the parts, but Ute sent them anyway, rather than run the risk of alienating the customer. Since that time Evans has opened a dive shop that has become the largest one in Fiji, and he buys heavily from Ute.

Ute has been married for 27 years to her husband Joe, who has provided the support that made Ute's career possible. Both Joe and her children made the sacrifices necessary to support her as a career "mom." Joe even took vacation time from his job to enable Ute to make many business trips.

To give something back to her community, Ute has been active in many different service organizations. These include the local Parent/Teachers Association in Orange County where she lives, Women in Sales, and the International Marketing Association .

Ute's advice for someone who wants to work in sales management is to get to know the company you work for as completely as possible. Realize that you will put in 10-12 hours a day, and that you must have drive and ambition to make this work.

SCOTT MCINTYRE

Scott McIntyre is the Vice President of Sales at Oceanic USA. Scott grew up in a family that was in the retail business, and earned a Bachelor's degree in Advertising Journalism in 1985. His minor was in marketing.

Scott earned his scuba certification in 1985, although he had been diving in Mexico every year for the previous ten years. His sister was a diver, and it was her influence that got him interested in the sport. Scott's family made frequent trips to Mexico, and the warm waters there provided the right environment to stimulate his interest in diving.

After graduating from college Scott worked for a large retail distribution firm, before moving on to a marketing and consulting group in Scottsdale, Arizona. When the marketing group decided to move to the San Francisco Bay area in 1989, Scott went along as the vice president.

Before the year was over, Scott was looking for a career change. He had been on the outside of the companies he consulted to, and felt it was time to work from the inside. He wanted to be involved with a company that manufactured consumer products. He also wanted to

Fig. 15.11 – Scott McIntyre discusses sales with sales representative Jon Hayes and customers at the DEMA trade show.

be closer to the retail end of distribution. After evaluating many firms in the food, toy, and software industry, Scott had found nothing that interested him. Finally, he realized that he wanted to work in an industry that was related to something that he enjoyed doing.

McIntyre began investigating the diving industry in an attempt to distinguish those companies that might be good to work for and could use his talents. He quickly identified Oceanic and sent a letter to Bob Hollis, president and CEO of the company. Initially he sent Hollis a letter, but no resume. After meeting Hollis on several occasions, Scott was hired to join the Oceanic team.

When Scott was first hired by Oceanic his starting position was "Special Projects Manager." In this job he evaluated several different markets for the company, particularly the wetsuit market. He also analyzed the internal structure of the company.

After his first year at Oceanic, Scott was promoted to Executive Director of Sales and Marketing. During this time, he became heavily involved in Oceanic's export sales. In 1991 Scott was promoted to Vice President of Sales at Oceanic. In his present position he has numerous responsibilities, including management of domestic and export sales, sales administration, and co-management of customer service. He reports directly to Bob Hollis.

Scott likes meeting with retailers and looking at how they approach the diving business in their area. He enjoys helping them with their problems.

Because Oceanic is a small company, each person is involved with many different things. For example, Scott participates in the test dives of each new product before it is released. As Scott puts it, "Oceanic is a hands-on company."

Scott doesn't enjoy the political environment of the diving industry, and would like to see a more cooperative effort between all the stakeholders in the business. While he realizes that this is improving, he still recognizes that the industry has a ways to go.

"Anybody who feels that there is any glamour in this business better look for something else to do," recommends Scott. His hours are long, with weekends frequently devoted to trade shows and travel.

McIntyre's advice to anyone thinking about working in sales management in the diving industry is to get either an educational or practical background before you enter the business. "This isn't a situation where you can learn as you go," he warns. "There is no buffer between you and the marketplace. You must know what you are doing, either from education or experience. You must come in with something to offer."

Experiences of a Company President in the Diving Industry

SKIP DUNHAM

Skip Dunham is the president of Diving Systems International (DSI), the largest manufacturer of commercial diving masks and helmets in the world. DSI manufactures a variety of products that are used by professional divers in military, scientific, public safety and commercial diving.

In 1967 Skip had just returned to Los Angeles from duty in the Navy. Upon his return Skip felt that Los Angeles had become crowded enough that he wanted to leave and live somewhere else in California. After a weekend trip to Santa Barbara, he quit his job in Los Angeles and moved there without a clear view of how he would support himself and his wife, or what their future would hold.

Skip went from business to business and pounded on doors seeking work. Through chance he landed a job with a small company known as the Kirby-Morgan Corporation, that was building a special mixed gas helmet known as the "Clamshell" for the Navy and SeaLab III. The company was also making heavy gear helmets and a lightweight fiberglass full face mask known as the KMB-6, or Kirby-Morgan Band Mask #6.

The Kirby-Morgan Corporation was run by two commercial divers, Bev Morgan and Bob Kirby. Morgan was a former lifeguard and helped found the Los Angeles County scuba instructor's program with the late Ramsey Parks and Al Tillman. Kirby had been a Navy diver and an abalone diver. Together they have

Fig. 15.12 – Skip Dunham writes up an order for an EXO-26® full face mask for a customer at Diving Systems International.

invented more commercial diving masks and helmets than anyone else in modern times.

In the early days of the Kirby-Morgan Corporation, Skip worked in all phases of production of the helmets and masks, including fabrication and assembly. It was a busy time for the company as the offshore oil industry was booming.

Skip learned to dive during his first year with Kirby-Morgan. Morgan was still diving commercially at this time, and Skip would go out as a tender on commercial diving jobs with him. Skip and Bev continued to do commercial work on the side until the end of 1973. This commercial experience gave Skip the knowledge to understand how the company's products were being used and the demands made on the equipment in the commercial field. He made many working dives with the band mask during this period.

In 1969 Kirby and Morgan sold the product line to U.S. Divers Co., who also purchased the name "Kirby-Morgan." Kirby and Morgan formed a new company, Deepwater Development, that was the same company with all the same people. U.S. Divers paid a royalty to Kirby and Morgan and bought their engineering time and expertise. Skip continued to work for Deepwater Development.

In 1975 Kirby and Morgan formed yet another company, which is the present Diving Systems International (DSI). Skip continued to work for DSI and in 1980 became the company president. Today the company has 25 employees and ships masks and helmets around the world.

To make the move from fabrication and assembly to president took time, but Skip recognizes that everything he learned about the business was necessary to do his present job well. During his years with the company Skip has held virtually every position and responsibility, from purchasing to shipping and receiving, from sales to test diving. "You must learn and understand all aspects of the business if you expect to supervise and make intelligent decisions."

Today Skip's responsibilities are extremely diverse. His responsibilities include overseeing the daily operation of the company, monitoring sales, long term planning, and working with the engineering and design groups. He regularly test dives all new equipment and product improvements.

Skip enjoys meeting and exchanging information with the divers who use the company's products. He finds that juggling the company's production capabilities to meet the customer's needs is a rewarding challenge.

Some of the major accomplishments of the company include the performance of their helmet, the SuperLite-17® during the salvage of Air Florida Flight #90. While other helmets froze and were unusable, DSI's SuperLite-17®, performed successfully during the salvage of the Air Florida plane from beneath the ice on the Potomac River. The U.S. Navy approved this helmet for use by their diving personnel.

The unpleasant aspects of Skip's job include having to ask customers for payment when their accounts are overdue, laying off staff when times are tight, and keeping track of the piles of paperwork that flow across his desk. These responsibilities frequently keep him away from diving.

Skip's advice to anyone who wants to work for a manufacturer is that they must know as much about the diving field as possible. In particular, you must understand how things work, like valves and regulators, and have good mechanical experience and knowledge. A background in business is also indispensable. He also points out the need to continue your education through night classes and special programs. "When you see an opportunity in a company developing you should get the additional training to qualify yourself for that job," observes Skip.

Suggested Reading:

Davidow, W. and Uttal, B. *Total Customer Service.* Harper & Row, New York, NY. 1989

Karass, G. *Negotiate to Close.* Simon and Schuster, New York, NY. 1985

McCormack, M. *What They Don't Teach You in Harvard Business School.* Bantam Books, New York, NY. 1984

ABOUT THE AUTHORS

Steve Barsky

Steve Barsky learned to dive in 1965 in a Los Angeles County scuba program, and completed his certification at Catalina Island, California. He was first employed in the diving industry in 1968, working part-time and during summer vacations through high school in a dive store. In 1970 Steve was certified as a diving instructor and moved to Santa Barbara, California to attend college. Steve has also worked as a dive guide in the Caribbean and Hawaii.

Fig. 16.1 – Steve Barsky has worked as a scuba instructor, dive guide, dive store employee, commercial diver, in dive equipment marketing, and as a diving photo-journalist.

From 1974-1976 Steve attended the commercial diving program at Santa Barbara City College and completed his master's degree at UCSB in diver performance and diving physiology. He was a research diver at the

University and was a member of the school's diving safety board for three years. Immediately following school, Steve went to work for SubSea International, a commercial diving firm. His deepest working dive for the firm was 580 feet.

After working in the North Sea and the Gulf of Mexico for seven years, Steve returned to Santa Barbara to work for Diving Systems International, a manufacturer of commercial diving helmets. He next worked for Viking America, Inc., handling all of their marketing and photography.

In 1989 Steve formed his own firm, Marine Marketing and Consulting, that produces advertising, technical manuals, and both topside and underwater photography for the diving industry. Steve's articles and photos have appeared in virtually every diving magazine, and he has authored three other books on diving topics. He also conducts specialized scuba training and does expert witness work in diving accident cases.

Fig. 16.2 – Kristine Barsky is a marine biologist and highly experienced diver.

Kristine Barsky

Kristine Barsky is an associate marine biologist and diver with the California Department of Fish and Game. She holds a Bachelor's degree in Zoology from Humboldt State University, and an A.A. in Wildlife Law and Conservation.

An avid diver since 1972, Kristine's diving experience includes dives along the entire California coast, the Caribbean, Hawaii, and Mexico. Kristine worked on the Department of Fish and Game's abalone enhancement project for eight years, logging over 250 dives annually at the Channel Islands and along the coast. She has authored several scientific papers and has spoken at many conferences.

Kristine's diving experience also includes the use of surface supplied equipment, full face masks, and extensive dry suit diving. She is certified as an assistant instructor and has been active in the organizational end of research diving.

She is currently the Department's marine resources manager for Santa Barbara and Ventura Counties. In this capacity she deals with both commercial and sport divers and anglers, marine collectors, and mariculturists (people who grow saltwater plants and animals).

If Kristine looks familiar, it's probably because you've seen her photo many times. As a model for her husband Steve, Kristine's image has appeared in numerous diving catalogs, books, and ads, including those for Viking, Zeagle Systems, Poseidon, DUI, and U.S. Divers.

Ronnie Damico

Fig. 16.3 – Ronnie Damico is a highly experienced diver and diving instructor who has worked in the scientific diving field as well as sport diving.

Ronnie Damico was first certified as a diver in Monterey, California in 1976. She attended a NAUI instructor training course in San Diego and was certified as NAUI instructor #5489.

In 1979, Ronnie started work as the assistant diving safety officer for the University of Southern California's (USC) marine lab on Catalina Island. She was promoted to the full-time position of diving officer in 1980.

At USC, Ronnie developed many specialized diver training courses, including programs in blue water diving (diving in the open ocean many miles from shore), and surface supplied diving. She also became a decompression chamber treatment supervisor and volunteered more than 800 hours in the treatment of diving accident victims at Catalina.

Ronnie has conducted numerous diving seminars and conferences. She has been the conference director for several of NAUI's most successful International Conferences on Underwater Education.

On the lighter side, Ronnie has worked as a stunt and support diver for the motion picture and television industry on such projects as the *Fall Guy, General Hospital, Rip Tide,* and *Friday the 13th.*

Ronnie was the Diving Safety Officer at California State University in Long Beach from 1985 through 1992. She currently teaches diving as an independent instructor, and is a member of the Board of Directors of the National Association of Underwater Instructors.

INDEX

A

B

C

D

E

I

J

K

L

N

T

U

V

W

X, Y, Z